Misha Glenny is the Central Europe correspondent of the BBC's World Service, based in Vienna. Before joining the BBC he worked for the *Guardian*, covering central and south-eastern Europe for three years, although he has been studying the area for over a decade. A speaker of German, Czech and Serbo-Croat, he has developed an inside knowledge of the countries that few other journalists possess. Before taking up journalism full-time he worked in publishing, having studied in Bristol, the Freie Universität in Berlin and Charles University in Prague.

MISHA GLENNY

———————

THE REBIRTH OF HISTORY

EASTERN EUROPE IN THE AGE OF DEMOCRACY

PENGUIN BOOKS

PENGUIN BOOKS

Published by the Penguin Group
Penguin Books Ltd, 27 Wrights Lane, London, W8 5TZ, England
Viking Penguin, a division of Penguin Books USA Inc.
375 Hudson Street, New York, New York 10014, USA
Penguin Books Australia Ltd, Ringwood, Victoria, Australia
Penguin Books Canada Ltd, 2801 John Street, Markham, Ontario, Canada L3R 1B4
Penguin Books (NZ) Ltd, 182–190 Wairau Road, Auckland 10, New Zealand

Penguin Books Ltd, Registered Offices: Harmondsworth, Middlesex, England

First published 1990
1 3 5 7 9 10 8 6 4 2

Filmset in Lasercomp Bembo
Printed in England by Clays Ltd, St Ives plc

To the memory of my father

'Du liebes Kind, komm, geh mit mir!
Gar schöne Spiele spiel' ich mit dir;
Manch bunte Blumen sind an dem Strand,
Meine Mutter hat manch gülden Gewand.'

from Goethe's *Der Erlkönig*

Contents

Acknowledgements

My motivation for writing this book was quite simple – I was worried about Eastern Europe. Nothing has happened in the few months since I started writing it to make me any less worried. On the contrary, my fears have been confirmed. There is little I can do to promote stability in the region, but I believe that, as an attempt to examine the new democracies in the light of their histories both pre-war and post-war, this book has some political value. Because I am considering contemporary politics some of this book may appear to have been overtaken by events. What I hope the reader will find is that, although I may not predict the precise course of the next few years, he or she will understand much better why Eastern Europe has developed in the way it has. If I have one regret about the book, it is that I have not provided footnotes. I must apologize and explain that it was written under great pressure; the majority of details in the book come from my memory (any uncertain figures or dates have, of course, been verified).

How I go about thanking the people who contributed to this book I do not know, as they did so largely in an indirect way over a very long period of time. But I must mention those who have either made a special contribution to my understanding of Eastern Europe or simply offered me the support without which I could not have continued. From the following people I have learned a great deal, and I would like to offer them my warmest thanks – Edgar de Bruin, Madla de Bruin, Oldřich Černý, Dana Vlčková, Tomáš Míka, Pavla Slabá, Kateřina Lukešová, Hejma and Vlček (together for the first time), Klement Lukeš, Béla Rásky, György Dálos, Luboš Jurík, Míla Flint, Věra Škraňková, Naďa Rybarová, the late Milan Hübl, Jiří Dienstbier, the late Milan Šimečka,

Acknowledgements

Miklós Sükősd, Gábor Kelemen, Julia Mátrai, Sorin Antioche, Ella Kasprzycka, Andrej Gustinčić, Milan Nikolić, Sonja Liht, Barney Petrović, Alisa Maliqi, Shkelzen Maliqi, Isuf Berisha.

I would like to thank the BBC, in particular the World Service News Desk under the leadership of Bob Jobbins, the *Guardian* and the *New Scientist* for feeding my craving for Eastern Europe.

I will never be able to thank Jenny Cole and Carol Hall enough for the support and friendship they afforded me in the most difficult of times. Similarly I will never be able to repay what I owe Peter Gowan for encouraging my interest in Eastern Europe over several years and for an invaluable discussion concerning the present volume. Imma Palme, Hans Ljung and Meckie deserve special mention for the wonderfully intelligent relief that they provide without fail.

The enthusiasm and vigilance of Jon Riley, my editor at Penguin, ensured that the book was written – without his confidence it would not have been. Without Sally Abbey's efficiency it would have been slower.

Many thanks to Alan Forrest and Roger Davies for holidays, the malt, golf and the Magnificent Seven.

Judy Dempsey was, predictably, totally indispensable; without her help this book would not have seen the light of day. To her and the following people I would like to say that, however depressing our profession becomes, their support and solidarity have seen me through, and I hope that one day I will be able to give them half what they have given me – Susanna Höll, Angela Leuker, Jolyon Naegele, Michael Montgomery, Laura Silber, Alison Smale, Mike Stewart, David Storey, Jola and Honza Žalud.

The following people are always in my thoughts – Big B., Colin Robinson (why Col, I'll never know, but there you have it), Carrie Harrison, Catherine Shepherd, Clare Conville and Justin Langlands – what a team!

Jack and Julie Sydenham, Elizabeth Purdy, Tamara Ehrlich, Paddy, Sandy and Alice Glenny, Leah Graham and Sarah Graham have played an irreplaceable role in the production of this book.

The last year has not been an easy one for me, but three people have made it tolerable – Tanya Sillem, Snežana Ćurčić and Miljan Glenny: my love and apologies to all three.

Acknowledgements

Finally, at this stage people used to thank their typist – I would like to thank myself and my Olivetti, (and, by extension, Carrie).

M.G.
August 1990

Introduction

In the weeks after the final revolution in Romania I returned to London for a visit. Everyone I met demanded detailed descriptions of what I had seen and done. I complied with their requests as best I could but found it difficult to recreate the excitement. Even a fortnight after three-quarters of the Czechoslovak working population had risen as one against single-party rule, my mind was elsewhere, trying to map out the uncharted territory that Eastern Europe was just beginning to explore. Although I had been moved, thrilled and, in Romania's case, appalled by the events, the revolutions had not taken me by surprise. Naturally I had no idea that everything would happen in 1989, but I had been working, visiting or living in Eastern Europe for almost fifteen years when the moment arrived. During this period I had watched closely how the refusal of the communist state apparatus to diagnose, let alone heal, social conflict with any instruments other than duplicity and repression had led to the development of a very painful and terminal cancer.

It was gratifying to witness the death of this political mutant. The tremendous dignity that forty years of neo-Stalinism had inadvertently generated in ordinary people had often been hidden behind the grey façade of these societies. But during the revolutions the essential human qualities, which most visitors to Eastern Europe since the war have encountered, were revealed for the whole world to see. In 1989 the qualities of simple kindness and courtesy took on a novel political form. But their essence was identical to that of the hospitality that most East Europeans had for a long time bestowed upon strangers. I have lost count of the number of people who, before the revolutions, provided me with a bed for the night, never having set eyes on me, despite the risks entailed in putting up a Westerner without registering with the local police. A guest in an East European home is invariably offered food and drink beyond the means of the host, and no amount of pressure would induce him or her to accept money or gifts in return.

The belief that courtesy could transcend the brutality of neo-Stalinism was sometimes shaken but never destroyed. It exerted a profound influence on the work of the opposition in Eastern Europe. Moral criteria frequently triumphed over ideological differences, the common goal of democratic rights smothering political divisions. At the beginning of 1990 I asked the Czechoslovak Foreign Minister, Jiří Dienstbier, why the new leadership of his country, which for four decades had been a third-class diplomatic power, was capable of having such a powerful impact on international relations within six weeks of the Czechoslovak revolution. Dienstbier explained that during the twelve years of the opposition Charter 77's existence the understanding between its supporters had grown so strong that nothing, and certainly not ideological disputes, could subvert it. All its signatories, from the right-wing Catholic Václav Benda to the Trotskyist Petr Uhl, were committed to an independent Czechoslovak foreign policy. But even more significant, Dienstbier believed, was the personal support that Chartists had received from one another, and continued to receive, after the revolution. The experience of imprisonment and persecution has brought the new leaders of Czechoslovakia closer together than any democratic political process ever could.

On occasions such personal bonds would link entire countries. From the East German uprising in June 1953 to the overthrow of Ceauşescu, post-war Eastern Europe has provided examples of popular solidarity that would be unimaginable in the West. The revolutions of 1989 bore majestic witness to this unity. They represented not only a complex victory of personal politics over the interests of a repressive state but also a straightforward victory of the rational over the irrational.

Despite feeling emotionally bound to these victories, on my return to London I was none the less distracted and disturbed by the implications of the revolutions. While I was describing to friends the dramatic moments of the previous six months, I was already grappling with the embryonic political inconsistencies and disputes conceived at the point of revolution. Above all I wondered how Eastern Europe's authoritarian and nationalist traditions would re-appear, having been refracted through the distorting prism of Stalinism, and how the devastated economies of the area, which with one or two exceptions had been weak and unstable before the war, could begin the process of reconstruction.

Nobody wants to deny the peoples of Eastern Europe their euphoria at having thrown off the chains of dictatorship. But those involved with the opposition in particular realize that sober political analysis is required now more than ever, as a failure to ensure a peaceful transition from dictatorship to democracy and from the planned economy to some form of market economy will have far-reaching consequences not only for the countries of East-ern Europe but for Western Europe as well. The revolutions are not over; they have only just begun.

The strongest impression that Eastern Europe leaves on visitors is the power and diversity of its cultural traditions, all the more striking in view of the enormous programme of social engineering begun in 1948, whose chief aim was to level diversity in the name of Stalinist internationalism. In one respect the architects of this artificial fraternity were successful – those outside Eastern Europe, including many Western governments, accepted this distorted image of the new socialist states as carbon copies of the Soviet Union. It was held that the relationship between Moscow and Warsaw or Bucharest was identical to the relationship between Moscow and Smolensk or Vladivostok. Naturally there was some truth in this perception of post-war Eastern Europe. Basic human rights, for example, have been systematically denied to millions in the socialist camp since the war. But the determination of many in the West to view the area as a cultural and political monolith was the product of a misapprehension.

Time and again the fabled omnipotence of East European states proved incapable of imposing its will on local populations. During the height of Polish Stalinism in the early 1950s, for example, many urban areas were terrorized by youngsters organized in gangs with such names as the 'Bloody Avengers' and the 'Golden Hand'. Their *Weltanschauung* was profoundly hostile to authority in general and Soviet socialist principles in particular. Their criminal activity included such practices as throwing people under trains, burning breasts with cigarettes, cutting eyes with razor blades and fastening mouths with safety pins. In many working-class districts police were unable to curb the work of these groups despite unprecedented powers to do so. In a number of villages in eastern Serbia it has always been considered desirable to marry at a very early age. There have been many cases of young boys and girls joined together as nine- or ten-year-olds. In several places the average age of young couples getting married is still between twelve and fourteen. The practice is entirely illegal, and several concerted efforts have been made by the authorities to put a stop to it, all to no avail.

In such ways the social reality of Eastern Europe during the past forty years has often diverged from the newsreel images of nations trapped inside a mammoth metropolis. In its own fashion it was a nightmare but much closer in conception to the unpredictability of Kafka than the mechanical certainties of Fritz Lang. The uprisings in East Germany, Poland, Hungary and Czechoslovakia from 1953 to 1981 were regarded as chance breakdowns that could be repaired by Soviet engineers. In fact, they demonstrated that the national political traditions of these countries were in the long term irreconcilable with Stalinism.

After Mikhail Gorbachev came to power in the Soviet Union the image of the monolith began to disappear. But the cultural diversity did not re-emerge in 1985 after forty years of hibernation. It had always been there, albeit hidden behind the leading role of the Communist Party and other political structures. In this sense the post-revolutionary states in Eastern Europe are not attempting to construct pluralism on a *tabula rasa*. There are over 120 million people in the area, divided into a multitude of nations, speaking myriad tongues. By comparison Western Europe appears relatively homogeneous. The economies of Eastern Europe range from the highly industrialized regions of Bohemia, Moravia and East Germany to the third- and even fourth-world conditions of

Romania and Kosovo in southern Yugoslavia. Some areas can boast powerful democratic traditions, while others have known only dictatorship and violence. In an ideal world Western policy towards Eastern Europe would be mindful of the extreme differences separating the individual countries, but it often appears that the image of the monolith continues to make itself felt.

The communist take-over of power was completed in 1948, and it was not long before the theologians of the people's democracies, as the states were called, had proclaimed a new dogma, according to which no fundamental conflicts, either within or between the socialist states, was possible, since their root cause (the bourgeoisie's ownership of the means of production) had been eliminated. In order to justify widespread repression, the doctrine warned that the enemies of socialism would stop at nothing to restore capitalism so that vigilance had to be maintained. But, despite this frequently pathological fear of imperialism, the new leaders were adamant that the people's democracies had embarked upon the construction of a utopian future and that there was no turning back the clock.

This political theory was as simple as it was nonsensical, but for good reasons it appealed to many in Eastern Europe, which historically had received few benefits from capitalism and had been devastated by Nazism and war. In the Yugoslav republics of Serbia and Montenegro Marshal Tito's army of communist partisans enjoyed enormous public trust. Mindful of pre-war unemployment and the division of Czechoslovakia by Germany, Britain and France at Munich, 40 per cent of the population in Bohemia and Moravia, the most developed industrial area in the region, voted communist in the elections of 1946. The Communist Party commanded considerably more support in Romania at the end of the war than is often believed, in particular among the Hungarian minority in Transylvania. Throughout the region there were more examples of communists successfully wooing large sections of the peasantry (with promises of land reform), the working class and the intelligentsia than have sometimes been remembered.

It is difficult to find fault with the millions who invested their passive or active political energy in the communists' utopian vision, based, apparently, on precise scientific laws. The overwhelming majority did so in good faith, but, with the exception of party activists and the intellectuals, they did so for particular local reasons. They were certainly not seduced by the idea of a broad, classless community of ethnic and national groups in which Bulgarian tobacco farmers would link arms with the miners of Katowice in resolute hostility to imperialism. Peace was welcomed everywhere, but little attention was paid to the causes of instability in Central Europe and the Balkans, especially nationalism. On the one hand Stalin and his vassals proclaimed that nationalism had been eradicated in one fell swoop once the capitalists had been expropriated. At the same time, however, the Soviet leader actually strengthened the national state system by blocking the creation of a Balkan federation as conceived by the Bulgarian communist leader, Georgi Dimitrov, at the beginning of 1948.

Initially there was popular support in most countries for the Red Army, which was regarded as a liberating force, and millions held Stalin in the highest regard. The new communist leaderships presented this popularity as unquestioning and mindless adoration. The cult of all things Soviet was allowed to permeate every aspect of life of the people's democracies with disastrous effects, which continue to take their toll to this day. Far from removing the historical national tensions, this cult injected into the area a virulent strain of chauvinism that sooner or later agitated violent national and racist passions throughout Eastern Europe.

Not all of these passions were negative, particularly when channelled against Soviet imperialism. The first, and – Albania excepted – until 1989 the only, successful manifestation of anti-Soviet sentiment conquered virtually all of Yugoslavia after its expulsion from the Cominform (the Communist Information Bureau, a short-lived political umbrella binding the Soviet Union's new East European allies with Moscow) in June 1948. The late 1940s and early 1950s were probably the only period in post-war Yugoslavia during which local nationalist conflicts were set aside in defence of the federation.

The dispute between Belgrade and the capitals of the Cominform made it abundantly clear that the political élites in Eastern

Europe would not hesitate to use nationalism both as a way of settling political accounts and in an attempt to improve their public support among a targeted section of the population. In the early 1950s Czech communists played on anti-Slovak feeling when purging some of Slovakia's most popular communist politicians, including the former Foreign Minister, Vladimir Clementis. In Romania the high proportion of Hungarians in the party and state leadership in the early post-war period was systematically reduced by the ethnic Romanian General Secretary, Gheorghe Gheorghiu-Dej. Not only did he lay the foundations for Ceauşescu's racist policy of Romanization but he also prepared the ground for Romania's independent foreign policy within the framework of the Warsaw Pact, which Ceauşescu would later use in order to justify, among other things, Stalinist domestic policies. Since the war most national or ethnic minorities in Eastern Europe have been victimized, none more so than the Jewish and Roma communities that have regularly had to bear the pain of systematic discrimination, often sponsored by the Communist Party, from Warsaw to Skopje.

Nationalism in post-war Eastern Europe has taken on various guises. The uprisings in East Germany in 1953, Hungary and Poland in 1956, Czechoslovakia in 1968 and again Poland in 1970–71 and 1980–81 gave vent to the mighty and popular hostility to Russian imperialism. Sometimes nationalist disputes were contained within the ruling bureaucracies, as in Czechoslovakia or Romania during the 1950s. Traditional popular prejudices have also survived well. Beyond Poland's borders there is a common view that all Poles are lazy crooks. East Germans are regarded as potential Fascists, Czechs as snobs and Hungarians as stubbornly weird. Outsiders, like the Vietnamese *Gastarbeiter*, have borne the brunt of the region's intolerance. The conflict between Hungary and Romania in the 1970s and 1980s and the resurrection of the Transylvania problem was played out on two levels: between the two national bureaucracies and between Hungarian nationals and the Romanian state. In most countries the state has used the Jewish and Roma minorities to divide and rule by encouraging popular racism in order to deflect political or economic discontent. The

Polish Communist Party, for example, under the influence of the Interior Minister General Mieczysław Moczar, unleashed a degrading anti-Semitic campaign, as a way of restoring order after student demonstrations throughout the country in March 1968.

Of course, the one thing that until recently united these various forms of nationalism was the adamantine denial issued by the communists that they existed. How could they, if nationalism was a purely capitalist disease? On those occasions when nationalism became so virulent that the bureaucracy had to confront the problem it was explained away as having been engineered by imperialist forces outside the bloc. Anti-Semitism, for example, was always characterized as anti-Zionism, although, as the following poem circulated by Moczar in 1968 demonstrates, this was patently ludicrous:

> A Fifth Column, it's true,
> Not so long ago so wisely someone said
> They're wont to look up to the Jews,
> These Polish blockheads.
>
> Onward brothers! Sabre in hand,
> Seize the Jew by his payee
> And – if you well understand –
> Hurl him over the sea.
>
> Poland, this land they spit at,
> Grants them favour albeit,
> Gulp your beer, you student,
> And for approbation wait.

None the less, when accused of being anti-Semitic, the Polish leadership exploded with indignation. Similarly Soviet and Hungarian political scientists maintained for years that the Hungarian uprising of 1956 was instigated by conservatives and fascists secreted into Hungary by the CIA. To justify both the erection of the Berlin Wall and the invasion of Czechoslovakia, the Soviet Union claimed that revanchist groups in West Germany were planning the forcible overthrow of the East German and Czechoslovak governments.

Throughout the history of the people's democracies the ruling

Communist Parties celebrated the supposed alliance between the Bulgarian tobacco farmer and the miner from Katowice. But for much of the period strenuous attempts were made to prevent the fraternization of people from different East European states. Most East Europeans who travelled within the Warsaw Pact in the 1950s and early 1960s did so either with official organizations, such as the Youth Leagues or trade unions, or in groups of tourists. Individual travel and the genuine cross-fertilization of different cultures were discouraged. On many occasions borders between Warsaw Pact countries were closed or blanket bans imposed on citizens travelling from one country to another within the bloc.

As a consequence, prejudice based on ignorance has been allowed to flourish, and popular awareness of how damaging nationalism and racism can be has remained at a low level in Eastern Europe. Those ethnic or national groups that have been the target of abuse, whether popular or inspired by the state, have had little opportunity to organize or express their grievances either politically or through the media. Although much of the democratic opposition in Eastern Europe has attempted to draw attention to the problems of racism, as an issue it has appealed neither to the masses nor to the intelligentsia. Anti-Vietnamese jokes are now commonplace throughout north-eastern Europe among social strata whose Western equivalents would never dare utter a derogatory word about minorities. Soon after the revolution in Czechoslovakia groups of Moravian and Slovak students began using the vehicle of local nationalist organizations to voice demands for the forcible repatriation of Vietnamese *Gastarbeiter*. Similar movements exist in what was East Germany. It was not long before popular resentment had translated itself into violence. Gang warfare between Moravians and Vietnamese, which included the use of knives and machetes, broke out soon after the revolution, while in several East European countries the Roma community has been identified as the most popular target of violent attacks by the growing community of skinheads.

Political pluralism and democracy are essential if the peoples of Eastern Europe are to find solutions to the numerous nationalist conflicts in the area, but they are no absolute guarantees. Indeed, in certain areas they represent a double-edged sword that must be handled with the utmost care. In the Balkans nationalism offers the greatest threat to stability and the possibility of conflagration. During the revolutions in Eastern Europe it was easy to forget just how precarious is the peace in southern Europe.

If only because of its large ethnic minority in Transylvania, Hungary belongs to the Balkans. Nothing testifies more eloquently to Ceauşescu's quintessential nastiness than the solidarity that developed between Romanians and Hungarians following the abduction of the Hungarian priest László Tökes by the Securitate in December 1989. For a few weeks one of the most intractable national problems of the area appeared to have been solved. But within a month of the revolution relations between Hungarians and Romanians began to deteriorate steadily, since when support groups based in Hungary have been extremely active in Transylvania.

As yet there have been no calls for the return of Transylvania to Hungary, either by any of the mainstream parties in Hungary or by the Democratic Union of Hungarians within Romania. Romania's claim to Transylvania is based on what many Hungarians refer to as the 'treachery of Trianon', the settlement that granted Romania possession of Transylvania after the First World War. Hungarian nationalists, who depict Trianon as a classic 'knife-in-the-back' arrangement much in the way that the German National Socialists did the post-First World War settlement, are particularly active in the governing Hungarian Democratic Front. The Transylvanian Hungarians must be guaranteed full cultural autonomy if the two countries' post-war borders are not to be called in question by organized political forces in Hungary. In rural districts, which exert an inordinately powerful influence on Hungarian politics, the so-called populists draw their strength from a belief in the essential goodness of the Hungarian peasant. This commitment to the *Nep* (People) has been exaggerated by Hungary's ethnic isolation, surrounded as it is by what the populists often regard as hostile Slav, Teutonic and Latin peoples. It is no coincidence that Hungary's new constitution insists that the government should rule in the name of *all* Hungarians, including those living outside its borders. Thus, according to Hungarian law, the government now has the right to intervene in the affairs of neighbouring countries in defence of the Hungarian minority.

For their part the Romanians must resist the temptation of pursuing Ceauşescu's policy of assimilation. This will not be easy. The Romanian people, and its intelligentsia in particular, have been brutalized and numbed for much of this century by authoritarian governments fired by mystical nationalism that bestows on the descendants of the proud Dacian race (surrounded by hostile Slav, Teutonic and Ugric peoples) a mission to civilize their uncultured neighbours. This is ironic, as, with the exception of Albania there is no country in Eastern Europe with such weak democratic traditions as Romania's. Since the revolution it has been instructive to observe the polarization of Romania's few dissidents under Ceauşescu. One leading adviser in the National Salvation Front, Silviu Brucan, emerged soon after the revolution as a proponent of the Khrushchevite communism that influenced him so deeply in the early 1960s. Doina Cornea, on the other hand, who displayed remarkable courage at the hands of the Securitate, has developed into a rabid conservative whose commitment to political pluralism no longer seems as impeccable as it did under the former dictator. Ironically, both became victims of Romania's curious political hybrid, the National Salvation Front, within a few weeks of the revolution.

All East Europeans encounter difficulty when trying to distinguish between popular will and the will of the *Nep*, the *Volk* or the *Narod*. In conditions of political or economic stress they have found the mythical idea of the 'people' easy to construct.

The law of probability suggests that if serious trouble is going to break out, it will be in the Balkans, and that if a book were opened on the question, the smart money would undoubtedly back the possibility that the territory occupied at the moment by the Socialist Federal Republic of Yugoslavia would be involved. Despite the trouble it has caused over the last century, the Balkans remain an area of great mystery to the West. This is not because the communities in the area still live in such a remote environment that to uncover their secrets one would have to spend years hiking around barren mountains. It is simply because traditionally people in the West (and, indeed, in parts of the East) have not cared a great deal for the Balkans. This has been particularly evident during the past two decades, when the bulk of Western political and cultural research into Eastern Europe has focused on the countries of north-eastern Europe, in particular Poland, Czechoslovakia and Hungary (West Germany, of course, devoted most attention to East Germany). The only revolution in the Balkans to receive widespread media attention in the West was the Romanian revolution because it was exceptionally violent and because Ceauşescu was exceptionally insane. Compare Western interest in the overthrow of communism in Bulgaria and the point becomes clear. If Ceauşescu had gone in an orderly palace *coup*, as the Bulgarian leader, Todor Zhivkov, was forced to, Bucharest would still be as unknown a capital as Sofia.

Despite the suffering and continued economic misery of the Romanians, they have become wandering pariahs in Europe. Most West European countries began refusing Romanians the right of entry soon after the revolution, and within six months East European countries adopted similar measures. The flirtation with Romania's misery had clearly lost its *frisson*. Evidently the misery of other Balkan countries is also secondary to the concern shown for north-east European countries. This lack of interest in the fate of Albanians, Serbs, Macedonians, Bulgarians and the many other national groups in the area is likely to backfire. War is still quite likely in the Balkans. This may bother the West less today than at one time because it would almost certainly not spark off another European war. But, aside from the humanitarian concern the situation ought to engender, it would make a mockery of the West's oft expressed desire for an integrated Europe. We ignore the Balkans at our own peril.

The national question in north-eastern Europe has taken on a very different form since the revolution in East Germany. The prospect of the creation of an economic and political Colossus in Central Europe has meant that German unification now dwarfs all other issues in the region. Certainly, there are local rivalries between ethnic and national groups, but these will not change the entire political geography of post-war Europe. The country most directly affected by unification is Poland. It is difficult to ascertain, however, to what extent Polish fears of a united Germany are based on Poland's economic prospects and to what extent on historical experience. Margaret Thatcher was quick to side with the Polish position in early 1990, and, as is her wont, she revived memories of Anglo-Polish solidarity at the beginning of the Second World War. In doing so, however, she was clearly motivated not by the threat of a possible German invasion of Poland but by the fear that has gripped Thatcher's cabinet about a general expansion of German power in Europe, as evidenced by the remarks of the former Trade and Industry Secretary, Nicholas Ridley, in the early summer of 1990.

Initially it seemed that Poles were worried as well by the economic consequences of unification, but their concern soon developed beyond this, largely because of Chancellor Kohl's crude electoral tactic of wooing the German right by refusing to give an immediate commitment to the inviolability of Poland's western border. Although this was later forthcoming, the fact that Kohl was prepared to use the border issue as a tactic was sufficient to agitate Poles. Warsaw's concern was exaggerated further by its initial exclusion from the 'Two plus Four' talks at which the two Germanies and the four powers occupying Germany and Berlin mapped out the road towards unification. In February 1990 the Poles offered observers an insight into their psychological response to German unification by ganging up, in a local election in Silesia, against the candidate of the Germans in Silesia, Henryk Krol. The election was unpleasant and a useful reminder of how quickly national relations in the area can deteriorate when the international climate begins to cloud over. In a remarkable twist, some political forces have turned to the Soviet Union for protection against any possible German claims on Poland. A minority body of opinion in Poland favours the continued stationing of the Red Army on Polish soil. Fascinating though this new-found love for the Soviet Union is, it comes at a most inappropriate moment, as the Soviet republics are busy dismantling the Union, which is unlikely to be in a position to guarantee any country's borders for much longer.

German reunification has posed a dilemma for the Solidarity-backed MPs and activists who make up by far the largest political grouping in Poland. During the years of opposition they insisted on the Germans' absolute right to unite if this was their democratically expressed wish. But popular mistrust of a united Germany is beginning to place a strain on this commitment.

The new Czechoslovak leadership, which is dominated by former opposition activists, was the first to recognize the inevitability of unification and, like Solidarity, welcomed it as both an expression of democratic will and an important contribution to the creation of a common European home. Czechoslovakia's postwar borders are not an issue for the Germans, although almost immediately after taking office Jiří Dienstbier and, later, President Václav Havel apologized for the expulsion of several million Germans from the Sudetenland after the war, indicating, perhaps, how keen Czechoslovakia was to get on well with Germany. Prague's confidence in a united Germany has been bolstered by Czechoslovakia's relatively stable economic structure. The government and President Havel have characterized Czechoslovakia as not having reached the crisis in which Poland and Hungary now wallow. However, they do warn that, despite appearances, Czechoslovakia hovers on the edge of that crisis. Economic cooperation between Germany and Czechoslovakia could well bring substantial benefits for both countries, whereas the relationship between Germany and Poland could become one of dependency.

Germany's neighbours all reject one of the solutions to the security problem that unification has created – a neutral Germany. Despite this, since the beginning of 1990 opinion polls have suggested that neutrality is supported by between 60 and 70 per cent of all Germans. As the Warsaw Pact began to disintegrate, Western governments insisted that a united Germany must belong to a NATO that may later expand not as a military but as a political alliance. As a way of controlling a united Germany this concept has united Paris, London and Washington. However, the West's forceful arguments neglect the political inclinations not only of the Germans but also of most of the new forces in Eastern Europe. For decades they have seen their lives ruined by the division of Europe into two hostile military blocs, and their dream – and, indeed, their stated political goal – has been the dissolution of both blocs. They express a resolute political and emotional aversion to both the Warsaw Pact and NATO.

In general the Czechoslovaks and, to a lesser extent, the Poles bear little resentment towards the West Germans, confident in their experience of democracy. Suspicion of East Germans and fear of a right-wing revival on the erstwhile territory of the GDR is, however, widespread in both Czechoslovakia and Poland. Within days of the East German revolution signs of neo-Nazi activity began surfacing throughout the country, although much of this was restricted to the alienated youth of Berlin, Leipzig, Karl-Marx Stadt (Chemnitz) and other cities. The strongest political tradition, which has almost certainly survived forty years of the Socialist Unity Party, is that of social democracy. The power of the East German CDU was created out of very weak traditions but very tempting promises made by Helmut Kohl, whose vigorous attempt to present himself as the political godfather of unification has proved remarkably successful. Within weeks of the revolution the East Germans were able to cast off their association with the rest of Eastern Europe. Although they suffered an extraordinarily rapid social collapse in the months between the revolution and unification, they were all aware that, in the long term, unification guaranteed a standard of living that most other East Europeans would only be dreaming of for a very long time to come.

While struggling to conjure up stable democracies, the East European states are also learning to juggle with the laws of the market economy. Political reform is a pre-condition for the transition to economic reform, but at the same time economic stability is needed to ensure a peaceful political transition. All the East European states are committed to some form of market economy, although Bulgaria and Romania have been rather vague in their commitment so far. Exactly what type of market economy will develop is likely to remain unknown for a long time, as even in Czechoslovakia, which undoubtedly has the brightest economic prospects (leaving aside East Germany's maverick situation), government economists believe that it could take at least ten years for the new economic system to function properly.

Western governments and supporters of economic liberalism appear to have underestimated the appeal that an extensive social security network exerts on the workforces of Eastern Europe. Although Hajek and Friedman have many disciples in the area, the Czechoslovak working class and the intelligentsia have long admired Sweden as an economic model. There is, of course, a certain irony in this at a time when the Swedish social democratic system appears to be running into terminal difficulties. None the less, it is unwise to ignore the value that East Europeans place on the right to work. Solidarity, the greatest political movement ever to emerge in post-war Eastern Europe, was informed by a powerful workerist ideology. As the economic reform now under way in Poland demonstrates, the very workers who crucified the Communist Party in 1980 are prepared to shoulder enormous hardships in an effort to establish a rational economic mechanism. But the prime minister, Tadeusz Mazowiecki, knows that their patience is finite and that his government will not be able to move the Polish working class around like a pawn if his austerity programme does not produce results.

Given the massive indebtedness of Eastern Europe to Western financial institutions and governments, the programme will not be easy to implement. Eastern Europe's economy still has a large agrarian base. There are many highly industrialized areas, but it is essential to remember that most of these were constructed at break-neck speed in the 1950s within the framework of Stalin's plans for industrializing Eastern Europe. As a consequence, many of the regions contain industries that are huge loss-makers, able to survive only because of state subsidies. Most people recognize that the subsidies, which account for up to 40 per cent of the budget in Eastern Europe, will now have to go. This, of course, will result in massive unemployment among workers whom it will be difficult to retrain even if new industries were to spring up to replace the old factories. Already in some areas of Poland it is possible to observe an extraordinary migration from cities to the countryside, a reversal of what happened in the 1950s, as recently unemployed Poles search desperately for ways of making a living. This bizarre phenomenon is also likely to emerge in Hungary, Romania and Bulgaria.

Czechoslovakia now resolutely refuses to accept foreign loans or aid. The new leadership is convinced that the only way in which the economy can develop is to attract foreign investment. It too faces the problem of dismantling useless industrial Leviathans, but in stark contrast to most of the region it can offer investors a highly skilled workforce and a communications infrastructure that works to an extent. Hungary, which began to implement economic reforms long before most other countries, is doomed to remain an economic backwater unless it modernizes its infrastructure in earnest.

In Bulgaria and Romania the economic priority is land reform. In the case of the latter this is a matter of extreme urgency. Ceauşescu's insane economic policies have succeeded in all but destroying Romanian agriculture, once the envy of surrounding countries. The country is permanently under threat of the food supply drying up, which poses an immediate challenge not just to Romania but to the whole of Europe. Peasants in the area find it hard to resist the temptation to hoard food, and, regrettably but understandably, the Romanian government has had to persist with Ceauşescu's Draconian laws, which were drawn up to discourage the practice.

In Bulgaria the problem is a political one. The Bulgarian Communist Party, now called 'Socialist', is proving the most stubborn in resisting political reform. Its tactics are most successful in the regions and the countryside, where the local communist bureaucracy has developed an ingenious, if damaging, strategy of buying off the population by ensuring short-term prosperity at the expense of urban areas. The result of the exodus of hundreds of thousands of Turks from Bulgaria in the summer of 1989 was that some branches of agriculture, particularly the lucrative tobacco industry, almost seized up. Now, however, local communist leaders are turning the labour shortage to their advantage by wooing workers from urban areas to take up work in the countryside. Reform of Bulgaria's collapsing economy is dependent on political change, but, in contrast to the rest of the region, this still looks some way off.

However enspiriting the East European revolutions have been, the soul droops in despair when confronted by the devastation caused by forty years of a planned economy. The dirt and inefficiency of the area's industry and agriculture sap the enthusiasm of the most hardened political activist. Subjecting these economies to the ruthless logic of a completely free market would result in social upheaval and a second, more threatening phase of revolution. It is unlikely that democrats would be the beneficiaries of a renewed revolutionary activity. In its own interest the West must be prepared to make economic sacrifices as it contributes to the reconstruction of the East European economies. In particular, it must beware of neglecting investment in some countries because of the easy money to be made in others. East Europeans are already competing with each other for Western investment, but with their economies in such a weak state such competition is not healthy; rather, it tends to exacerbate local political prejudices.

'What you have to realize,' I was once told by a Yugoslav friend, 'is that during our entire lives we have been raised to believe that the noblest goal in life is to work as little as possible and at the same time to make as much money as possible.' Social consciousness in Eastern Europe is deeply corrupt. And although millions have been dreaming of freedom for decades, most are very suspicious of politics and politicians. They are also inexperienced in thinking for themselves. Of course they are able to decide if something is right or wrong, but few like taking decisions, as they are so used to accepting orders, particularly in the work place, and then acting upon them. It is one thing no longer to fear being picked up by the police for criticizing the government or party (although this still happens in parts of Eastern Europe); it is another to establish not just democratic mechanisms but a rule of law whereby institutions act as safeguards on behalf of citizens to protect them from the abuse of political power. It was, for example, quite breathtaking, after six months of freedom in Eastern Europe, to note how atrocious the standards of journalism were throughout the region, partly because of crude manipulation by politicians, which was particularly disturbing in Hungary and Romania, and partly because journalists found it impossible to liberate themselves from the role of court flatterer. The obsequious attention still paid to President Havel in the Czech press, for example, is a travesty of everything that the playwright stood for before the revolution.

Large parts of the urban intelligentsia absorbed Western liberal values before the revolutions, and indeed dissidents like Václav Havel and Adam Michnik have made a substantial contribution to the debate about state and society. But the influence of the progressive intelligentsia in the largely agrarian societies of south Eastern Europe remains small. Even in Czechoslovakia, which has the most sophisticated political culture in Eastern Europe, the post-revolutionary parliament passed a law on political parties and an electoral law that to an extent defined the new democratic order in terms of restrictions and duties rather than possibilities and rights. A political movement is allowed to register as a party only if it can produce 1,000 signatures in support of its application. The electoral law is more restrictive still, as only parties with a membership of 10,000 or more are allowed to stand at elections. No Monster Raving Loony Party for the Czechoslovaks.

Once freely elected MPs can take their seats in parliaments throughout Eastern Europe, the new democracies will face their stiffest practical challenge: confrontation with the state and party apparatus left behind by the old regimes. Since the collapse of the leading role of the Communist Party these networks have continued to control local and regional government as well as most economic life in Eastern Europe. They represent the very heart of communist rule, and to an extent they are irreplaceable – a fact of which people working in the structures are well aware. Not unnaturally, they wish to hang on to the privileges granted to them by undemocratic governments. The newly elected governments realize that they cannot simply dismantle the bureaucracy overnight, and indeed the more honest among the post-revolutionary governments admit that they will have to maintain large parts of it. At the same time they face tremendous pressure from the electorate to destroy these structures, which are popularly, and often accurately, regarded as responsible for a great deal of misery. The only option available to the new administrations is to assimilate the bureaucracies into the democratic structures of government and prune them where possible.

This will have a significant effect on Eastern Europe. The new democracies are likely to evolve structures similar to those in Austria, where an enormous bureaucracy assumes many of the functions that in the United States and Britain, for example, would be the prerogative of the judiciary and legislature. This would militate against the development of a 'civil society', which the Hungarian, Czechoslovak and Slovene opposition always regarded as an essential safeguard, preventing centralism on the one hand and a rampant free market on the other. If the bureaucracies do remain largely intact, this will certainly pose a major obstacle to the supporters of Hajek, Friedman and Thatcher.

Most of the new political parties can trace their political roots back to the inter-war years or, indeed, the nineteenth century. In Czechoslovakia and East Germany it appears quite likely that social democracy and Christian democracy will emerge as the decisive political forces, but every country in the region will witness the development of powerful nationalist parties.

A novel type of political organization has grown up in response to communist dictatorship. This is the large front organization like Solidarity in Poland, Civic Forum in Czechoslovakia and the UDF in Bulgaria. In Hungary the opposition alliance that negotiated the transition to democracy never fused; indeed, hostility between the opposition parties has been intense. Eventually Solidarity, Civic Forum and the UDF will break up into their constituent elements, but for the moment they consider themselves the most reliable guarantor of the restoration of democracy.

In Poland and Hungary the rump Communist Parties are sliding rapidly towards electoral insignificance. In Bulgaria the communists remain the most powerful political force, while in Romania there is a strong suspicion that the National Salvation Front is merely the reincarnation of the party, although clearly in a much more acceptable form than existed in the days of Ceauşescu. In Czechoslovakia the Communist Party has retained its name and is clearly intent on cultivating the strong tradition of left-wing social democracy in both the industrial and the agricultural areas of Bohemia and Moravia.

This is the new Eastern Europe – a labyrinth whose winding paths are beyond the comprehension of the most skilled cartographer. During the past forty years vicious Minotaurs have stood arrogantly in the middle of the main thoroughfares. They have not disappeared, however. They now merely lie in wait at the end of numerous dimly lit cul-de-sacs.

I CZECHOSLOVAKIA

The Glorious Revolution

The revolutions of 1989 engendered a number of clichés. One of the most popular proposes that Czechoslovakia will have fewer problems than any other East European country (if the GDR is recognized to be a special case) as it attempts to establish democratic institutions, to join the European mainstream and to install the mechanisms of a market economy.

In contrast to its neighbours, Czechoslovakia has a democratic tradition, albeit one that has been in hibernation for fifty years. Largely thanks to its intelligentsia and to some of its sporting stars, many Europeans already consider Czechoslovakia a welcome addition to their ranks. And its reputation as an important and healthy regional economic force is bettered by those of none of its former Warsaw Pact allies (the GDR, of course, excepted). On the surface the transition would appear relatively easy, but, as many leading politicians in Czechoslovakia agree, the country is beset by a number of debilitating diseases that can be cured only by drastic intervention.

The Czechoslovak revolution has few parallels in history. External and internal conditions had matured to a point at which revolution was both inevitable and bound to be successful. There were moments when some of the participants feared a counter-revolutionary *coup* by the army or the secret police, but these fears were based on the natural mistrust of a people that had laboured for twenty years under the uniquely gloomy communist regime of 'normalization', the consolidation of neo-Stalinist rule in the 1970s. They were not the result of considered, rational reflection.

By the time Czech security forces lit the spark of revolution on 17 November 1989 by brutally dispersing a huge demonstration on

National Street in Prague, the fate of Czechoslovakia had already been determined by two events. The first was the fall of Honecker in East Germany, the greatest ally of the Czechoslovak communist leadership. The second was the decision made by the leadership of the Soviet Communist Party to denounce as a grave political error the invasion of Czechoslovakia in 1968 by five Warsaw Pact countries. These two events swept away any remaining speck of legitimacy to which the leadership of the CPCz (Communist Party of Czechoslovakia) may still have been clinging. While it is true that the Soviet announcement was not made until after the revolution began, enough people in Prague knew about it to fuel the confidence of the revolutionaries.*

Despite the advantages that the forces of change enjoyed, the revolution could still have been a messy and long-drawn-out affair. Instead its course was plotted and executed with text-book precision. This was guaranteed by the courage of the students, the tactical brilliance of Civic Forum's leaders and the extraordinary solidarity shown by over three-quarters of the country's entire workforce during the general strike that took place on Monday, 27 November. The transition from Husák's presidency to Havel's was swift.

Czechoslovakia was thus the only country in Eastern Europe where the government was firmly in the grip of the opposition within days of the revolution. Poland suffered several months of painful negotiations before the former Communist Party chief, Mieczysław Rakowski, finally gave up the struggle in August 1989 and allowed the Solidarity activist Tadeusz Mazowiecki to form the government. Significantly, however, Solidarity did not even then feel confident enough to engineer the dismissal of President Wojciech Jaruzelski, the man who imposed martial law in Poland in 1981. In East Germany first Egon Krenz, and then as Prime Minister Hans Modrow, the head of the SED in Dresden, steered the country between Honecker's fall and the elections.

---

*I was in Prague almost a year before the revolution, and I first heard then of the working group set up by the Soviet Party's Central Committee to reassess the Soviet-led invasion.

Miklós Németh, Rezső Nyers and Imre Pozsgay enjoyed a long interregnum before Jozsef Antall of the MDF was finally able to wrest power from the pro-reform communists in Hungary. The democratic forces in Czechoslovakia, however, leapfrogged over their peers elsewhere. They did not have to wait for elections before assuming their newly won power. Within six weeks of the start of the revolution the Communist Party had lost control of almost all key political functions to supporters of Civic Forum or its Slovak counterpart, Public Against Violence (VPN). Those communists still in power, including the current federal prime minister, Marián Čalfa, and the interim Slovak prime minister, Milan Čič, had made it quite clear that they would diligently carry out the orders of Civic Forum and VPN. The Government of National Understanding, as it was called, was thereby able to examine in detail the main problems facing Czechoslovakia and to lay the foundations of the transition to democracy and a market economy before the elections.

The election of Václav Havel to the presidency for an interim period while elections were organized led to Czechoslovakia's being showered with much flattering publicity abroad. For several months Havel was the toast of the establishment from Berlin to Washington. The bumbling playwright with a cute, embarrassed smile won the hearts of millions. Journalists looking for a new angle to the story trumpeted that his new regime at the castle in Prague comprised a team of comics completely lacking in political experience. Havel himself often reiterated that he was a writer without political experience and that he did not want to remain in office long. Political analysts inside Czechoslovakia, however, were quick to spot that the new Czechoslovak president was not a buffoon but a very shrewd and experienced negotiator. Indeed, Havel is still the most powerful individual in any East European country.

The influence of Charter 77 activists on the development of Czechoslovakia after the revolution was substantial. The Charter had come into existence in January 1977, during one of the darkest periods of normalization. Its signatories spanned the spectrum of those who had been politically dispossessed by the Communist

Party during normalization. The Charter's aim was to monitor abuses of human rights as defined by the Czechoslovak constitution and the international agreements and conventions that the government in Prague had signed. It never attracted very many signatories but, together with other dissident organizations, became the focus of political opposition in Czechoslovakia and, not surprisingly, the primary target of organized repression by the CPCz. For thirteen years before the revolution some of Czechoslovakia's best intellects worked in public (conspiratorially), in prison and in exile. They formed alliances within their movement, and some even kept in touch with representatives of the party and state who sympathized with them clandestinely. Some informed for the secret police; others exposed them. Many were sentenced to long periods in jail; some of them died there; some, it is thought, were even murdered. The signatories and their sympathizers came from all walks of life, including a healthy number from the working class.

In the most awkward and difficult circumstances Charter 77 signatories lived and breathed politics. They may not have been charged with administering a state, but that was the only aspect of politics that was unfamiliar to them. The objective conditions in Czechoslovakia in November 1989 were set for a successful revolution, but it was thanks to the experiences of the Chartists and other opposition movements that the collapse of communist power was carried out so neatly and so efficiently. The network of close personal friendships that grew up around Charter continues to exert a substantial effect on politics in Prague.

The Great Illusions

More than any other country in Eastern Europe the new Czechoslovakia associates itself with the state created after the First World War, the first independent Czechoslovakia. The memory of Czechoslovakia's inter-war democracy, and in particular the personality and philosophy of its founder, Thomas Garrigue Masaryk, provides a positive national tradition with which the majority of the population is still eager to identify. The revolutionary forces in 1989 constantly refer to Masaryk's heritage, and once he had been elected president, Václav Havel ostentatiously adopted some of Masaryk's presidential habits, including learning to ride, in order to reinforce the continuity between the first republic and the new Česko-Slovensko Federativní Republika (ČSFR).

The inter-war republic had proved a unique success. While the timid democratic structures elsewhere in central and south-eastern Europe degenerated into dictatorship from the mid-1920s onward, Czechoslovakia's multinational state survived as a relatively healthy body until it was dismembered by Hitler, with the approval of France and the United Kingdom, six months after the notorious Munich *diktat* of September 1938. None the less even before Czechoslovakia fell victim to Nazi aggression the foundations of Masaryk's state had been threatened by a number of political problems, in particular the national question. The existence of a huge German minority was the excuse that eventually led to the demise of Czechoslovakia, but tension between the two major national groups, Czechs and Slovaks, was also a source of considerable friction during the inter-war period.

These difficulties naturally became acute during periods of economic depression when the structures of the first republic were found wanting. Largely because of economic mismanagement in the 1920s and early 1930s Czechoslovakia was slower than other industrialized European countries to shake off the consequences of the great economic depression that followed the Wall Street Crash of October 1929. The exception to this was the armaments industry of the Czech lands, which greedily fed on the arms race. Ironically, this race would claim Czechoslovakia as one of its first victims. A significant number of Czechs and Slovaks believed that Germany, Britain and France had allowed their country to be carved up as part of a pact devised by international capital. Thus although, as Václav Havel has often pointed out, the communist misrule of the past forty years has rendered the concept of 'socialism' meaningless, large parts of Czechoslovak society have retained a deep suspicion of capitalism because of the experience of the collapse of the inter-war republic.

Before the depression of 1929 Czechoslovakia's 3-million-strong

German minority voted almost exclusively for parties participating in the government and supporting Czechoslovak statehood. During the 1930s, as the economy foundered, German and Slovak irredentism grew steadily in strength, while calls for Fascist, radical nationalist and clerical regimes became louder among all ethnic groups except, understandably, the Jews and the Roma.

None the less, Czechoslovakia was able to resist the allure of dictatorship in the 1920s and 1930s because, despite economic mismanagement, its citizens still enjoyed a higher standard of living than was available elsewhere in the region. The inter-war republic was considered to be about the tenth most powerful economy in the world, thanks in large part to the German-owned industry concentrated in north and western Bohemia, Prague, Brno and northern Moravia. Czechoslovakia was famous for its light industry but also for its engineering and arms plants, notably Škoda in Plzeň, ČKD in Prague and Zbrojovka in Brno. Despite this success, critics have pointed out that the Czechoslovak economy survived through luck rather than judgement. Among the industrially developed countries Czechoslovakia was one of the most backward at the end of the First World War. In the period until 1938 it was unable to make up this ground, alienating large parts of the workforce, usually into nationalist camps, and thereby facilitating the break-up of the country.

The pronounced tendency of Czechs today to glorify the first republic has developed as a response to the experience of Nazi occupation and forty-one years of Stalinism. The first republic signifies independence, democracy and the genuis of Masaryk, but beyond that powerful symbolism the memory of the first republic has few concrete solutions to offer the new Czechoslovakia – although over-sentimental Czechs will argue otherwise at great length. Slovaks were never so enamoured of the first republic. The failure to strengthen the Slovak economy in the inter-war period, together with the colonial attitude of Czech administrators in Slovakia, have meant that Slovaks perceive the inter-war democracy as having been designed to subordinate their interests to Prague, the capital of both Bohemia and the federal state. Since the revolution of 1989 Slovak suspicion of the Czech lands has once again developed into a significant political force, although it has yet to don the cloak of clerico-Fascism that it assumed in the late 1930s.

Czechs and Slovaks are often accused of being supine. Unlike the Poles and Hungarians, it is said, the Czechs and Slovaks have never been prepared to fight for their freedom. Even the lateness of the Czechoslovak revolution in 1989 is sometimes cited as an example of their cowardly attitude – they were prepared to take to the streets in large numbers only once it was clear from events in other socialist countries that the game was up for the communists everywhere. But the argument most frequently heard (it has even been taken to the conclusion that Czechs and Slovaks do not deserve an independent state) rests upon their relatively passive response to the Soviet-led invasion of 1968 and, even more important, their capitulation after Chamberlain and Daladier betrayed Czechoslovakia at their meeting with Hitler and Mussolini in Munich on 29 September 1938. The Munich agreement accepted the German demand for the annexation of the Sudetenland, where most of the Czechoslovak Germans lived. Its implementation would have led immediately to the end of the republic. The Czechoslovak government's initial response to Munich was to order the mobilization of the army; a broad popular political coalition, including the communists on the left and the radical Czech National Democracy on the right, had agreed to fight. In the end the government and President Eduard Beneš, who had succeeded Masaryk in the office in 1935, decided to capitulate. It was a difficult decision and one clearly influenced by the fact that Czechoslovakia had been deserted by all its allies. (In addition, both Poland and Hungary had taken advantage of German pressure on Czechoslovakia to make their own territorial demands.) The likelihood of a Czechoslovak victory was negligible; but had the country fought and not won, this would certainly have led to enormous loss of life, given that Hitler's plan for Czechoslovakia was to Germanize Czechs with the requisite racial characteristics and expel the rest.

If a criticism can be levelled at the Czechs and Slovaks, it should be directed at the weakness of the resistance during the war and the absolute passivity of most of the population. Historically an independent Czechoslovakia has been able to survive only if its two powerful neighbours, Germany to the West and Russia to the East, have allowed it to. The close cooperation between Czechoslovakia and Poland on issues of European security since the revolutions is a significant reflection of this reality. Such cooperation is likely to continue well beyond the construction of a new European security system.

The desire for change after the war was fuelled by the utopian vision of the CPCz and the depressing but clear memory of the pre-war collapse of Czechoslovakia. On reflection, people observed a confluence of the political betrayal at Munich and the interests of foreign capital. Czechoslovakia's existence, it seemed to them, had been dependent upon the fickle ambitions of profit-hungry Westerners. In addition, towards the end of the war the communist resistance movement in Czechoslovakia had achieved several important victories, while the Red Army had liberated the country. Post-war Czechoslovakia corresponded more closely than any other country in history to Marx's vision in which a mature proletariat would articulate its considered hostility to capitalism. In the last free elections, held in 1946, before the communist *coup* of February 1948 the CPCz won 38 per cent of the vote country-wide. In Bohemia and Moravia this figure even reached 40 per cent. In relation to the size of the population, the CPCz was the largest and most influential Communist Party outside the Soviet Union. Its electoral victory afforded its tacticians considerable advantages when Stalin decided, in the middle of 1947, that it was time to consider the subversion of Czechoslovak democracy, which was duly executed in the Prague *coup* of February 1948.

When, in his New Year's speech of 1990, President Václav Havel accused Czechs and Slovaks of bearing considerable responsibility for the forty years of communist rule in Czechoslovakia, he was referring in one sense to the election of 1946 and the militant enthusiasm with which the *coup* of 1948 was greeted. At the time, it must be remembered, the programme and organization of the CPCz was infinitely more persuasive than those of the opposition. In addition, until the middle of 1947 the CPCz appeared keen to pursue a 'national' road to socialism, which implied a certain independence from the Soviet Communist Party. Leaders of the CPCz were upbraided by their Stalinist counterparts for apparently deviating from the common path. After the communist take-over, however, the CPCz quickly developed into a model Stalinist monster, and the forty-year existence of 'Absurdistan', as Jiří Dienstbier has called it, began.

The Burden of Normalization

The healthier inter-war traditions of Czechoslovakia re-emerged during the Prague Spring of 1968. This development suggested that Czechoslovakia was deserving of its reputation as the most politically sophisticated country in Eastern Europe. The liberalization under First Secretary Alexander Dubček offered hope to anti-Stalinist socialists around the world, as the declared aim of the reformers was the creation of a 'third way', a market socialism that encompassed political pluralism. For well over a decade the concept of the 'third way' enlivened the debate on East Europe's future, but for Czechoslovakia the optimism was short-lived. Soviet tanks put a stop to it. The invasion was followed by one of the most crushingly tedious and spiteful forms of Stalinism to have emerged in Eastern Europe – normalization. A small group of Czechs and Slovaks, led by Gustáv Husák and ably supported by the appalling trio Vasil Bil'ak, Alois Indra and Miloš Jakeš, offered convincing proof that Czechoslovakia could still call on the tradition of petty dictatorship.

The destruction wrought by the normalizers over twenty years was impressive. Indeed, it was striking that immediately after the revolution of 1989 the situation in the country was referred to, by a broad spectrum of public figures, as one of 'moral, political, ecological and economic devastation'. Within weeks of the revolution Czechs and Slovaks used the word 'devastation' to express both its original meaning and a novel one – 'the situation in which we find ourselves'. While the CPCz had spent four decades busily trying to persuade Czechs and Slovaks that they were heading steadily towards a communist utopia, the

Czechoslovak economy was marching with equal resolution backwards from tenth position in the world to around fortieth. According to some individual indicators, the jewel in the socialist community's crown now lies behind Nepal and Sri Lanka.

The moral devastation of which Czechs and Slovaks speak includes the development of obedience towards authority and the readiness to execute any task, however absurd, provided it has been requested by a superior. In this way the 'normalizers' were able to build upon the Habsburgian traditions of Czechoslovakia. It is interesting to note that the stamps, the language, the procedures and other instruments of bureaucracy in Czechoslovakia are identical to those that administer Austria and Hungary, betraying their common political heritage. Although German-speaking and Jewish, Kafka's grotesque visions were inspired by Habsburgian Prague. The primary function of the most abiding figure of twentieth-century Czech literature, Švejk, was to mock the Habsburg military bureaucracy.

Given the deeply rooted petty-bourgeois traditions of many Czechs and, increasingly, Slovaks, the normalization of the country after 1968 proved relatively easy. After the Soviet Union had applied a big, powerful stick in the shape of 200,000 troops, the Czechoslovak communists who took control after the invasion dangled a moderately appetizing carrot from which people could take bites by exerting a minimum of effort. This was the deal of normalization during the 1970s – Czechs and Slovaks were offered one of the highest living standards in Eastern Europe, and in return they renounced political activity. Unfortunately the carrot was placed so close to the donkey's jaws that in the meanwhile the beast has forgotten how to walk. As a result, the once proud Czechoslovak economy will now have difficulty competing with Western markets, although the country does not labour under the burden of a foreign debt to the extent that Poland or Hungary does.

None the less, Czechoslovakia will need generous friends. It is heavily dependent on imported raw materials, and its dependence will grow. The country's energy supply is frighteningly dependent on indigenous brown coal stocks, which have a low calorific value and therefore produce large amounts of the pollutant sulphur dioxide. Sixty per cent of all electricity in Czechoslovakia is produced by about six main power stations in the black belt of northern Bohemia, which stretches 60 kilometres from Chomutov in the west to Ustí nad labem and Litoměřice in the east. With a population of 15 million, Czechoslovakia annually pumps out an astonishing 18 tonnes of sulphur dioxide per square kilometre (the principal cause of acid rain). This is twice as much SO_2 as West Germany produces with a population of 60 million. Almost three-quarters of these emissions come from the chimneys of northern Bohemia. Nowhere beats northern Bohemia in scope, but Prague, northern Moravia, western Bohemia, Bratislava and eastern Slovakia were all officially characterized in the final years of communist rule as 'ecological disaster zones'. The long-term consequences of industrial pollution in Czechoslovakia are unknown, but the short-term effects have already proved quite catastrophic. Over 30 per cent of the country's forest stocks, one of the economy's bedrocks, has been irreparably damaged. Another 50 per cent is suffering from partial damage. The population's health has been badly affected by pollution and poor dietary habits. The lifespan of Czechs and Slovaks has been steadily decreasing in recent years, and for males it is now three to five years lower than in neighbouring countries. In northern Bohemia life expectancy is three to four years lower than elsewhere in the country; infant mortality is estimated to be at least 12 per cent higher than in other regions; while during the winter the entire area is blackened by smog when a process known as 'temperature inversion' occurs. All the fumes and smoke from the area become locked over the entire 60-kilometre stretch by hot air.

These areas are the power house of Czechoslovak industry upon which the country's relative affluence is built. All political forces in the country now accept that pollution is one of the most serious problems facing the country. Indeed, almost immediately on taking office after the elections of June 1990 the government announced that, following consultations with the regional authorities in northern Bohemia, some of the power stations would be closed down.

The Soviet Union has already begun to reduce its promised oil exports to all of its former East European allies because of what it claims to be increased domestic demand. Within the first six months of 1990 the Soviet Union cut supplies to Czechoslovakia by one-third, according to the finance minister, Václav Klaus. His immediate response was to throttle consumption by imposing a 50 per cent increase on the price of petrol, which was already the second highest in Europe. Thus Czechoslovakia is now more dependent on buying oil on the open market with money that, until the crown is fully convertible, it simply does not have. After the Iraqi invasion of Kuwait in August 1990, and the subsequent blockade of the two countries the situation became even more critical.

The cut in oil stocks has also encouraged the development of Czechoslovakia's nuclear-power network, a policy that has encountered hostility both at home and abroad, in particular from one of its most important trading neighbours, Austria. Despite criticism the Minister for the Environment, Josef Vavroušek, has indicated that the nuclear programme will have to be maintained, although he stressed that Czechoslovakia, one of Europe's most wasteful countries, must concentrate on saving energy. The Prime Minister, Marián Čalfa, pointed out early in 1990 that Czechoslovakia's energy consumption was 30–50 per cent higher than that of West European countries, whose citizens enjoy a much higher standard of living. Interestingly, some government members and leading supporters of Civic Forum who were implacably opposed to the expansion of nuclear power in the past have now been converted to enthusiastic support of the Soviet-designed VVER stations. Securing a cheap and reliable energy supply, while slashing industrial emissions, is one of Czechoslovakia's most challenging economic problems in the long term.

At the end of 1989 the Czechoslovak debt stood at US$7.9 billion, which, by comparison with Hungary's and Poland's, is an impressively low figure. None the less, that debt is steadily rising, while the price of Czechoslovak exports on the world market is falling. In some heavy engineering products, where traditionally Czechoslovakia has been the leader among the socialist countries, it has been overtaken by Hungary, Poland and even Bulgaria. Over half the Czechoslovak debt could be covered by hard-currency loans and credits made in favour of Syria, Libya, Iraq, Burma, Cuba and Nicaragua. One of the last foreign-policy interventions of the CPCz General Secretary, Miloš Jakeš, was to travel around the Middle East asking in vain for the return of some of the money. But Jakeš was unable to secure its return, and the swift commitment made by President Havel and Czechoslovakia's new government to enforcing trade sanctions against Iraq and Kuwait during the Gulf crisis ensured that the debts would have to be written off for the foreseeable future. At the same time Czechoslovakia has to extract itself from COMECON's 'economic merry-go-round', as it has been described, and to divert exports either to the West or to the developing world. Over two-thirds of the country's foreign trade takes place within the framework of the 'socialist common market', which brings in neither hard currency nor goods of an acceptable quality.

In so far as a coherent economic policy existed during the period of normalization, it guaranteed the short-term maintenance of living standards. During the last ten years of communist rule, however, real wages in Czechoslovakia registered a steady decline, graphically illustrated by the number of hours Czechoslovaks had to work in order to be able to afford certain consumer items as compared with their counterparts in West Germany. For everyday groceries they had to work 2.5 as many hours; for a colour television 9–14 times as many; for a hi-fi system 33–40 times as many; and for a simple pocket calculator 65 times as many! (Not forgetting, of course, that the quality of goods bought by the Czech or Slovak is incomparably worse than the equivalent purchased by the West German.) Despite this gloomy state of affairs, Czechoslovaks were never afflicted by the dramatic fluctuations and collapse of wages that affected the Polish, Hungarian or Romanian workforces. This partly explains why Czechoslovakia was one of the last countries to mount a revolution. Now the chronic exploitation of resources undertaken to ensure stability will create enormous difficulties as the new government tries to resuscitate this sickly economic entity. The technology of production in Czechoslovakia is between five and fifteen years out of date compared with the West, while plant and machinery is on average between five and seven years older than elsewhere in the industrially developed world.

Despite its seductive external appearance, the revolutionaries in Czechoslovakia have inherited a weak and tatty economic mechanism. They also have a workforce that was more pampered than any other in Eastern Europe except that of East Germany during the period of communist rule. Although these people are prepared to make sacrifices, their patience is not without its limits, as the tense debate about the new economic policy suggests.

The Devil and the Deep Blue Sea: Economic Strategy

By the time Marián Čalfa had announced his government's programme to parliament in Prague on 3 July 1990, the so-called Balcerowicz plan in Poland was running into serious social and political difficulties. Despite substantial good will towards Prime Minister Tadeusz Mazowiecki, the uncompromising austerity programme named after the Finance Minister, Leszek Balcerowicz, but in reality conceived by the IMF was beginning to test the patience of many Polish workers to the limit. The programme of the Čalfa government included a provision, unique in Eastern Europe, that guaranteed both a minimum standard of living for all Czechoslovak citizens and, in addition, a legal minimum wage for all those in employment. Indeed, Čalfa outlined substantial welfare provisions and a number of major projects aimed at protecting the environment. It is increasingly clear that not only does the maintenance of a considerable social security network enjoy the support of President Havel but the overall philosophy probably stems from his office. In his keynote speech just prior to Čalfa's announcement of the government programme the president was at pains to express his determination to protect the population from the predicted effects of economic transformation: 'Our economists must accept our oft declared commitment to introduce reform so that it does not result in great social shocks, rapid inflation or even the loss of basic social security. In this regard "It won't work" is not an acceptable answer.' President Havel, whose influence in government and among the population is paramount, has made it clear that Czechoslovakia will not be a playground for liberal economists.

Indeed, the new economic mechanisms that the government has said should be completed in 1991 are relatively modest – the internal convertibility of the crown, a thorough price reform and the first moves towards denationalization and privatization. During the parliamentary discussion on the government programme several MPs made the point that, for a government committed to a radical transformation of the economy, its programme is disturbingly vague. Both the Finance Minister, Václav Klaus, and Vladimír Dlouhý, in charge of the newly formed Economic Ministry, have explained that it will take them time to formulate their concrete policies ready for parliamentary discussion. Klaus and Dlouhý are both unhappy with the cautious moves towards reform associated with Havel and, by extension, Prime Minister Čalfa. Despite the deep differences in government, most cabinet members recognize that Klaus's position as Finance Minister is of great importance in stimulating Western confidence in Czechoslovak economic policy. There was a move to ease Klaus out of the government (it is rumoured that this was engineered by the president's office) and name him head of the state bank instead, but the minister resisted this.

The struggle between the liberal economists and the liberal intellectuals in the government will be a major factor in determining what type of society Czechoslovakia develops into. There is a strong traditional commitment among working people to a degree of egalitarianism, most frequently articulated in their support for 'the Swedish model'. Already independent trade-union organizations are putting down strong roots, and the prime minister has been keen to point out that the government wants to work closely with the unions. Indeed, initial economic decisions will be taken only after extensive discussions with representatives of management and unions, a strategy that in Austria has, since the war, crystallized into an entire system of corporate economic management. This corporatist state, which is substantially different from most West European models, holds many attractions for the uncertain democracies in Eastern Europe. As far as can be ascertained, Western policy advisers see in it a threat to the interests of capitalism. Those in Czechoslovakia, like Václav Klaus, who wish to see a relatively pure capitalist model introduced quickly will find it difficult to argue their case, given the caution of their colleagues in government. But if overall economic performance continues to decline as the next elections approach in 1992, their hand will be strengthened.

As Czechoslovaks began to appreciate the extent of their country's economic decay in early 1990, a serious conflict arose that will remain the central political issue in the country for some time to come. At its heart lie the nature of the Czechoslovak state and relations between the two major national groups, Czechs and Slovaks. It is a complex and often opaque problem that is largely ignored not only by the West but also by many Czechs. By the summer of 1990 the national question had begun to call in question the very existence of a federated Czechoslovak state.

Czecho-Slovakia: Hyphen Warfare – the Nationalist Threat

One of the deepest wounds of the Stalinist 1950s that provoked the growth of reformist tendencies within the CPCz a decade later was the Slovak question, as it was called. Among the victims of the internecine trials in the early 1950s were a group of Slovak communists led by the widely respected former foreign minister, Vladimír Clementis, and including Gustáv Husák, that was condemned for the crime of bourgeois nationalism. This was the most dramatic expression of what Slovaks considered the chronic centralization of the state after 1948, during which Prague administered all political and economic affairs, including the budget for Slovakia. Resentment at the arrogant attitude of the Czech comrades surfaced among Slovak communists in the mid-sixties. Alexander Dubček, the leader of the Prague Spring, became noticed in the Communist Party's Central Committee in the mid-1960s not for his outspoken liberalism but for his resolute defence of Slovak interests. Following the Soviet invasion Dubček, who was the first Slovak to lead the CPCz, was replaced by another, Gustáv Husák.

When Husák came to power many believed that, because he had been wrongly imprisoned during the 1950s, he would attempt to salvage what he could from Dubček's reform programme while simultaneously placating the angry Soviet communists. In fact, the only item implemented by Husák and his neo-Stalinist colleagues was the federalization of Czechoslovakia. This led to the creation of a Slovak government with its seat in Bratislava and, on paper, wide-ranging powers of autonomy that were never realized to their full extent. Instead Husák's 'solution' to the national question merely led to greater mutual resentment between Czechs and Slovaks. The former believed that Husák was syphoning off large amounts of investment from the Czech lands to his friends in Slovakia, while the Slovaks continued to perceive themselves as second-class citizens because their republican government in Bratislava was nothing more than an impotent symbol. Because of state repression and the triumphalist rhetoric of the regime, tension between Czechs and Slovaks was only ever expressed obliquely in public.

None the less, mutual suspicion has been the most pernicious sore to fester under the repressive dressing of the last two decades. Relations between the two peoples under normalization were complicated. Czechs, who generally live in Bohemia and Moravia, outnumber the inhabitants of Slovakia by about two to one. The two peoples are very closely related. They speak separate languages, but these are mutually comprehensible without the slightest difficulty, although older Czechs in particular will occasionally scoff at Slovak ('that foreign language'), which is used as frequently as Czech on television in Bohemia and Moravia. Broadly, the Czech tradition has been most strongly informed by secular thinking and the achievements of the industrial revolution, while Slovakia is one of the strongholds of political Catholicism in Eastern Europe and still a predominantly agrarian society. The most committed believer in the idea of a single Czechoslovak nation was Masaryk. Despite his efforts to unite Czechs and Slovaks, the new nation never emerged, but the two peoples have gained greatly from their cooperation in both the first republic and the post-war socialist republic. Unfortunately deep, lingering resentments were strengthened during the period of communist rule and these have found ample expression in some of the new parties to have emerged since the revolution.

The curious relationship between Czechs and Slovaks within the state and Communist Party apparatuses found a strange mirror image in the uncertain ties binding the two people's opposition movements. Charter 77 was in essence a Czech affair. Some of its key signatories, notably Milan Šimečka, a Czech living in the Slovak capital, Bratislava, and Miroslav Kusý, a Slovak historian, ensured that there was contact with Slovakia. Significantly, Jan Čarnogurský, the most important Slovak dissident in the period leading up to the revolution, did not sign the Charter, although he maintained close contacts with many leading Chartists. Trained as a lawyer, Čarnogurský comes from a family of Slovak nationalists. A devout Catholic, he was one of the intellectually most gifted dissidents, while his moral authority in Slovakia was tremendous. Like many Slovaks, he found channels other than Charter 77 to express dissent. For many discontented Slovaks the most important of these was religion. An underground Church has existed for a long time in Slovakia, and some of the annual pilgrimages, notably to the shrine at Levoča, could attract over half a million of the Slovak faithful. Slovaks felt that Charter 77 was another manifestation of the cultural and political dominance of Czechs. The weighty issues addressed by the Chartists in Prague and Brno were of little value to the Slovak peasant. It must be remembered that throughout the twentieth century Czechs have treated Slovak culture and language as secondary and inferior to their own and other European cultures. As a result – and this has undoubtedly been true within Chartist circles as well – they have never considered Czech–Slovak relations as a problem. If Slovaks wanted to join in, the Czechs believed, all they had to do was sign the Charter.

After the excitement of the revolution, suppressed tension between Czechs and Slovaks began to impose itself on political life. After being elected president in July 1990 for a two-year term Václav Havel said that his most important task would be to oversee the promulgation of three constitutions, one for the ČSFR, one for the Czech republic and one for the Slovak republic. The essential difficulty confronting parliament lies in determining the degree of autonomy to be enjoyed by Slovakia. But although on a number of issues the governments of the Czech and Slovak republics are at odds, they both wish to see granted to the republics extensive economic and even diplomatic powers that would emasculate the role of the federation. In the Czech republic the surprise electoral victory of the Moravian/Silesian nationalist movement (HDS) in the elections highlighted the discrimination widely felt by Moravians, who are Czech speakers. The HDS is a force powerful enough to ensure that the prime minister of the Czech republic, Petr Pithard, will have to satisfy some of the programmatic demands if he is to prevent Moravians from propelling the right to self-determination towards one of its more absurd conclusions. In order to pacify the separatist forces represented in the Czech parliament, the government of the Czech republic has not given the federal authorities all the support that they might wish.

Despite the considerable tension that existed between Czechs and Slovaks after the revolution, one of the most striking results of the elections of June 1990 was the victory in Slovakia of Public Against Violence (VPN), which has a clear 'Czechoslovak' orientation. Jan Čarnogurský's Christian Democratic Movement (KDH) did worse than expected, coming second, and he decided to remain in Bratislava to lick his political wounds as Slovak deputy prime minister instead of taking up Václav Havel's offer of joining Marián Čalfa's federal cabinet in Prague. None the less Čarnogurský's party, the KDH, did agree at least to participate in it after a long period of hesitation.

Although VPN beat the KDH into second place, the extreme nationalist Slovak National Party (SNS) did well, gathering 13 per cent of the votes overall and, in some areas (especially in areas where many members of the Hungarian minority live), gaining over 20 per cent of the vote. The SNS's programme is unashamedly separatist and clearly hostile to the 700,000-strong Hungarian minority. In public Čarnogurský's supports the federation with the Czechs. Many Czechs and Slovaks, however, are of the opinion that Čarnogurský is working towards a separate Slovak state. Just as Czechs will have a better idea about how the new political spectrum is developing at the next elections in 1992, so will Slovaks. And many believe that the VPN will split for the same reasons as Civic Forum did. If the Slovaks want to attempt to leave the federation, then this will happen after the elections. Much depends on how the issue is treated by Čarnogurský's KDH.

Slovak separatism presents a very real threat to the CSFR as it is presently constituted. Within the range of nationalist enmity in Eastern Europe the conflict between Czechs and Slovaks appears mild, never having degenerated into violence. But the Czechs' dismissal of Slovak national sentiment has often been unwisely insensitive. Czechs also consider the aim of an independent Slovakia to be a manifestation of small-minded nationalism, inappropriate at a time when small European countries should be moving towards the greater whole. In economic terms the Czechs undoubtedly have a strong case. Occasionally they find it hard to avoid using patronizing language. Slovaks have accused many Czechs, including two rather influential ones, the author Ludvík Vaculík and President Havel's press secretary, Michal Žantovský, of making anti-Slovak remarks in public since the revolution, and both have contributed to a radicalization of Slovak intellectuals. In both cases it has been interesting to note just how sensitively Slovaks have reacted. Resentment at Czech arrogance is a significant social force.

The Slovak nationalists respond to the argument that separatism has no economic future, rather as the Croats in Yugoslavia would. They would like to see an independent Slovakia join in a Europe of regions. They also believe they can succeed by encouraging investment and soliciting economic help from the reservoir of Slovak emigration while maintaining close trading links with Austria, the Soviet Union and, indeed, the Czech lands. This economic programme is unrealistic, not to say slightly absurd, but it would be wrong to underestimate the political potential of Slovak nationalism.

Zdeněk Jičinský, a reform communist in 1968 and later a Charter 77 signatory, is the man charged with co-ordinating the creation of the federal constitution. Jičinský maintains that

during work on the new Czechoslovak federal constitution it will be necessary to solve the dilemma . . . Local political representatives believe the political focus should be the [two] republics, which would then decide with what powers the federation should be entrusted. But at the moment Czechoslovakia, if it wishes successfully to attach itself to the processes of European integration, must do so as a whole, as a relatively strong state . . . So far some of the provisional proposals for a new constitutional order do not respect this and are oriented more towards a confederation.

Jičinský treats the subject delicately because he understands well that the issue of republican powers is an explosive one, especially in Slovakia, which, if roughly handled, could provoke the rapid growth of what is already a significant separatist movement.

The debate exploded in the summer of 1990, setting a tough agenda of struggle for those forces that wish to maintain a federation. At a secretive meeting between representatives of the Czech and Slovak republican governments and the federal government the Slovak prime minister, Vladimír Mečiar, who belongs to VPN, demanded that all key economic ministries be devolved from the federal to the republican level. This would effectively have rendered central government redundant, divorcing the overall economic strategy from the needs of the federation as a whole. The dispute was seized upon by an increasingly confident front of Slovak nationalist organizations, led by the Slovak National Party, which used it to advertise their demand for a separate Slovak state – daily a more realistic prospect. The dispute highlighted just how ignorant the Czechs and Slovaks are of each other's cultural and political aspirations, and the presses of both republics became the mouthpieces for bitter campaigns of mutual recrimination.

A by-product of the debate about federalization and the Czech–Slovak relationship has been the minorities question. The vote of the radical SNS was highest in those areas where the Hungarian minority in Slovakia is most populous, and political activity among the minority is frequently regarded as a preface to territorial claims – which, of course, none of the Hungarian groups operating in Slovakia makes. While Slovaks can produce ample historical evidence of overweening behaviour by Czechs, claims for statehood and integral Slovak borders are based on much less certain propositions. The only Slovak state to exist was a puppet construction led by Dr Josef Tiso whose borders, which did not include a number of important areas now part of Czechoslovakia, were guaranteed by Nazi Germany. A group of Slovaks caused consternation and upset in July 1990, when they unveiled a commemorative plaque to Tiso in the town of Bánovce nad bebravou. Apart from this dubious legacy, the only document outlining Slovakia's borders is the treaty of Trianon, one of the post-First World War settlements signed in 1920 and still regarded today by an overwhelming majority of Hungarians as a treacherous agreement. If, within their political struggle aimed at achieving equality with Czechs, the Slovaks pressurize the Hungarian minority in the area, they will be in danger of galvanizing the Hungarian nationalist movement across the border that still regards southern Slovakia, the *Felvidék*, or Uplands, as an integral part of Hungary.

The Roma community in Czechoslovakia is much more exposed than the Hungarians, having no 'mother country' to look after its interests. The racist response of Czechs in particular to the Romanies was typified by an article in the new tabloid newspaper *Expres*, headlined 'Population explosion of the Romanies'. The piece contended that, according to current statistics, there would be 6 million Romanies in a hundred years' time and only half the number of Czechs. This would lead, it continued, to the renaming of the Czech Republic the 'Romany Republic'. It might be easier to dismiss the growth of this tin-pot racism if it were not also accompanied by regular incidents of Czech skinheads attacking Romanies and other foreigners. The violence that has cast a disturbing shadow over post-revolutionary Czechoslovakia is an important reminder that this society does not merely comprise thoughtful intellectuals and jolly, beer-swilling workers. The tensest situation of all is in Moravia, where there have been armed clashes between Vietnamese *Gastarbeiter* and local Moravians. Some of these have been provoked by the Vietnamese, but the emergence of violent racist propaganda among some of the Moravian separatist groups is a frightening phenomenon. The Czechoslovak Foreign Ministry is negotiating the return of the great majority of the 70,000 Vietnamese workers in the country. As the reality of economic reform begins to bite in Czechoslovakia, asylum-seekers and other less well-off foreigners will provide a rigorous test for the tolerance of the 'velvet revolutionaries'.

The Havel Factor

The realization that Czechoslovakia was making the transition from being a big fish in a small pond to being a sickly, adolescent trout in a hatchery coincided with some rapid political developments before the elections of June 1990. These continue to exert a significant influence after the landslide victory of Civic Forum and Public Against Violence. During and after the revolution Václav Havel was still protesting that he was a writer and not a politician. As calls for his election to the presidency became louder, he reiterated that he did not want the job, but if it was in the interests of Czechoslovakia, he would assume it for a limited period of time.

When Havel first accepted office he said, quite justifiably, that he would stay only until free elections had successfully been held. He would then have to reconsider his position. Immediately on taking up office, however, it became clear that he intended to take the Czechoslovak body politic by the scruff of the neck. He travelled extensively abroad. Among other foreign trips he went to both Germanies, the Soviet Union, France and the United Kingdom, and he made a triumphal visit to the United States. Together with his trusted associate from Charter 77, the new Foreign Minister Jiří Dienstbier, Havel began to make his mark on foreign policy. The conclusions to the long debates within Charter and between Charter and its allies and critics in the West could now be put into practice. Havel's commitment to a bloc-free Europe whose security should be guaranteed by a new set of permanent institutions has been an important contribution to the discussion about Europe's future, even if it has not been always welcome to some participants, most noticeably the United States and the United Kingdom.

Despite his devastating schedule, Havel was similarly determined to play a crucial role in domestic policy. He was prepared to speak his mind about any issue. His comments themselves carry considerable political significance, and his opponents claimed that by publicly supporting Civic Forum and Public Against Violence during the election campaign he was giving them an unfair boost. Havel responded to this by pointing out that neither President Mitterrand nor President Bush attempted to conceal their political affiliation. Of course, Havel could have cited the West German President, Richard von Weizsäcker, whose background in Chancellor Kohl's CDU plays no role in his work, but he didn't. Instead he chose to indicate that the Czechoslovak presidency would be one with an executive function. But he has contradicted himself on this issue by saying that Czechoslovakia does not have a tradition of an executive presidency and that when the new constitution is drawn up his presidential powers should be defined by it. Zdeněk Jičinský, writing in June 1990, pointed out:

at the present time the actual role and weight of the personality of the president goes beyond how the constitution perceives them. If a parliamentary republic is preserved, it will be necessary to renew the relations between parliament, the president and the government regarding the division of labour, which in the present constitution is oversimplified.

It is striking that Jičinský even mentions the possibility that a parliamentary republic may not be preserved. However, it is most likely that the new constitution will define the president's role as, first and foremost, symbolic. Despite this, President Havel appears determined to influence everyday politics in Czechoslovakia, and he has fashioned his office accordingly. One of the most important political conflicts in Czechoslovakia as it struggles to regain democracy and economic respectability will be precisely the triangular relationship between Havel's castle or *Hrad*, the cabinet and parliament. At the moment Havel's power clearly goes well beyond that of the cabinet and parliament. Soon after the elections he announced a reorganization of the presidential office. Eight policy-making councils would be created, each headed by a secretary. Havel stressed that these would not function as a shadow cabinet. He is probably right but only inasmuch as the *Hrad* has greater ambitions than merely to play the role of an opposition cabinet. The *Hrad* has two ways of influencing government policy; in both cases Havel is the key. First, a number of cabinet ministers, including the Prime Minister, Marián Čalfa, are unswervingly loyal supporters of Havel. A crucial ally of Havel in the cabinet is the Deputy Prime Minister in charge of the economy, Václav Valeš. He will play the foil to the only man capable of mounting political opposition to Havel, the Finance Minister, Václav Klaus. The latter is a supporter of a more radical road to a market economy than is Havel.

Apart from having very direct lines into the government, the president has a controlling interest in Civic Forum, the movement that he co-founded on 19 November 1989. Civic Forum and its Slovak sister organization, VPN, have resisted the temptation to transform themselves into political parties. They are broad churches indeed. In theory, Civic Forum is controlled by a council elected by a pyramid of democratic bodies known as assemblies. In fact, the decisive policy-making bodies within Civic Forum lie outside this structure. The first is known as the Circle, an informal discussion body that includes the top Civic Forum activists, some of Havel's old friends from Charter and, of course, the president himself. The Circle is a loose formation to which people can be co-opted or asked to make specific contributions. It is essentially a consultative body. Above this stands the Inner Circle, which includes Havel and three or four other leading activists. This was the undemocratic brain of Civic Forum until right-wingers scored a significant victory when Finance Minister Václav Klaus was democratically elected Civic Forum's chairman in October 1990.

Havel's influence has on the whole benefited the country. He is well aware of the most sensitive issues confronting Czechoslovakia and displays an uncanny ability to anticipate them and deal with them before they become political problems. However, the cult which has emerged around him, whether of his making or not, is distasteful. The Czechoslovak media follow his itinerary with pointless precision, while leading politicians like nothing better than to be photographed with him. The obsequiousness towards him that is displayed by parts of the Czechoslovak press is depressing in a country where so many fine writers were gagged until recently.

Havel has one characteristic that, in politics, is an Achilles heel – the loyalty he shows to friends. On occasions Havel's position has almost been compromised because of his belief in those whom he trusts as friends. He now has a large and powerful entourage surrounding him at the castle. Despite his insistence that he does not wish to remain president and would prefer to write, Havel has shown himself to be an enormously intelligent politician who appears to be more comfortable wielding power than he himself has suggested. The key question is whether, after he has guided the country's democracy through the foetal stage, Havel will give up the office of the president or succumb to the taste of power.

The Rise and Fall of Civic Forum

Despite the considerable influence that Havel enjoys in Civic Forum, most of the organization's supporters believe that its days are numbered. Its main historical function was to overthrow communism and to guide the country towards a functioning multi-party democracy. As a revolutionary organization it was simultaneously a mass movement and a tightly welded vanguard, directing events. The movement stayed together to stand at the elections in June 1990 in order to fulfil the second part of its historical role, the establishment of a stable democracy, which is also the task which Havel has set himself. But Civic Forum is doomed. It includes politicians as far to the left as the Trotskyist Petr Uhl, while on the other hand it boasts men like Pavel Bratinka, a committed supporter of the English conservative philosopher Roger Scruton. The tensions caused by this political Babylon are already evident, and many leading supporters predict the breakup of the parliamentary caucus of Civic Forum in the near future.

The constituent elements of Civic Forum are likely to crystallize around some novel form of social democracy, while others will be drawn to the existing Christian democrat movements. As is the case elsewhere in Eastern Europe, social democracy, once a powerful movement in Czechoslovakia, is faced with a major problem as it tries to revive. The majority of Civic Forum activists, including Havel himself, together probably with most of its supporters, believe that the transformation to a market economy must be balanced by the maintenance and, in certain areas, the expansion of the country's social security network. In many respects their programme is close to Western social democracy, but nobody has yet had the courage or the ability to organize an explicitly social-democratic programme. When Civic Forum collapses, one of its rumps may finally be forced to undertake this task.

The biggest political loser in Czechoslovakia since the revolution has been Christian democracy. Together with the other 'major political forces', as they are called, the Christian democrats agreed to limit those parties represented in parliament by erecting a 5 per cent hurdle that has to be crossed before seats are allotted. This measure was to prevent a repeat of the situation in the first republic when all Czechoslovak governments were composed of huge coalitions that included all sorts of tiny parties. Now only five main groupings are represented in parliament. Before the elections many predicted that the Christian democrats would run neck and neck with Civic Forum, largely because of the enormous support that they were presumed to enjoy in Slovakia. But, apart from being obliterated by Civic Forum in the Czech lands, nation-wide the Christian democrats were beaten into third place by the CPCz, the one Communist Party in post-revolutionary Eastern Europe that has defiantly refused to dilute its name. The CPCz scored a consistent 13 per cent in almost every region of the country, showing that it still enjoys a firm constituency. The main problem for the CPCz in the next few years will be sustaining that support, given that the great majority of communist voters in the elections were over fifty years old.

That Civic Forum, with its conciliatory rhetoric, came first and the Communist Party, with its unbending commitment to social welfare, second points to an important factor in Czechoslovak politics: people are wary of what the future may bring and, in addition, they are clearly scared of the two main evils associated with the transformation to a market economy – inflation and unemployment. Already a strong independent trade-union movement is emerging in the Czech lands, in particular in northern Moravia, northern Bohemia and Prague. While the more desirable industrial plants, notably Skoda in Plzeň and the vehicle factory in Mladá Boleslav, have managed to attract a large number of weighty Western companies, some of the state conglomerates central to the Czechoslovak economy have not, and workers in these areas appear ready to fight for their jobs. The post-war model to which Czechs have always been most attached is Sweden, which illuminates the mood and certain traditions of the Czechs and goes a long way to explaining why VPN did so well in Bratislava and Košice, the two most heavily industrialized areas of Slovakia.

Civic Forum may disintegrate happy in the knowledge that a democracy has been established, but President Havel will not disappear in a puff of smoke unless he decides to. The current parliament has a mandate until 1992, as do most East European governments. Following the next elections parliament will once again elect the president. Havel has said that he does not want to remain in the office for ever. For the foreseeable future, however, it is unlikely that any major policy decisions will be implemented unless they have the approval of the playwright whose personal story would appear too far-fetched even for one of his own plays.

Czechoslovakia clearly enjoys a stability and an economic potential that the other East European countries can only envy. But it is easy to be seduced by the beautiful capital Prague, by the legendary Czech humour, by the wonderful skiing slopes in the Tatra mountains and by the country's dazzling new president who, for many, incorporates the absurd contradictions of Central Europe. Czechoslovakia has been shaken and shattered by neo-Stalinism as much as any other country in the area. There is no guarantee of a complete recovery, and in no circumstances could it be painless.

2 POLAND

The History Men

Throughout Eastern Europe history has claimed a much more substantial role for itself in daily politics than it could elsewhere in the industrialized world. In their short lives the existence of East European nation states has been threatened with forces far greater than any aiming to undermine Western countries. Hitler never claimed that he wanted to destroy the people and culture of Britain and France, but he was frank about his intentions east of the Elbe. He wanted first to subjugate and later to eradicate the Slavic sub-races. He addressed the Polish question with special verve – he wanted nothing less than the liquidation of the Polish nation. During the two years from 1939, after the signing of the Molotov–Ribbentrop pact between Nazi Germany and the Soviet Union, Stalin also decided that the European order could happily dispense with a sovereign Poland. Within days of its start the Second World War had developed into the ultimate Polish nightmare in which the nation is shredded by both of its hungry and powerful neighbours.

No country in Europe witnessed such a sustained programme of barbarism during the war as Poland. After the bulk of its territory was ravaged by the *Wehrmacht* what remained in the East was swallowed up by the Red Army. The Polish population was decimated: an average of 3,000 citizens lost their lives every day of the war. Six million Poles, roughly half of them Jewish, were slaughtered during the occupation, while Hitler chose Polish territory on which to erect the instruments for his 'final solution of the Jewish question' – the death camps at Oświeçim (Auschwitz), Majdanek and Treblinka.

History is therefore communicated from generation to generation in Poland (and elsewhere in Eastern Europe) as an essential aid to national survival and hence forms an integral part of political dialogue. This often results in rather vulgar historical generalizations that are usually used to underpin nationalist mythology. Some Serb historians, for example, have created the exclusive category of 'historical nation' (to which, of course, the Serbs belong). The 'historical nation' is supposed to have contributed, in an irreplaceable way, to the development and survival of European culture. Similarly many East European nations, including Poland, Hungary, Serbia and Albania, trumpet as their finest hour the time when they stopped the Ottoman Turks from breaking through Europe's eastern borders to overrun Christendom.

Poles are as guilty of such exaggeration as anyone else in Eastern Europe, but they will correctly point to a substantial difference. The Polish kingdom enjoyed a 'golden age' that was long and prosperous. For two centuries after the union of Poland and Lithuania in 1386 the Jagellonian dynasty guided Poland to the status of a great European power that dominated the political landscape of north-eastern Europe. In 1440 the Polish king Ladislaw III accepted the Hungarian offer of its crown, thus laying the foundations for the powerful historical bond between the two nations and extending Polish power to the Black Sea. The memory of this period has meant that, more than any other East European nation, the Poles regard their national struggle as a challenge. Their quest is a return to a state of grace from which they have not fallen but been unfairly removed by their fickle and hostile neighbours.

Never have Poles risen to this challenge better than in the face of apparently overwhelming odds, most notably during the Second World War. Another remarkable example of this was the growth and consolidation of Solidarity in 1980–81. This organization was able to mobilize over half of the adult population in the country despite the extensive apparatus of repression in the hands of the Polish United Workers Party (PUWP), as the communists called themselves. No other East Europeans were capable of mounting a political opposition of such extraordinary sophistication and power, drawing on such diverse social traditions. Although Soviet-backed neo-Stalinism survived for another ten years in Eastern Europe, Solidarity marked the beginning of its end.

Just as Solidarity exposed the extent of discontent with single-party rule in Eastern Europe and the potential of opposition to communism, it was inevitable that Poland should be in the vanguard of those East European countries pushing to break communist power once and for all. Together with Hungary, Poland showed the way to East Germany, Czechoslovakia, Romania and Bulgaria. It was clear, even before the final political struggle that developed in Poland during the spring of 1989, that this was not another attempt to reform and redefine Communist Party power but the beginning of a movement that would abolish it. Once the party had agreed, at the round-table negotiations, to the weird form of power sharing that would give Solidarity a real stake in the political process, all efforts made by embittered party loyalists were more or less doomed to failure.

Resistance of the old guard was especially weak in Poland for two reasons. First, the country was economically a complete failure. Inflation was shooting out of control, while central government was finding it ever more difficult to assert its authority over the large mafias administered by the regional party bosses whose profligacy ran the economy still further into the ground. The złoty was worthless, and some shops had begun to sell their goods for hard currency only or at least for a combination of hard currency and the złoty. Strikes were ripping through the country, and a young, more radical working class was confronting the exhausted authorities with maximalist demands. Secondly, the political experience of Solidarity gave the opposition enormous advantages over the apparatus even if, as an underground organization, it had fragmented considerably. Long before the government had conceded defeat, the Polish press had gone much further in its exploration of *glasnost* than any of its counterparts among the Warsaw Pact allies.

With undisguised pride the Polish opposition became the first to smash the party's control over the state, and by the middle of August 1989 the first government headed by someone not sponsored by the Communist Party since 1947 was being formed. President Wojciech Jaruzelski had entrusted Tadeusz Mazowiecki with the job. He was one of Solidarity's leading lay Catholic intellectuals and editor of the weekly *Tygodnik Solidarność*. The appointment of Mazowiecki set off an avalanche of historical ironies that would smother all Eastern Europe during the following year. As the man who imposed martial law in Poland, President Jaruzelski had been responsible for the arrest and internment of Mazowiecki in December 1981; now he was conferring on him the power to govern. Poland had taken a big leap towards fulfilling its historical quest of regaining its dignity and independence.

But just as Poles appear capable of astonishing acts of selfless heroism when the collective back is against the wall, history has also indicated that when they approach the holy grail of democracy and independence, they are likely to fall prey to a destructive bout of intolerant squabbling. In this century Poles have survived more misfortune than many nations may expect to encounter in a millennium. Although politically the country's prospects have never seemed brighter, many observers express a foreboding about the Poles' ability to establish a social order that will not be threatened by powerful malcontents feeding on the low life that the cesspit of Poland's economy inevitably breeds.

The Looking-glass Democracy

The appointment of Tadeusz Mazowiecki was confirmed by one of the most curious parliaments in European history. Just over a third of the lower house, the *Sejm*, and the entire senate had been elected in a free vote according to the round-table agreement signed in early April 1989. Sixty-five per cent of the *Sejm*, however, had been reserved for communist-backed MPs, and after much tortuous argument Parliament finally elected Wojciech Jaruzelski as state president. In the half-rigged elections of June 1989 Solidarity massacred the Communist Party, winning all of the seats earmarked for open contest and all but one of the Senate seats. Even in those seats where other genuinely independent candidates stood against Solidarity almost all the candidates personally approved by Lech Wałęsa won.

Because the Polish deal was such a pioneering arrangement the negotiators had reserved four years for a full transfer to parliamentary democracy and the final end to any undemocratic claim to power by the Communist Party. Perhaps understandably everybody assumed that the deconstruction of neo-Stalinism in Eastern Europe was something that would have to be carried out, step by step, over a period of time so as to avoid rocking any boats. By the end of 1989, and three revolutions later, it was clear that by dint of its very path-breaking role Poland would be denied general elections for a longer period than anyone else. After the Polish agreement both the Hungarian government and opposition soon made it clear that they were negotiating a timetable for free elections with no strings attached. And once the SED and the CPCz were overthrown in East Germany and Czechoslovakia it was clear that the revolutionaries were not interested in anything except full free elections. Although many Poles envy the other East Europeans who have participated in free and fair elections, the turnout of just over 42 per cent at the local government elections held in late May 1990 suggested that Poles had already developed a profoundly indifferent attitude towards democracy, although the final proof can only be given in general elections. Figures for the participation in the local elections were especially disappointing, as the turnout for the semi-democratic elections of June 1989 had been a paltry 62 per cent. Oppression may create unruly subjects, but it does not necessarily breed responsible or eager democrats.

While the Communist Party was being systematically removed from governments and ministries all over Eastern Europe, in Poland its members were still involved, if not at the very centre of power then certainly close to it. However, the influence of the communists steadily waned after the formation of the Mazowiecki government, which initially enjoyed enormous popular trust, as the Prime Minister made it plain that he would be introducing a programme of reforms that would bury the undemocratic power base of the party.

Mazowiecki had the full backing of Solidarity and its leader, Lech Wałęsa, who, following the formation of the government, claimed that he would be retiring to Gdańsk, where he would concentrate on his work as a trade unionist. By now Solidarity had grown well beyond its original form, and its Citizens Committees, which had been founded during the round-table negotiations, had developed into an embryonic political wing of the movement. These found their clearest political expression in the OKP, the Citizens' Parliamentary Club, which grouped together the Solidarity-backed MPs in parliament.

As Mazowiecki's government programme began to take shape, the political dominance of Solidarity became daily more evident. From afar it looked as though even without general elections the authority of Solidarity and Mazowiecki was so great that it would steer a stable and easy course towards the promised land of the market economy. And indeed attempts by the Communist Party to sabotage it were not co-ordinated. Members of local *nomenklature* were accused of trying to exploit the transition to capitalism by using their position to buy into profitable enterprises, but they were not accused of trying to subvert the process. The power of the regional mafias in Poland, which in certain industrial areas is still a formidable force, is now being confronted by the new municipal and district councils. Following the May 1990 elections, these are now largely controlled by Solidarity members or their sympathizers, who are determined to break the power of the bureaucracy. Paradoxically, although Mazowiecki could not claim the full democratic mandate, there were few East European governments, even after the elections, which commanded so much sympathy as Mazowiecki's.

This was just as well. Soon after coming to power Mazowiecki indicated that the Polish government was not going to dally as it examined the various paths at whose distant end the market economy beckoned. In February 1990 the path had been chosen and named after Mazowiecki's Finance Minister, Leszek Balcerowicz. It was the most drastic economic plan in post-war Europe. In comparison the price rises that had sparked off strikes and riots in 1970 and led to the downfall of Stanisław Gomułka were mild medicines; the price rises that sparked off strikes and sired Solidarity in 1980 and led to the downfall of Edward Gierek were merely cosmetic. The deflationary programme of fiscal recovery embarked on in February 1990 was the most unforgiving ever visited on the Polish working class, but political support for Mazowiecki was so substantial that the government believed it could take the risk.

The Cold Bath

The plan was tied to a $1.5 billion loan granted by the IMF and, in fact, could be more accurately called the IMF plan than the Balcerowicz plan, as the Finance Minister, with his coffers bare, did not have much choice but to accept the conditions imposed by the IMF. The primary aims were, first, to reduce inflation, which in 1989 had shot over 100 per cent and hovered maliciously on the edge of the hyper-inflationary spiral, and, second, to restore confidence in the local currency, the złoty, which by the end of one-party rule was popularly believed to be marginally less valuable than the paper bag.

The main budgetary victims of the Balcerowicz plan were the enormous state subsidies earmarked primarily for food but also for housing, transport and a variety of other social services that the planned economy kept at artificially low prices. Excluding the Soviet Union, these subsidies swallowed more public funds in Poland than anywhere else in Eastern Europe. At one point in the 1970s food subsidies accounted for 40 per cent of the state budget, although by the end of 1989 the figure for all the subsidies had dropped to between 32 and 34 per cent. Combined with these budgetary cuts was the introduction of a new system of progressive taxation that would penalize wage rises, thus breaking the inflationary spiral. It is important to note, however, that these fiscal measures were a first step. Only later would legislation follow that was designed to privatize Poland's industry (90 per cent of which was owned by the state).

The plan appeared to achieve most of its aims within the first six months. In fact, in certain respects the Polish economy was no longer recognizable, so dramatic was the change. Whereas before Poles had surplus cash and nothing to buy with it, now the centre of Warsaw was overflowing with quality Western goods that nobody could afford. What is more, those goods could on the whole be purchased with the revived złoty, which had stabilized around 9,600 for US$1, even pushing the American greenback out of its traditional place as leading currency in Poland. Inflation had been beaten and by July 1990 was only just over 5 per cent, in itself a temporary hiccough as the annual rate was heading for below 3 per cent.

But in other respects the plan had worked too efficiently. The deflationary tactics led to a 20–30 per cent drop in productivity. Once productivity dropped the government was faced with the problem of how to raise it again without resuscitating inflation. Not only did the new tax system militate against the bonus system in the factories but also these were not yet competing according to market rules, as ownership had not passed from state to private hands, and dilatory management was as endemic as ever. With the fall in productivity there was a much more serious collapse of living standards than had originally been predicted. It must be remembered that before the Balcerowicz plan had been implemented, living standards in Poland were among the lowest in Eastern Europe (comparable with those of Bulgaria and the Yugoslav republic of Serbia).

Littered as it was with former Solidarity activists, the government was very much aware that this squeeze of living standards could unsettle the Polish working class. Although it made no sign of changing policy mid-stream, the government, and in particular Tadeusz Mazowiecki, stepped up their efforts to persuade the West to consider cancelling some of Poland's $41 billion debt. This remains the most insurmountable stumbling bloc to the successful convalescence of the Polish economy (if, indeed, such a recovery is possible). In May 1990, while on an official visit to France, Mazowiecki made an appeal to the West to reconsider its refusal to cancel any of Poland's debt, about two-thirds of which is funded not by private banks but by Western governments. Once again the West politely declined to consider Mazowiecki's plea, although by this time there were signs of growing nervousness about Poland's economic difficulties.

The Threat

In the 1950s the PUWP unwittingly created, and then nurtured, what was theoretically its very *raison d'être*: a mighty, educated and politically adept working class. It did this for various reasons but chiefly because Stalin told it to build a great many factories.

The Polish party leadership also used the opportunity to weaken what until then had been Poland's most powerful social group, the peasantry. Instead of providing the party with an impregnable fortress of resolute support, the working class behaved as Marx and Engels had predicted it would under capitalism. In the early 1970s it fired a powerful warning shot across the bows of the ship of state by rising in the Baltic ports to protest against price increases. The blood of dozens, probably hundreds, killed by security forces formed an indelible stain on the memory of the Polish working class, which drew on the experience first in 1976 and above all in 1980.

But by 1990 a process of differentiation had occurred within the Polish working class. Solidarity membership had not recovered and did not show signs of doing so. Whereas at its peak in 1980–81 it could boast 10 million members, after its legalization for the second time in 1989 it rose to only 2 million. In many industrial branches younger workers kept their distance from Solidarity both before and after the Communist Party relinquished power. In addition, despite its appalling reputation, the OPZZ – the official union set up during the martial-law period and led by the widely disliked Alfred Miodowicz – still commanded support among parts of the workforce, particularly because it invariably supported wage demands, a practice that it sustained even more vigorously after the Mazowiecki government had been sworn in.

By May 1990 parts of the working class were losing patience – and not only with falling living standards. At first the unemployment statistics reflected those people who were officially unemployed (including a large number of housewives) but who were now eligible to claim benefit (including, happily, many of the housewives, although it was uncertain how long that particular dispensation would continue). But as economists and politicians started to agree in public that unemployment would probably rise to around the 2 million mark before stabilizing, the workforce began to feel insecure. The result of this uncertainty and the falling living standards was a plethora of strikes, which broke out in various industrial branches although they were restricted mainly to the traditionally militant north of the country.

One strike in particular, led by rail workers in the town of

Słupsk, threatened to bring Poland's vital coal and steel exports to a halt. The Mazowiecki government refused to negotiate with the strikers over their demands (which included one for a wage increase) until they went back to work. The strikers not only refused to do this; in addition they threatened an all-out strike of transport workers around the country, which would have paralysed Poland at a time crucial for the success of the Balcerowicz plan. At the very last minute, and quite unexpectedly, Lech Wałęsa, whose political reputation had begun to look a little jaded, mediated in the dispute for a second time and persuaded the strikers to return to work. He added rather menacingly, however, that if the government were not able to redress the grievances of the strikers, he would lead them into a strike the next time.

The strike was a psychological turning point. The divisions that had been encroaching on Solidarity's unity for a long time spilled out into the open, and the potential instability of Poland's temporary political order was exposed not only to the Polish public but to Western governments as well. The long-term ideological disputes that had been fermenting in Solidarity initially expressed themselves in a rather dramatic personal showdown between Wałęsa and his advisers on the one hand and, on the other, Mazowiecki, the government and leading figures on Solidarity's liberal wing, most prominently Adam Michnik, the editor of the daily, *Gazeta Wyborcza*, which theoretically belonged to Solidarity's media stable. It was soon after this dispute that the Centre Agreement group was formed among Wałęsa's supporters in the OKP. Before long they had demanded the resignation of President Jaruzelski and the holding of nationwide presidential elections —their candidate was, of course, Lech Wałęsa. Just as Havel in Czechoslovakia had professed his unwillingness to take on the burdensome office of president in Czechoslovakia, so Wałęsa said he had no desire to take on the office in Poland.

The Wałęsa Factor

Lech Wałęsa is a remarkably skilful politician who is able to make blunders, then shrug them off before preparing another offensive. When the government of Mazowiecki's predecessor, General Czesław Kiszczak, lost the confidence of the *Sejm* it dawned on Poles that Solidarity would choose the next prime minister. The first name to be raised high was that of Wałęsa. He coyly refused and instead played the role of kingmaker, bullying, cajoling and negotiating with a variety of characters, including Jaruzelski, the party leader Mieczysław Rakowski, Cardinal Józef Glemp and, through the media, Mikhail Gorbachev. Two Solidarity activists, Mazowiecki and the well-respected Professor Bronisław Geremek, were put forward as candidates. Geremek was the favourite of Solidarity's liberal wing and at the time Mazowiecki appeared closer to Wałęsa. Later Wałęsa's advisers strongly denied that the Solidarity chairman had agreed to drop Geremek's candidacy at the request of Cardinal Glemp on the grounds that the professor was Jewish. None the less Mazowiecki was clearly acceptable to the Church, and initially many believed that Wałęsa would be able to manipulate him with ease. As Mazowiecki's close friends had warned, this assumption was erroneous. It soon became clear that Mazowiecki had no intention of being Wałęsa's lapdog. Following the strike of the Słupsk railway workers, Wałęsa and Mazowiecki fell out in a quite public fashion. It was at this point that Wałęsa revealed his intention to fight for the presidency. After some soul-searching Mazowiecki announced in September 1990 that he would stand against his old ally.

Wałęsa explained that he did not want to stand for president, but if he was requested to do so, he would for the sake of the country. He even went so far as to say that, if it was necessary, he would be prepared to rule by decree. Despite Wałęsa's denials, it is not unreasonable to assume that he wanted the presidency very badly. His refusal to travel to Warsaw to meet President Havel in January 1990 revealed both his desire to match Havel's standing and his occasionally peevish behaviour, which could not be excused by the vaguely distasteful charade of Havel's welcome by General Jaruzelski. The men who champion Wałęsa's cause most vociferously are his advisers, a curious bunch of whom three, the former head of Radio Free Europe's Polish section, Zdzisław Najder, and the two Kaczyński brothers, Jarosław and Leszek, are probably the most influential. Some admirers of Wałęsa, and even some of his opponents, believe that his intentions remain pure. By contrast they see in his advisers a group of evil councillors determined to exploit the good name of the Solidarity chairman. But it is much more likely that Wałęsa is, in fact, the architect of his strategy, the aim of which is the Belweder Palace, the seat of the Polish president. It is perfectly possible that, by the time this work is published, he will have replaced the General as president or at the very least be preparing his election campaign. According to the round-table agreement, Jaruzelski's term still has several years to run, but Wałęsa is using the growing discontent in the country, combined with an almost universal unhappiness with the present incumbent at the Belweder, to force an early presidential election. After mediating in the railway strike, Wałęsa's popularity rocketed. He soon started to behave as if the presidency were his by right, and as his determination to be president by the beginning of 1991 strengthened, opposition to his apparently overweening ambition grew.

It was quite characteristic of Wałęsa to refuse the job of prime minister in 1989. The office would have involved spending much time behind a desk trying to reach diplomatic solutions to very serious problems. Wałęsa has never hidden his dislike of cabinet structures and has in the past been criticized for his undemocratic tendencies. Being prime minister would have cramped his style; being president would be a very different matter. Mazowiecki clearly felt uncomfortable deciding to run against Wałęsa. This was partly because there was no obvious choice to replace him as prime minister. But he also knew that he might beat Wałęsa in the election. So he had to decide which was the lesser of two evils – a populist Wałęsa as a president threatening to rule by decree or a malcontent trade-union leader whose wrath would increase after an electoral defeat by his former adviser, Mazowiecki.

When Wałęsa launched his attack on Mazowiecki and other former colleagues, notably Henryk Wujec, Adam Michnik and Geremek, he accused them of having acted too slowly. 'Acceleration' became his buzz word. In the political sense, this goal was straightforward. He demanded that Poland move towards elections, both presidential and general, much faster than the round-table agreement foresaw, and he positively encouraged the fissions that were destroying the unity of Solidarity and the Civic Committee, as these would lead to 'pluralism', which is, after all, at the heart of democracy. At the same time his vision of a strong presidency clearly included a threat to pluralism, although the democratic election of a president would be consistent with acceleration. According to Wałęsa, Mazowiecki (and, of course, Balcerowicz) had failed Wałęsa's constituency, the workers, by not reforming the economy quickly enough. This is nonsense. The workers are unhappy precisely because the Balcerowicz plan has had such a devastating effect on the Polish economy in such a short time. The strikers, with whom Wałęsa came to be closely associated in the public mind, wanted less Balcerowicz and not more. Wałęsa's economic argument, riddled with inconsistencies, was developed as a populist tactic to strengthen his political claim on the presidency. To judge by the fear of his former colleagues, the plan has worked well.

The historical parallel between Wałęsa and the inter-war Polish leader Marshal Józef Piłsudski is hard to resist despite inevitable deviations. The political origins of both men are to be found in the workers movement, Piłsudski as an early socialist, Wałęsa as the leader of Solidarity. Both played a crucial role in the creation of a democratic Poland, after which their actual political power diminished. In 1926, alienated from the young democracy, Piłsudski put an end to it by military means and ruled as president together with a restricted parliament until his death in 1935. Piłsudski reasoned that his so-called *sanacja* regime was necessary for the sake of Poland and Poles (an appeal that did nothing to bolster the confidence of the country's substantial Ukranian, Byelorussian and Jewish minorities). It is absurd to believe that Wałęsa would call on the army to gag Mazowiecki's government, but he is quite prepared to consider authoritarian solutions to Poland's problems, especially if he is involved with their execution. In an interview that he gave in June 1990 he called for 'a president with an axe, decisive, tough, straightforward, who doesn't mess around and doesn't get in the way of democracy but fills in the holes immediately. If he sees people profiting from the change of system, stealing, he issues a decree, valid until the parliament passes a law. I would save half of Poland if I had such powers.' Initially Wałęsa's newly won enemies from the ranks of Solidarity brushed aside his intemperate language, but gradually concern mounted. By the beginning of August 1990 Jarosław Kaczyński was casually dismissing those whom Wałęsa would allow to remain in government and those whom he would not when he became president.

In the Polish context this is stern stuff, closely reminiscent of the *sanacja*. Many Poles admire Piłsudski as the true father of modern Poland, but Wałęsa is also quite captivated by his political strategy, which became ever more hostile towards democracy as the Marshal aged. Since the most recent transition to democracy began Wałęsa has developed a remarkably pompous and cocksure populist style that, in times of economic hardship, is designed to appeal to several constituencies. His ability to communicate with impoverished workers is unparalleled, and although Mazowiecki's saintly, avuncular style has won the support of many Poles, only Wałęsa has the ability to mobilize the masses. Whether Wałęsa hopes to emulate Piłsudski is not the question. It is certainly possible that he could rule by decree as an authoritarian populist in the name of Polish interests, but he is not specifically seeking to do so. The question is: with Wałęsa as president, will Poland's democracy be strong enough to prevent him from being tempted to resort to Piłsudski's tactics? It is a serious mistake to believe that, after forty years of single-party rule, Poles will not countenance another form of authoritarian rule. Poland's post-communist order does not derive its strength from popular democratic fervour if the turnout at the two elections in 1989 and 1990 are a reliable guide (by contrast, Czechoslovakia's, which can boast an enormous electoral turnout, does). Instead it must look to the competence of its government and parliament and the related economic performance of the country.

If the Balcerowicz plan locks Poland into a recession, then the possibility of a populist or authoritarian solution will arise. This may not necessarily accommodate Wałęsa, but it probably will. While Poland's economy remains shattered and unhealthy,

Wałęsa is a powerful *potential* threat to democracy. The key sentence during his interview in June was 'If he sees people profiting from the change of system, stealing, he issues a decree . . .' Therefore a President Wałęsa's perception of the economy would determine the style of government in Poland. Of course, this also means that if Poland were to show signs of prosperity, a President Wałęsa would feel much less inclined to intervene.

The End of Solidarity

While supporters and opponents of Wałęsa continued to squabble about when the president should be elected and how (whether parliament or the country should vote on the office), one thing became clear: Solidarity, the starter motor of revolution in Eastern Europe, was finished as a political movement. There were already nascent divisions before the battle between Wałęsa and Michnik and Mazowiecki broke out, but the two main movements to emerge during the summer of 1990 were products of this personalized dispute. The first, formed in May, was the Centre Agreement, masterminded by the indefatigable Jarosław Kaczyński. This is an organization that links most of Wałęsa's supporters in the *Sejm* and the Senate, who together number about 125. Despite its name it is generally agreed to be to the right of centre, although within the current Polish context this is an unhappy designation, particularly given the strength of working-class support for Wałęsa. The prime mover behind the opposing Civic Movement–Democratic Action (known by its Polish acronym ROAD) is Władysław Frasyniuk, one of the most gifted and politically astute leaders of the union during its heyday in 1981. ROAD joins together many of Solidarity's great intellectuals, above all Michnik but also men such as the film director Andrzej Wajda. Michnik's programme is undoubtedly left of centre. It can be compared most closely with West European social democracy.

This presents a problem for Michnik, however. He cannot call himself socialist or social democratic, partly because the former Communist Party grabbed the sobriquet of social democracy for itself and partly because the terms socialist or social democrat remain, for the moment, sure-fire vote losers. This is an important reason why Michnik and his friends attempted to prevent the split in Solidarity for as long as possible. He desperately needed a political concept with which he could counter Wałęsa's Centre Agreement. Michnik's colleague, Frasyniuk, circumvented the problem of political description by referring to ROAD not as left of centre but as west of centre. This rather cheeky formulation fits comfortably with Michnik's concept of ROAD and, indeed, the Centre Agreement, which he sees as representing the second of two broad strands of Polish history. The first is the ideology of the modernizers and Europeans, the second that of the xenophobes who glory in Poland's historical past and wish to recreate its mythical success. This dichotomy is very similar to the more clearly defined split in Hungarian society along the lines of populists and urbanists. While such broad brush strokes are clearly visible in Polish society, there are many parts of the canvas where the two overlap and become indistinguishable. None the less these two nascent political parties are likely to play a substantial role in Polish politics over the next few years.

The collapse of unity among the ranks of former Solidarity colleagues should not be mourned. Clearly there is a degree of personal sadness, as the people who mounted such a brave challenge to the Communist Party in the early 1980s now spend much time exchanging insults, but that is an unavoidable consequence of democracy. In addition, while Solidarity remained a political monolith, it clearly hindered transition to a recognizable form of democracy. In May 1990 one opinion poll showed that 49 per cent of those questioned around the country supported Solidarity; another 49 per cent answered that they supported no political party; and all other parties together received just 2 per cent of the public's support. For a society attempting to generate political debate such statistics are a disaster. Although some of the many political parties that have been formed since the end of communist rule enjoy localized support, until the banner of Solidarity was rolled up their practical value in Poland's democratic development was negligible. Solidarity will almost certainly continue to function as a trade union. If Wałęsa fails to get elected as president, then it will clearly remain in its present form, as the union continues to be his most reliable power base. But even if he is elected, he may find it useful to maintain the closest of links with his union organization.

While Solidarity as a political unit withdraws from the game, there is a large number of organizations that hope to fill the gap. These have been aware of the vacuum being created for a long time, of course, and in many instances they have attempted to work through existing Solidarity organizations to gain a foothold within the political establishment.

Beyond the Centre Agreement and ROAD, probably the best-organized movement with representation in the *Sejm* and the Senate is the Christian National Union (ZChN), which draws on the traditions of the National Democratic Party or *Endecja*. Throughout 1990 there has also been a steady growth in popular support for the ZChN, which is closely linked to parts of the Catholic hierarchy. In the inter-war period the National Democratic Party, which was led by the charismatic anti-Semite Roman Dmowski, was the most influential movement opposing Marshal Piłsudski. The *Endecja* comprised conservative nationalists whose practical influence in the republic was often greater than that of Piłsudski himself. In addition to its powerful anti-Semitic tendency, the National Democratic Party was hostile to all other minorities and violently anti-German. It was also the political home of the Catholic Church. With the exception of Ireland, there is no country in Europe where the political influence of the Church is so telling as in Poland. Throughout the communist period the Church has been one of the central pillars in Polish political life, a privilege enjoyed by no other organization outside the control of the Communist Party in Eastern Europe.

Since the collapse of one-party rule the Church has been searching for a new role. On a social level the inherent conservatism of Polish Catholicism has been demonstrated by its campaign for the reintroduction of compulsory religious education in schools. It has also been lobbying against such evils as pornography. Communist puritanism invariably coincided with Catholic abhorrence in respect of pornography, and this is one aspect of the revolution that is not welcome in church circles. Indeed, the Polish Pope, John

Paul II, warned early in 1990 that Eastern Europe is now exposed to the risk of moral subversion that is so prevalent in the West. In some countries, notably Yugoslavia and Hungary, the relaxation of censorship has led to an almost uncontrollable growth in the publication of pornography. Indeed, in Yugoslavia the public display at news stands of hard-core pornography is quite enough to shock most urban Westerners visiting the country. The Church is determined to prevent such an explosion in Poland, although both men and women have shown some curiosity in the products of the 'sex industry' in other East European countries.

While communists and Catholics may have agreed on this, they were sharply critical of one another on the issues of contraception and, in particular, abortion. Whereas Christian political parties in Slovenia and the Czech lands, for example, have decided to adopt a low profile on abortion because opposition to it is a confirmed vote loser, it is a powerful political weapon in Poland. (Women, of course, may have different opinions on the matter, but, as is the case elsewhere in Eastern Europe, their influence within the emerging political parties is not great.)

Some members of the clergy appear to believe that since democracy is being introduced into Poland, their political function has come to an end. Others, including the primate Cardinal Jósef Glemp, clearly think that this is no time to stop being involved in high politics. Although he has not done so publicly, it is believed by some that the ZChN enjoys the support of Cardinal Glemp, and he certainly favours Wałęsa as president. Glemp himself is not a very popular character, but he has a powerful grip on parts of the Polish clergy. If a consultative role cannot be found for the Church within either the Centre Agreement or ROAD (it is highly unlikely that such an arrangement could be reached with the latter), the ZChN is likely to become home for an influential section of the clergy.

If Wałęsa's ambition represents one possible authoritarian threat to Polish democracy, then the increasing power of the new *Endecja* is a second. One advantage that their opponents enjoy is the difficulty that the two face in finding a compatible working relationship. None the less the traditions of the National Democrats should not be underestimated. Already large parts of the Solidarity organizations in the south of the country have committed themselves to supporting the movement, which is also augmented by a plethora of small and rather lunatic extreme nationalist organizations. It is the strength of the ZChN that ensures the absence of a stable and primarily secular Christian Democratic Party along German or Italian lines. If not checked, Poland's political Catholicism, a source of inspiration in the past, could become a destabilizing force in the near future.

If the *Endecja* is to become a serious political force, it will have to play the national card. Although anti-Semitism is still a powerful current influencing much of Polish society, the country's Jewish community is small and ageing, and it is likely to receive all the support it needs from central government. Even despite the post-war bonus of the western Polish territories that were given up by a defeated Germany, many Poles still believe that vast tracts of the Ukraine, Byelorussia and Lithuania (where there are substantial Polish minorities) should be returned to Warsaw. Relations with Lithuania may become particularly sensitive when that country achieves its independence, as seems likely. The Polish Foreign Minister, Krzysztof Skubiszewski, has given Lithuania firm assurances that Warsaw does not seek any border revision, and at the moment it seems unthinkable that Poland might dispute the eastern borders. However, as the Soviet Union breaks up into smaller units Poland may again begin to play a determining economic role in north-eastern Europe, as it did many centuries ago, and unscrupulous nationalists could resuscitate mutual resentments.

The great political constituency that seems destined not to be able to assert itself in democratic Poland is the peasantry. Although historically the peasantry has often been at the core of Polish politics, its political representatives have emerged from communism badly divided among themselves and unable to offer a coherent voice with which to promote the interests of farmers in parliament. So ineffective have they been that a group of farmers resorted to occupying the Agriculture Ministry in Warsaw early in the summer of 1990 in order that their grievances concerning the structure of food subsidies might be addressed.

Ironically, and indeed tellingly, Polish agriculture – which consists mainly of numerous small private holdings – is one of the most inefficient in Eastern Europe. Given that Poland has the largest population, however, and that a significant chunk of hard-currency exports depends on agricultural output, the peasantry is a constituency that the Polish government ignores at its peril. In recognition of their weak position, rank-and-file members of the main peasant organizations, the NSZZ Individual Farmers Solidarity, the Polish Peasant Party Solidarity, the Polish Peasant Party – Rebirth, and the Polish Peasant Party – Wilanów, are increasingly burying their differences in order to construct a united front despite the continuing mutual hostility of their leaders. As urban unemployment grows, Polish farmers are also having to come to terms with an increase in the emigration of first- and second-generation urban dwellers to the countryside. Historically Polish farmers have proved effective in cutting off food supplies to the cities in order to drive home their demand for a more sympathetic hearing from the government. After the failure of the occupation of the Agriculture Ministry (which was cleared by the police), they may well consider resorting to similar tactics again.

The real heir to Polish social democracy is Adam Michnik, although, as we have seen, he chooses not to identify himself publicly with the ideology. Elsewhere those claiming to be the inheritors of the Polish Socialist Party (PPS) are hopelessly split into warring factions. There are three organizations now claiming the title PPS, each as electorally insignificant as the others. Most of the older socialists, including some who were members before the war, belong to a group headed by one of the most enduring characters of the Polish opposition, Jan Jósef Lipski. Some of their former comrades split on a range of social issues (including differing approaches to the Church) to form the Provisional National Committee of the PPS, while the PPS–Revolutionary Democratic has developed a programme of socialist self-management that is violently critical of the transition to capitalism. Although the social democrats are weak for the moment, they have gained some support as discontent with the Balcerowicz plan has grown. None the less in the minds of many Poles they are too close to the dreaded Social Democrats of the Republic of Poland (aka communists) to warrant support. The latter draw their strength largely from the ranks of former bureaucrats, even if, under a rejuvenated leadership, they are trying against the odds to lay the foundations of the 'modern European left'. Social democracy will begin to increase its political purchase on Polish society only if the warring factions of the PPS can develop a dialogue not only among each other but also, more important, with Frasyniuk's and Michnik's 'west-of-centre' ROAD. This is likely to be a long time in coming because of the fundamental differences between the PPS and ROAD concerning the government's economic policy.

Paradise Found, Paradise Lost

Poland has always succeeded in capturing the minds of Westerners better than all other East European countries. While Chamberlain could dismiss Czechoslovakia as 'a far-away place of which we know nothing' in 1938, Britain was prepared to go to war on behalf of Poland a year later. The heroic struggle of Solidarity in the early 1980s also contributed, without doubt, to the love affair between Westerners and Poland. Now, however, after the great struggle is over, Poland, the largest country in the region, is one of the saddest and most depressed in Europe. The infrastructure of the Polish economy is one of the most desperate and hopeless in the area. The impoverishment of ordinary Poles has accelerated since the end of communism (though that hardly seemed possible, given the enfeebled state in which the communists had left the population), and despite the incisive efforts of Mazowiecki and Balcerowicz the economy is on its knees. Although the currency has been stabilized, little progress, if any, is being made with the development of market mechanisms that would affect the huge heartlands of Polish industry. These are themselves horrific monuments to the insane extreme Leninist commitment to technology and progress. Eastern Europe offers an endless list of ecological nightmares, but Poland takes the unenviable biscuit. The highest concentration of acid rain in Europe falls on the blighted city of Chorzów, north-east of Katowice. Poland has the highest concentration of water deemed unfit for human consumption in Europe, and its once proud rivers have the highest concentration of toxic chemicals in all of Europe. As a result Poland is the worst polluter of the Baltic Sea, while almost all its beaches are considered unsafe for bathing. The country's social fabric is visibly torn and tattered, while criminality and deprivation is on the increase. Poland looks a complete mess, a place from where it is most sensible to escape. With complete freedom to leave the country that is what many Poles are trying to do, although finding a Western country that will accept these 'economic refugees' has become almost impossible.

One depressing but significant side-effect of all this has been growing political apathy among Poles, exacerbated by the fierce outbreak of political divisions within Solidarity and the pretensions to power of some leading political figures. Polish democracy will flourish only if apathy is replaced by a strong civic commitment. Despite the great efforts of some political forces in the country this is for the moment an impossible goal. Poland simply does not have the resources or the money to reconstruct its moribund economy. It has, however, issued an important warning to the West that should not go unheeded: if the countries of Eastern Europe are allowed to rot in the economic quagmire first nurtured and then bequeathed by the communists, these countries will revert to their old political habits, which bear little resemblance to democratic ones and will benefit nobody. In economic terms they have tended to exaggerate existing problems, while politically they have encouraged regional destabilization.

Such a political development is not inevitable in Poland. Although some forces actively promote the authoritarian solution, the overwhelming majority of Poles would prefer to live in a stable democracy. This remains the only long-term solution that will allow Poland to emerge from the catastrophe in which it now finds itself. It can succeed only if Poland receives substantial economic help from the West. At the moment there is little sign of that.

3 HUNGARY

The Politics of Backwardness

Populism and Urbanism – the Hungarian Face
Behind the European Mask

Like most East European countries, Hungary is neurotic. But
although the four decades of Communist Party rule nurtured this
neurosis diligently, its roots lie outside the garden of Stalinism. As
Hungarians grow up they are attracted by a series of cultural
traditions that pull fiercely in opposing directions. Many suffer a
crisis of identity as they attempt either to reconcile or to choose
between these conflicting traditions. This is reflected both on a
mundane, if disturbing, social level by the incidence of suicide in
Hungary, which figures in Europe's top three every year, and on a
national political level, where people have always been easily
seduced by soothing gestures and symbols that are often regarded
as satisfactory substitutes for sound policies – indeed, in the eyes of
many they are considered superior. As Gáspár Miklós Tamás, one
of the leading members of the Association of Free Democrats
(SZDSZ), told me a few weeks before the Hungarian elections in
March 1990, Hungary's democracy 'will have the brightest colours,
the most majestic heraldry, the jolliest bunting but very little
substance'. Hungary may have a proud history, but its democratic
traditions would barely fill a school exercise book.

With the exception of the Stalinist rump, the Hungarian Socialist Workers' Party, all political parties in the country sport the
same colours – red, white and green. This almost unconscious
commitment to the Hungarian flag is assumed to be an essential
ingredient in any successful political mix. In addition it generally
signals a political programme strong only on patriotic rhetoric and
lyrical denunciations of the enemy, whoever that may be.

The origin of Hungary's cultural contradictions lies in the Hungarians' ethnic and linguistic heritage. Related to Finnish and Estonian, Hungarian belongs to one of Europe's very few language groups that are not Indo-European. Its speakers are the descendants of Mongol nomads, the Huns, who arrived in Europe in the middle of the fifth century. This distinct background has intensified the struggle for survival that most small nations in Central Europe have been waging for the last two centuries. Hungarians regard their culture and language as uniquely vulnerable to corruption, yet remarkably well preserved, particularly among certain Hungarian communities in the Soviet Union and Romania that have been largely untouched by outside influences. The attachment of young people to old Hungarian traditions is striking. No West European country can match the passion with which young Hungarians soak in and disseminate Hungarian *folklor*, and as a consequence Hungary is a fertile country for historians, ethnographers and anthropologists.

Nobody can ignore this special and invariably fascinating Hungarian identity. Arriving in Budapest for the first time is a strange experience. It seems like a normal central European capital with everything in its correct place, but there is something that disturbs and unnerves. Finally it hits you: not one single word makes any sense – there is no variation on *lait*, milk or *moloko* that you remember from the three great European language groups. Hungarian is at first glance absolutely incomprehensible. Later on you can recognize certain peculiarities of the language that help to illuminate some of the Hungarians' behavioural traits. The word *ő* in Hungarian means either 'he' or 'she'. When speaking English or German to Hungarians such confusions as 'She was talking to his husband' crop up regularly. But behind this apparently egalitarian approach to gender lies a system of address that is probably the most complicated in Europe and goes a long way to explaining Hungarians' obsession with social form and rank. To some extent this is breaking down in cities but not in the countryside, where a rigid patriarchal hierarchy still obtains in public. Whenever possible, Hungarians cling to their language and culture.

It is, of course, quite natural for a nation to want to preserve its cultural identity, but in Hungary there are two distinct and apparently irreconcilable traditions, the populist and the urbanist. Both claim to work towards the same end but by very different means. Described crudely, the populists believe that in order to survive Hungarian culture must remain pure, while the urbanists consider it essential to integrate Hungarian culture with European patterns. An important sociological difference is the large number of intellectuals and Jews who are involved with the urbanists. As a result Hungarian populism has often, but not always, been infected by anti-intellectualism and anti-Semitism.

Hungarian Stalinism and, later on, Kádárism did not destroy these currents of thought; instead the state ideologies informed, and in turn were influenced by, these traditions. Since the collapse of communism the populists and the urbanists have been swift to re-emerge publicly. They have found direct political expression in the country's two dominant forces, the Hungarian Democratic Forum (MDF) and the Alliance of Free Democrats (SZDSZ). Although both organizations are forced to cooperate with minor parties, the rise of the two in the eight months preceding the general election in March 1990 was remarkable. The MDF and SZDSZ now account for 257 out of the 386 seats in the Hungarian parliament, which is elected by a system of proportional representation. Other parties survive, but they have assumed the form of narrow interest groups incapable of representing a broad spectrum of Hungarian society. Some parties have been eclipsed altogether by the MDF/SZDSZ constellation. The Greens, for example, have been virtually wiped out as an organized force despite the critical role played by the environmental movement in prising open the Kádár regime from 1984 onwards.

The struggle between populism and urbanism will have a decisive influence on the new Hungary and will determine the success or failure of the democratic experiment. If the MDF, which is by no means a monolith, does not break down into its constituent ideological elements, and if right-wing populism is able to tighten its grip on power in Budapest, Hungary runs the risk of remaining isolated from Europe, neurotic and defensive.

The division between populists and urbanists influences most aspects of Hungarian society. Yet, although the Democratic Forum has received strong backing from conservative and Christian democratic parties and the Alliance has attracted the support of liberal and social democratic opinion in Western Europe, populism and urbanism are not simply Hungarian synonyms for right and left. Originally Hungarian populism itself boasted a left wing and a right wing, while the urbanist writers were supported by city professionals and the liberal, and especially the Jewish, bourgeoisie.

After 1956, however, both populism and urbanism experienced some fundamental changes. The powerful left wing of the populists declined, while some of the most outspoken urbanists of the 1960s began their political career as critical Marxist intellectuals before settling down to become what is known as the Democratic Opposition in the late 1970s. This group was the only one that dared speak out consistently against Kádár's dictatorship, and, like Charter 77 in Czechoslovakia, it paid the price for doing so, albeit not quite such a high one. In contrast to his treatment of these urbanists, Kádár attempted to integrate the populists with his establishment. In return for their passive support, Kádár allowed them to publish on their favourite subjects – the evils of Hungary's suicide rate, the increasing rate of alcoholism among Hungarians, Hungary's declining demographic rate and the high incidence of abortions. Above all, from the late sixties onward Kadar permitted them to explore the idea of Hungarianness (*Magyarság*), a word that in many circles still invokes the same respect as the word *Deutschtum* did among Germans at the turn of the century. The central position that *Magyarság* occupies in the discourse of conservatives in Hungary means that their relations with West European Christian democratic parties may appear warm on the surface but are rarely more than skin-deep. Such Hungarians are unashamed nationalists who prefer to keep all foreigners at arm's length.

During the general election campaign the MDF accused the SZDSZ of harbouring Marxists (a term that is synonymous with Jews for many Hungarians). They based their claim on the intellectual (ethnic) origins of leaders like János Kis and Miklós

Haraszti. The MDF has largely ignored the fact that Kis, Haraszti, Gáspár Miklós Tamás and other leading SZDSZ activists became the most energetic advocates of the multi-party democracy during the 1970s, risking their liberty in the process, yet the SZDSZ leadership fears the effect of this populist tactic on the electorate. A month before the elections one of the SZDSZ leaders, Péter Tölgyessy, felt it necessary to declare that as his party had grown and matured the influence of Jews and intellectuals within the SZDSZ had declined. 'Today,' he explained 'more than 50 per cent of our members are not intellectuals.' None the less the majority of its leaders are Jews and intellectuals or, like Tölgyessy himself, both.

In response to the tactics of the MDF the SZDSZ attempted to link the populists with the former communist apparatus. During the election campaign dozens of MDF posters were defaced with the simple formula MDF= MSZP (the Hungarian Socialist Party). While accusing each other of extremism, the two parties were busy presenting themselves to the outside world as centre liberals (SZDSZ) and centre conservatives (MDF) to fit in with European patterns. In some respects these labels are accurate, but the essence of Hungarian politics remains the urbanist/populist split from which there follows several other divisions that often defy the simple pattern of liberal and conservative.

In economic policy, for example, the Alliance is more committed than the Forum to an unrestricted market economy. The populist tradition is wary of outside influences that may infiltrate Hungarian life. This caution is born of the fear of cultural contamination, but inevitably it has economic and political implications as well. I have asked several rank-and-file members of the MDF whether they believe McDonald's should be allowed to open more outlets in Hungary, and they have all rejected the proposal categorically, not because they fear that fast food may undermine the health of Hungarians (although it is surely only a matter of time before the populists hit on that idea) but because they regard McDonald's as a gaudy threat to Hungarian culture. Such critics of the great American burger (which, ironically, owes its world-wide fame to a Czech) may be small-time nationalists, but they will not be the only East Europeans to regret Western consumer culture's invasion of Eastern Europe. However polluted and miserable the region appeared under neo-Stalinist rule, many areas were able to retain a certain majesty, or at the very least quiet beauty, that billboards and modernism had long since swamped in the West.

It is precisely this late capitalist culture the MDF finds vulgar and unbearable, which is why the vocal support given to the MDF by Margaret Thatcher and other European conservatives is slightly curious. Politically they clearly have much in common, but in economic terms the Tories and their West European allies are much closer to the SZDSZ. It also helps to explain the MDF's electoral success. The Democratic Forum stressed in its programme that it would not allow Hungarians to suffer a radical and painful transition to the market economy. Before the collapse of communist power in Hungary its citizens were already feeling the pinch of severe recession associated with Kádár's legendary economic mess, goulash communism. The MDF's narrow nationalism coincided with the deep fear of many Hungarians about the effects of the free market on their living standards.

The Politics of Intolerance

Hungary was the first country in Eastern Europe to renounce the system of one-party rule and prepare for multi-party elections with no strings attached. To the chagrin of many Hungarians, the East German government was forced to bring the elections in the GDR forward to 18 March 1990, one week before the Hungarian elections were due. The spectacular revolutions in East Germany, Czechoslovakia and Romania had already diluted the splendour of Hungary's path-breaking achievement in forcing the Communist Party to relinquish its monopoly on power. Now the country was denied the chance to be first to hold free elections. But despite the astonishing events in East Germany, Czechoslovakia and Romania, it would be a grave mistake to underestimate the importance of the Hungarian and, later, the Polish reforms in setting the revolutionary agenda in Eastern Europe and provoking the collapse of single-party rule throughout the region.

The death knell for existing socialism in Hungary rang out loud and clear in May 1988. At a special conference of the Hungarian Socialist Workers' Party (MSZMP), held to discuss the growing political and economic crisis in the country, a curious coalition of radical reformers and conservative technocrats outmanoeuvred János Kádár comprehensively. Together with his ageing praetorian guard Kádár, the man who had dominated the country since the defeat of the revolution in 1956, was politely deposed.

The final assault on Kádár had been led by three men, Károly Grósz, János Berecz and Imre Pozsgay. The first two clearly believed that the maintenance of single party rule, and hence their grip on power, could be secured by modernizing Kádár's benevolent dictatorship, which has best been described as 'the happiest barracks in the camp'. Pozsgay, however, was developing a different strategy. Together with the *éminence grise* of reform communism in Hungary, Rezső Nyers, and two bright young politicians, Miklós Németh and Gyula Horn, he wanted to replace the one-party system with a multi-party system. Once these four had effectively wrested control of the party from Grósz and Berecz they were able to start dismantling the system. Nyers had no ambition beyond the desire to sustain the traditions of left social democracy in Hungary, but Németh, Horn and Pozsgay were evidently determined to secure their own positions in the new Hungary by forging the historical sword of transition. Pozsgay was in some key respects the godfather of the MDF, while Németh and Horn quickly adopted liberal Western positions after being named prime minister and foreign minister as the country awaited elections.

But these three great reformers miscalculated too, assuming that Hungarian citizens would thank them for having devised the multi-party system by supporting their new party, the Hungarian Socialist Party (MSZP), which emerged from the ashes of the MSZMP in October 1989. While Németh secured a large personal vote in the elections, Horn narrowly failed to win his constituency, while Pozsgay, once the darling of Hungarian politics, was pulverized by the opposition. If one person could be held responsible for the collapse of Kádárism in Hungary, it is Pozsgay. But transparent ambition led to his downfall. He was not devoured by the revolution, but it left him severely maimed.

The party reformers played an absolutely crucial role in the construction of Hungary's democracy, but even greater respect must be accorded to the Democratic Opposition, the small group of Hungarians, based mainly in Budapest, who fought for democratic rights throughout the 1970s at a time when their realization was just a dream. These people suffered persecution, physical attacks and imprisonment for many years, thereby exposing the vicious side of Kádárism that many people in the West preferred not to see. Without the Democratic Opposition Hungary's road to democracy would have been much less smooth. It was they who kept alive Hungary's fragile democratic consciousness during the great era of resignation when Brezhnev's ghastly gerontocracy appeared bent on keeping Eastern Europe in its political strait-jacket for eternity.

The Alliance of Free Democrats, which was officially formed on 13 November 1988, is the direct descendant of the Democratic Opposition. Its leaders, like Gábor Demszky, Miklós Haraszti, János Kis, Gáspár Miklós Tamás and László Rajk, became well known in the late 1970s and early 1980s for their work as human rights activists. At first the Alliance's activities were overshadowed by the initial success of its main rival, the Hungarian Democratic Forum, which had been founded over a year earlier in September 1987. But the MDF made a serious tactical error by supporting the socialist party's proposal for direct presidential elections just before Christmas 1989. At the time Pozsgay was undoubtedly the most popular politician in the country, and many people predicted that he would win a popular election. The Alliance, together with other smaller opposition parties, successfully staged and won a national referendum that postponed the election of a new president until after the general election. The MDF's decision to boycott the referendum left many believing that its links with the Socialist Party were closer than it claimed, and as a consequence the Alliance won support at its expense.

The stage was then set for the general election, with the opposition parties united in their hostility to the former Communist

Party but otherwise bitterly divided. In the first round the MDF won about a quarter of the national vote; the Alliance was about three points behind. The Smallholders' Party, one of the few parties that had existed before 1948, running under the conservative slogan 'God, Home and Family, Wine, Wheat and Independence', won 12 per cent of the vote. The Socialist Party scraped together 10 per cent of the electorate, while the remarkable FIDESZ (Federation of Young Democrats) secured 8 per cent beating the Christian Democrats into sixth place.

Until the last moment the second round looked as though it would be as close. Then the slumbering bear of Hungarian populism awoke from its hibernation, and the MDF conquered all in sight, leaving the political activists from the SZDSZ particularly shattered by a most bitter defeat. They were deeply disappointed that the turnout in the second round had slumped to just over 40 per cent compared with just under 65 per cent in the first round. The figure of 40 per cent hardly inspires faith in Hungarian attitudes to democracy. The second round was crucial in deciding the composition of parliament, yet almost two-thirds of the electorate could not find the energy to vote. This is a reflection of four decades of apathy under the communists and is consistent with the Hungarians' pre-war commitment to democracy. Even more demoralizing for the SZDSZ was the apparent defection of FIDESZ voters to the MDF. In the last two weeks of campaigning there was evidence that FIDESZ was becoming rather impatient with the SZDSZ's arrogant assumption that FIDESZ voters actually belonged to the Free Democrats.

In trying to explain the defeat the SZDSZ accused the MDF of running a dirty campaign before the second round, playing on nationalist sentiment. But the SZDSZ's almost messianic commitment to radical free-market policies also played a substantial role in its defeat. The MDF was at pains to stress during the election campaign that it would not tolerate wholesale deprivation during the transition from socialism to capitalism. The SZDSZ foolishly trumpeted the need for everybody to prepare for the approaching economic drought.

One striking aspect of the election was the regional spread of the vote. The populist MDF vote dominated much of the countryside, as had been predicted, but the urbanist Alliance fared worse than expected in some cities, including Budapest. Apart from a few anomalous pockets where working-class support swung behind the socialists and even the Stalinist MSZMP, the east of the country was solidly behind the MDF. The traditional homes of Hungarian nationalism, like the southern country of Csongrád, have become mighty strongholds of the MDF. With the exception of some traditional conservative pockets, the west of the country, which in recent years has benefited considerably from the growing economic traffic with Austria, was firmly in the grip of the SZDSZ.

This sharp geographical division in the election results suggested that the voters were well aware of the ideological origins of the two main parties despite their bland programmes. Both the MDF and the SZDSZ are at pains to stress their commitment to the political centre while accusing each other of secretly harbouring extreme left-wing or right-wing positions. They also outbid each other on the issue of who is the more anti-communist. As far as one could ascertain from their programmes at the time of the election, and the MDF's was particularly vague, neither group had drawn up a hidden agenda. Both organizations have developed stronger profiles as political parties than the front organizations like Civic Forum in Czechoslovakia, but their seductively anodyne policies indicate a plethora of tendencies within their ranks. As the pressures of government and responsibility mount, so too will the internal divisions.

The SZDSZ's claim to the centre rests on its avowed commitment to the creation of democratic institutions based on the rule of law and human rights. It is uncompromising in its support for rights of minorities in Hungary, in particular for one of Europe's least well-treated groups, the gypsies, and expresses concern for Hungarians living outside the state. It has also formed links with the West European liberal parties, a bonding that has been helped by the reputation of its leaders during their time in the Democratic Opposition. But with the important exception of its policy on domestic minorities, the SZDSZ's attempt to claim the centre ground for itself is spurious. The party's economic policy is far more radical than the MDF's and has much more in common with Thatcherism than with the more measured policies of West Germany or France. As a governing party the SZDSZ would be prepared to countenance mass unemployment and unrestricted access of foreign capital to Hungarian markets. Paradoxically the Alliance's politics are perceived as being left of centre, taking up the ground that social democracy occupies in most of Western Europe.

The MDF's determination to provide for the Hungarian people and not to allow the ruthless logic of the market to affect their standard of living will lead to problems, particularly since its supremely uncharismatic prime minister, Jozsef Antall, and his economic advisers have begun to link economic policy to nationalism. This is dangerous, as Hungary has to compete with its former East European allies for money and investment. The MDF wants to see a cautious and bureaucratic programme of privatization, which may well stall the initial unpleasant side-effects of rapid transformation but runs the serious risk of allowing the economy to stagnate still further.

Politically the MDF stands clearly to the right of centre. Dr Antall, whose grip on power is secured largely by the respect accorded by all political forces to his father, has frequently had to dismiss as mere aberrations the anti-Semitic or extreme reactionary sentiments of some of his followers. But the populist base of the Forum exerts a significant influence on policy. Soon after his appointment as prime minister Antall and his cabinet appeared to break the mould of populism by offering to cooperate with the SZDSZ in parliament. The most important fruit of this *rapprochement* was the virtually uncontested election of the writer Árpád Göncz, a member of the SZDSZ, to the office of president. It seemed as though Antall would be able to keep his rabble-rousing, xenophobic activists under control.

It was not long, however, before cracks started emerging in the newly formed friendship between the urbanists and populists. By the summer of 1990 Antall began to reveal himself to be quite as radical as some of his more vociferous colleagues in the party.

Against the spirit of liberalization, he presided over the introduction of specifically Catholic religious instruction into the school curriculum. Hungary is not a uniformly Catholic country, as Poland is, and some see the move as a political slight aimed at the SZDSZ, whose supporters include a high proportion of Jews. On the economic front it became clear that the MDF's caution was informed more by paranoid nationalism than by concern for the plight of the Hungarian worker. In August 1990 Antall replaced the head of the Hungaraton, the country's main recording company, with an organ player, István Ella, who had no business experience but who was instructed by Antall to promote Hungarian music, which, he claimed, had been neglected by Hungaraton. In the course of this intervention Antall insisted on the scrapping of a deal just clinched by the old management with EMI that would have given Hungaraton access to some of the best recording facilities in Europe. The MDF decided that the maintenance of the Csárdás was more important.

The respected Swedish newspaper *Dagens Nyheter* had agreed to buy one of Hungary's main dailies, *Magyar Nemzet*, before Antall stepped in to block the sale. The MDF decided that *Dagens Nyheter* had been hostile to the party during the election campaign and so would not be allowed to buy into the Hungarian newspaper market. Such crude political manipulation of the media is reminiscent of Hungary's recent communist past. However, because the MDF believes it is manipulating the market for the benefit of Hungarian culture, it clearly does not consider the action morally offensive. (It became absolutely clear that Antall was one of Eastern Europe's most eccentric prime ministers when he appointed seven teachers from the secondary school where he used to teach as under-secretaries of state in various ministries.)

Before the elections many Western reporters had detected a xenophobic attitude in the MDF leadership and, among rank-and-file members, obvious anti-Semitism. Antall and his colleagues continue to deny that anti-Semitism exists in the MDF, yet before the first round of the elections one of Hungary's most respected populist poets, István Csurka, made some explicitly anti-Semitic remarks on a radio broadcast concerning Jews and the media in

Budapest. In response to concern voiced about such tendencies, the MDF retracts its head into its shell. Immediately after its election victory it held its annual congress. The entire event was closed to outsiders, a decision that bred little confidence in a new democracy.

The MDF is faced with two dilemmas. First, it does not have a single, coherent ideology. To some extent it has the character of a front organization with great regional and ideological differences. As a consequence its policies are vague; should they be better defined in the future, they may force a split among the Forum's various factions. Thus the MDF's major problem is to forge for itself a clear political image without undermining its very base. Its second difficulty concerns those elements in the party that embrace xenophobic, nationalist interests and want to impose strict controls on Europe's influence in Hungary. Even if the MDF wanted to embrace Europe openly, it would need to develop a very cautious policy, appropriate for a country that is not psychologically prepared to be swamped by Western capital.

The Hungarian Socialist Party (MSZP), successor to the Communist Party, was humiliated at the elections. The newly formed Social Democrats, who assumed the mantle of the inter-war organization, were obliterated in the first round. The Hungarian left, it seems, has been destroyed. As was the case everywhere else in Eastern Europe, the end of single-party rule was accompanied by a rush of anti-communist and anti-socialist sentiment as people bellowed out frustrations that had built up over many years. Conservatives in both West and East have since been dancing on what they believe to be the graves of socialism in Warsaw, Berlin, Prague, Budapest, Bucharest, Sofia and Belgrade. This makes for excellent theatre, but the left's demise is an illusion. As large parts of the population are being affected adversely by the introduction of new economic conditions, they will have to find ways to defend their interests and improve their situation, which is in many cases quite pitiful.

Such a new left may well avoid all association with the classic vocabulary of socialism, but its emergence in political life is assured. Because of its past, however, it is unlikely that the MSZP, which calls itself a party of the modern European left, will reveal itself as the saviour of Hungary's dispossessed. Instead there are tendencies within both the MDF and the SZDSZ that are voicing their concern for the fate of the 'small man', in particular the peasant and the worker. The agrarian socialism of the early Hungarian populists is bound to return if the MDF's planned land reform fails to satisfy the aspirations of the peasants. The mass unemployed who are already filling Hungary's understaffed and inexperienced dole offices will have to find a voice through some political party, probably the left of the SZDSZ.

Having been at the forefront of reform for many years during the period of communist rule, Hungary now runs the risk of becoming an extremely provincial backwater, prepared to sacrifice the spirit of European integration for the sake of a uniform cultural and racial identity. In stark contrast to much of their electoral rhetoric, the MDF and the new Hungarian government are steering the country towards a position of nervous isolation. In the process it appears to be making a substantial contribution to the worsening of relations with its neighbours, Romania and Czechoslovakia.

The National Question: Hungary's Achilles' Heel

The birth of Hungary's democracy was accompanied by pain and blood. In the week before the electorate was due at the polling stations for the first round, at least three Hungarians living in Transylvania were killed as Romanian nationalists provoked running street battles with Hungarians in Tirgu Mures/Maros Vásárhely. The Hungarian media, still extremely poorly disciplined, reported rumour as fact and generally added to the tension. Despite this, ordinary Hungarians and, most surprisingly, all the major political parties behaved with impeccable restraint and dignity during the campaign for the first round, aware perhaps that intemperate language would inflame the nationalist hysteria that had gripped the Romanians. The SZDSZ accused the MDF of breaking, in its final TV advert two days before the election, the unspoken rule that kept Transylvania out of the campaign, but by Hungarian standards this was a small transgression.

In the second round, however, the MDF launched a much more aggressive campaign, which was clearly designed to appeal to the baser instincts of Hungarians. This, together with the shamefully low turnout of 40 per cent, ensured the MDF's landslide victory, and a distinctly nationalist approach to relations with Romania emerged. One of the greatest tests facing the MDF government is the exercise of restraint on the issue of Transylvania and the subduing of some of its more vocal and charismatic nationalists. If it reacts immoderately, Transylvania could explode. Although the minority in Transylvania is clearly oppressed, the power of Hungarian nationalism should not be underestimated.

One evening six years ago I was sitting in a pub drinking beer with several young sociologists from Budapest University. I was explaining to three of them some work in which I had been involved on youth culture in Czechoslovakia, East Germany and Hungary. One bearded man asked me how I could begin to understand anything about Hungarian culture if I did not speak the language fluently. I replied that even without language it is possible, through study and observation, to draw some conclusions about other cultures. He then denounced me publicly for daring to write anything about Hungary. The conversation was happily diverted for a few minutes until I mentioned the name Košice. My bearded friend turned round at this point and smashed his beer glass down on the table. 'What did you say?' he roared at me, silencing the entire table.

'Košice,' I replied.

'And what is this "Košice"?' he continued, foaming at the mouth.

I told him that it was a city in eastern Slovakia, as he very well knew.

'Oh,' he said 'our English friend means Kassa but obviously finds Hungarian pronunciation difficult.'

I continued to call it Košice, but for the remainder of the evening this man, who was about to become a doctor of sociology, glared at me as though I were sub-human. It was not my first encounter with the irrational nationalism of the Balkans, and certainly not my most depressing, but it was important. This Budapest intellectual, who spoke excellent English and German and in any other conversation would have appeared to be an enlightened cosmopolitan, behaved like an irrational pig when the discussion touched upon *Magyarság* and its sanctity.

In public the Hungarian political parties do not seek a return of the Felvidék (southern Slovakia) or Erdély (Transylvania), but in private an enormous number of Hungarians are convinced that these areas belong to Hungary and should in time be restored to their rightful owner. The existence of the minority in Transylvania guarantees that Hungary will not escape the quagmire of Balkan politics: the fate of an estimated 2 million Hungarians is probably the most emotive issue in Hungarian society. But the only way in which Hungarians living in Hungary can contribute to a positive solution in Transylvania is to exchange their emotional response to the problem for a rational one. In this important sense the SZDSZ and its allies are the bearers of hope. The record of the Democratic Opposition on Transylvania was excellent. They were as tireless in defending the Hungarian minority against the abuses of Ceaușescu's Romanization policy as the populists; indeed, in contrast to some leading nationalists, they were not cowed by Kádár's police. But for the SZDSZ the question of borders is not an issue – they do not wish to annex Transylvania, a policy that is crucial for regional stability. Publicly the same applies to the MDF and the national camp, but it requires only one evening's drinking with rank-and-file members of the MDF to convince the observer that the border question is very much a matter for debate within the party. A conflict with Romania over Transylvania would do more damage to Hungary than any other event since the defeat of the revolution in 1956.

After Transylvania, southern Slovakia and the fate of the 300,000 Hungarians living there is the favourite topic of conversation of Hungarian nationalists. The position of these Hungarians is incomparably better than that of the Transylvanian Hungarians. None the less relations between Slovaks and Hungarians have soured in the first few months since the revolution. Liberals from both nationalities cooperate well within Public Against Violence, Civic Forum's sister organization, but elsewhere in the political spectrum there is much mutual hostility between the two. In southern Slovakia much depends on developments within the Slovak rather than the Hungarian community. Here, in the first year since Czechoslovakia's revolution, there has been a marked radicalization, leading to growing calls for the creation of a separate Slovak state outside the Czechoslovak federation. Anti-Czech feeling in Slovakia has stoked traditional suspicion of Hungarians, which in turn has fortified Hungarian nationalists in Hungary. The Hungarians in Slovakia have good reason to be concerned about the growth of Slovak nationalism. However, their case is weakened (as is the case of the Translyvanian Hungarians) by the chauvinist response registered in Hungary itself. Czechoslovakia and Hungary are reputed to be two of the more peaceful East European countries, with civilized European traditions. It must not be forgotten that they are trapped by the same nationalist traditions as other East European countries, and since the collapse of neo-Stalinism these have burst out almost as powerfully as anywhere else in the region.

The moral justification for intervention in the affairs of Hungarians living outside Hungary's borders is greatly undermined by Hungary's treatment of one of its own minorities. Eight national minorities (Germans, Slovaks, Romanians, Serbs, Slovenes, Croats, Jews and Gypsies) now have automatic seats in Hungary's parliament, and, given the region's intolerance, the respect afforded to Hungary's Romanian, Serbian, German and Slovak minorities has been relatively impressive both under Kádár and since his demise. But to enter the home of one of Hungary's 350,000 Gypsies is to encounter conditions comparable with some of the worst in the developing world. The Gypsies are discriminated against both socially and politically. They are only partially nomadic, many having settled in poor ghettos usually situated on the outskirts of industrial towns or in villages where they alone live. Large families occupy cramped homes while Hungarians blame them for poor housing conditions. Many Gypsy communities will be devastated by the transition to a capitalist economy and in particular by its attendant unemployment. Under the government of the MDF the Gypsies cannot expect any great improvement in their life style. Socially and politically disaffected, they are at the bottom of Hungary's pile and hence represent no threat to the country's stability, only a blot on its reputation. If a country is to be judged by the treatment of its minorities (as Václav Havel would have it), Hungary's Gypsy community should be observed very closely.

The Economy

In the elections all major parties loudly broadcast their determination to build a modest but cosy room with easy access to all other living areas in the common European home. Because of its gradualist revolution Hungary has a head start over many other East European countries hoping for acceptance in the West European empire. It has excellent trade relations with Austria and West Germany. Its tourist industry is much better developed than its northern neighbours, Czechoslovakia and Poland, while its diplomats have been wooing the West unashamedly and with great success since well before Kádár was deposed.

Having arisen from the cosmopolitan traditions of the urbanists, the SZDSZ and the Federation of Young Democrats (FIDESZ) can hardly wait for Budapest to be mentioned in the same breath as Vienna, Stockholm or Madrid. For these two parties the Communist Party in power denied Hungary its rightful position within the European commonwealth of nations. The SZDSZ argues convincingly that Hungary can survive, economically and politically, only in Europe. To shut the door to outside cultural influences, as many members of the MDF would prefer, would be to banish Hungary to the stagnant backwaters of European development together with Romania, Bulgaria, Macedonia and Kosovo.

None the less some of the SZDSZ's members fear that the party is making a mistake by selling Hungary to another master so soon after it has bought itself out of Moscow's service. The historian György Dalos was formerly a leading member of the Democratic Opposition and is now a critical supporter of the SZDSZ living in Vienna. He believes that the shock to a Hungary that for so long has been cosseted against the influences of the outside world could lead to violent reaction, most notably in the form of urban social decay. This position, covertly supported by one powerful tendency in the SZDSZ, is not born of the xenophobia that circulates in the MDF; instead it is inspired by the concern that the SZDSZ leadership has brightly skipped over the social instability that the practices of an unfettered market economy will bestow on Hungary's neurotic society.

The centre of Budapest is one of the most deceptive sights in Eastern Europe. Adidas, Benneton, Pierre Cardin and Sony mix easily with the well-dressed members of the so-called *uj burzsoázia*, the new bourgeoisie. Traces of communist rule are still to be found in working-class districts and factories, but they have long disappeared from the areas frequented by tourists and businessmen. Budapest's hotels are comfortable and efficient, and most visitors return from Hungary's capital to Western Europe under the impression that Hungary has already arrived. One or two things undermine that conviction. Trying to make a telephone call out of Hungary is an exasperating task during the daytime. Hungary's retarded exchanges ceased to cope with the country's daily telephone traffic a long time ago. In many parts of central Budapest the waiting list for a new telephone to be installed is five years. In much of the countryside one telephone is shared by as many as two hundred families. Before the country can claim its place as an attractive target of foreign investment its entire telephone system must be replaced. It may be able to offer the West cheap and hard-working labour, but, unlike Taiwan, it cannot offer as many faxes or computer lines as the businessman may desire. The Hungarians are already working on changing their telephones, but the project's progress remains frighteningly slow.

Despite appearances on Budapest's fashionable shopping boulevard, Váci utca, Hungary's economy is in an advanced state of sclerosis. The country has an enormous foreign debt of over US $20 billion, one of the ugliest relics bequeathed to the new Hungary by Kádár. For many years the real size of the debt was kept secret not only from the Hungarian population, which was told that it was about $6 billion less than it actually is, but from Western banks and governments as well. The annual servicing of the debt costs Hungary in the region of $2.5 billion, while its actual repayment will last well into the next century. As Hungary began to loosen up in the early 1980s, inflation began to take off, and it now stands at over 20 per cent. Until a few years ago inflation had been artificially repressed by the price system of the planned economy, and open acknowledgement of its extent was a shock. Looking to the south of Hungary, economists were able to see the chaos that high external debt and swiftly accelerating inflation had wrought in Yugoslavia. This is the primary economic task now confronting the new Hungary: the prevention of hyper-inflation combined with an end to the billions of forints paid out in government subsidies in order to sustain unprofitable enterprises.

Hungary enjoys a head start over most other East European countries because its economic reforms, albeit incomplete, began well before those of every other country. Services are much better developed than in Czechoslovakia despite the economic muscle of its northern neighbour. Light industry, with a low capital base, is also proving successful in parts of western Hungary. Even taking these advantages into account, however, the country now faces an uphill struggle as it tries to convince Western investors to enter the market. International banks have indicated clearly that Hungary's poor debt management has dissuaded them from lending more money in order to service its overdraft. Foreign capital must pour into Hungary to offset the effects of the huge cuts in public spending that the transition to a market economy inevitably demands. The government of the MDF is thus faced with a very serious problem. The Hungarian population is poor. Over a quarter of families, about 3 million people altogether, live on or below the breadline, and in the countryside many are reliant upon an uncertain life of subsistence farming. In addition to the chronic poverty, there is also the extreme wealth of the *uj burzsoázia*, which has expanded considerably since the days when it was an anomalous novelty in the communist world in the late 1970s. While many welcome this wealth differential, it is also a source of resentment among the country's less well-off, and the government must attempt to reconcile this imbalance.

Although unemployment has not yet reached the scale it has attained in Poland, it is already visible as an inevitable offshoot of economic reform. Those losing their jobs are mainly in heavy industry in centres like Győr, Miskolc and Budapest. The steel industry in Miskolc was expanded grotesquely by Hungary's first communist leader, Mátyás Rákosi, when Stalinist industrialization was in full swing. The workers now being laid off are often first- or second-generation immigrants from the countryside. These people are now returning to farming on the *Puszta*, beginning an extraordinary, systemic re-emigration to the countryside that has no comparison in modern European history. In Hungary there is considerable doubt about whether the rural economy can bear this influx from the cities.

This adds up to an enormous social security bill for the government at a time when it has promised to axe subsidies everywhere. Hungarians have been suffering a loss of real wages for several years, and they are now faced with further cuts in living standards. The MDF fell far short of the SZDSZ's promises of a radically free-market economy. But in order to cope with the discrepancies of income and expenditure, the government will almost certainly have to approach Western governments and banks at a time when the country is already up to its neck in debts. Like all East European countries shaking off the dead skin of the East European trading bloc COMECON, Hungary must negotiate new bilateral contracts with the Soviet Union to secure a large range of raw materials, in particular energy. Along with its neighbours, Hungary has relied upon the fixed annual oil quota that the Soviet Union has delivered in exchange for consumer goods and agricultural products. It remains to be seen whether the Soviet Union will wish to continue selling oil to its former allies at prices that are generally below its world market value.

Hungary has expressed a clear interest in developing close political and economic relationships with Czechoslovakia and Poland, partly for sentimental reasons. Poland and Hungary have a history of popular friendship that stretches back into the last century and beyond. In 1956, when the two countries became the first in Eastern Europe to revolt, the slogan 'Long Live Polish–Hungarian Friendship' was one of the most memorable. Hungarians deeply regretted the decision of János Kádár to send troops into Czechoslovakia in 1968, and more recently there was extensive coordination between the three dissident communities that helped to pave the way for revolution. A loose confederation of the three states makes sound political sense and, for Hungary and Poland, economic sense as well. But Hungary wants to extend this central European union still further. It is particularly concerned to integrate its most important Western friend, Austria, as well as the more prosperous areas of Yugoslavia, Croatia and Slovenia, and northern Italy. Although Hungary is a close trade partner of Germany and enjoys excellent political relations, it must help to construct alternative economic alliances if it is to avoid being sucked in by the German whirlpool.

If the MDF keeps its promise, Paks, Hungary's only nuclear power station (a Soviet VVER 440), will survive. Paks is as risky a proposition as any of the Soviet-designed reactors in Eastern Europe. The VVER is not the same type of reactor that melted down at Chernobyl, but most of the East European stations have suffered dozens of small break-downs since their installation, although it is still impossible to know precisely how safe they are because of the excessive secrecy that still shrouds their operation. There is an anti-Paks movement in Hungary, but, like the rest of the Green movement, it has suffered a setback since the revolution.

The struggle in Hungary against the Gabcikovo–Nagymaros river barrage scheme, one of Europe's most ambitious and absurd river-diversion projects, resulted in one of the most impressive political victories ever achieved in Eastern Europe. For a period of almost two years from 1984 the region's best-organized environmental movement forced the Hungarian government to renege on a treaty with Czechoslovakia that committed it to participate in the construction of a massive hydro-electric power-station system stretching 120 miles eastward from Bratislava to Nagymaros. Tens of thousands of Hungarians mobilized to prevent the dams from being built. They were ultimately successful, although not before Czechoslovak, Hungarian and Austrian firms had devastated one of the most crucial ecological areas of the Danube.

To an extent the Hungarian Greens (or Blues, as they were later called) were an essential part of the revolution. Their collapse as a political force has been remarkable. In the elections they failed miserably, although this was partly due to organizational problems and splits in the party. But, just as in the rest of Europe, all other parties have leaped on to the ecological bandwagon and offered extensive commitments to cleaning up the environment. Cities like Budapest have dreadful local pollution problems caused by industry, motor vehicles and sewage. At the height of a particularly noxious attack of smog one foreign ministry official referred to East Germany's two-stroke Trabant cars as 'mobile chemical weapons that ought to be tabled at the Geneva talks on chemical-weapon disarmament'. Surrounded by hills to the north, Budapest is prone to attacks of temperature inversion when warm air above the capital traps cold polluted air in the city. But perhaps the Greens have failed politically in Hungary because the country does not suffer from the terrifying impact that pollution has on the so-called 'triangle of death' in East Germany, Czechoslovakia and Poland or the chemical gas chambers masquerading as the cities of Giurgiu and Ruse that glare at each other poisonously from either side of the Danube on the Romania–Bulgaria border. Gabcikovo-Nagymaros was perceived to be the most serious threat to Hungary's environment; following its solution, ecological problems have been shunted into the background for the moment. They will surely return.

No country can claim to be more Central European than Hungary. Physically it is right in the middle of Europe, while culturally it is a bridge between Russia and the East on the one hand and the West on the other. It also marks the divide between the historically powerful countries of north-eastern Europe and the unstable Balkan nations in the south. It can easily claim to belong to any of these political and geographical areas and, for different reasons, is drawn to all of them. Now freed from the Soviet imperative,

Hungary stands in the middle of these diverse cultures, stroking its chin and pondering which way to turn.

The road south-east towards Transylvania looks the most treacherous; none the less it must be negotiated. Even in the face of extreme provocation by Romanian nationalists, Hungary must remain level-headed. It must represent the interests of the Hungarian minority abroad without upsetting the *status quo*. If Hungarian democracy wants to win the respect of its newly found colleagues, it has to resist the temptation of demanding a revision of the post-war borders, as the Romanians would interpret this as nothing less than a declaration of war.

Nobody expects Hungary to ignore the fate of the minorities living outside the country, but the key to Hungarian success lies on the road facing west. Hungary had clearly benefited from its recently formed ties with Western Europe, but it needs some assurance that European integration will mean more than just a surplus of computer games, hamburgers, soft pornography and a circulation battle between Rupert Murdoch and Robert Maxwell. So far there is little evidence to the contrary, and in particular the West has refused any substantial help on the issue of debt cancellation. For many Hungarians the horizon looks gloomy, and the promise of mass unemployment is unsettling much of the country. But in the long term only Western capital, including American and Japanese, can resuscitate one of Europe's most seriously disabled economic cripples. Hungary desperately needs an economic revival. It would not be a panacea capable of healing all Hungary's problems, but it would go a long way towards ridding Hungarian society of the fear of contamination. If, on the other hand, the country's neurosis is allowed to grow unchecked, feeding on deprivation and insecurity, Hungary will survive only as a weak and unreliable partner that other Europeans would do well to avoid.

4 ROMANIA

The Frying Pan and the Fire

If most East European countries were drab satellites sluggishly orbiting Moscow's dying sun, Romania was a weird mutant asteroid weaving its own unpredictable path while never quite leaving the Soviet star system. Everything that grew on this fertile asteroid was denied to the inhabitants, whose main purpose in life was to suffer while being forced to applaud the insane activities of its omnipotent ruler. Travelling in Romania from the early seventies onward, when Ceauşescu's idiosyncratic style began its descent into raving lunacy, was the most depressing experience that Eastern Europe could muster – and the range on offer was extensive.

It is hard to pinpoint any single reason why Romania appeared quite so miserable because Ceauşescu succeeded in devastating most aspects of life. The country's glorious scenery was blighted everywhere by the enormous Dickensian pipes that burst out of the ground. These hideous forms still run for scores of kilometres along the side of the road before rising and blending into depressing industrial sculptures. Art was transformed into a nightmarish parody as terrified court poets prostituted their craft in a hopeless attempt to satisfy the insatiable vanity of Nicolae and his wife Elena. Those who sought to uphold independent traditions and ideas were bullied and tortured by the Securitate. Billions of dollars were poured into useless Stalinoid industrial projects and buildings designed to bolster Ceauşescu's prestige. In front of the shops and outside the markets people would form obedient queues in all weathers to receive the starvation rations left over for them after the bulk of the produce had been sold for export.

Sitting across the table at the Intercontinental Hotel in the winter of 1986, the loathsome Mr Tsiutiu, whose job it was to bully and sneer at most Western journalists, explained everything to me. 'I know the Romanian people. They are a greedy, primitive bunch. You offer them two chickens and they'll hoard them. They'll stuff their fridges full with them so we have to make sure that their greed doesn't destroy the economy.' Mr Tsiutiu then proceeded to lecture me on the folly of writing untruths about Romania, which was 'Europe's most prosperous land. You will never see a more beautiful underground system anywhere else in the world.' Instead I wrote that the deconstruction of the Ceauşescu dictatorship would be a bloody affair. As a result I was not permitted to return to the country until the blood of those lousy, greedy chicken hoarders whom Mr Tsiutiu despised so deeply was running in the streets.

After the revolution Romania's road to democracy looked quite the most treacherous in Eastern Europe. For the briefest of periods (it was literally a matter of days) Romanian citizens rejoiced as one, their ethnic origins and political differences forgotten in the melting pot of revolutionary fervour. Their victory was the most magical of achievements in a year of miracles, but it was not long before the burden of Romanian history began to confuse the revolutionaries as they embarked on their painful and probably impossible search for normality. Within days of the outbreak of revolt in Timişoara, Romanian nationalists in Transylvania were accusing members of the Hungarian minority of trying to hijack the revolution by demanding the creation of a Hungarian university in Cluj/Kolozsvár. Within three months street clashes between Hungarians and Romanians in Tîrgu Mureş/Maros Vásárhely left at least three Hungarians and three Romanians dead. Soon after relations between these two ethnic groups in Transylvania had begun to sour, another conflict emerged in Bucharest. The opposition parties accused the National Salvation Front (NSF), the newly installed revolutionary government, of assimilating the entire power structure of the Communist Party. The headquarters of the NSF were stormed before its loyal supporters could be brought in from outlying areas. The NSF foot soldiers proved even less discriminatory in their use of violence. It was an unedifying process, which inspired little confidence in Romania's drive for democracy.

Four days after the Romanian elections, which were held on 20 May 1990, the fluent commentator Florin Gabriel Mărculescu wrote in the daily newspaper *România Liberă* that the electorate was the first to 'install a communist government in a free vote'. The Romanian Communist Party (RCP) had been made illegal soon after the revolution, but, according to Mărculescu and many other critics, the NSF was a phoenix that had risen effortlessly from the ashes of Ceauşescu's RCP. Among disgruntled intellectuals, students, ethnic minorities and the dispossessed this theory gained tremendous purchase in the months leading up to the elections. By contrast, the overwhelming majority of workers and peasants scoffed angrily at the suggestion. As soon as the Front was established, its supporters claimed, the new organization began the task of ensuring an equitable distribution of food and promising social security for all Romanians. This, as far as the workers and peasants are concerned, adds up to the most convincing refutation of the opposition's theory. They remember the RCP's main function as being to make their life as difficult and miserable as possible. The NSF clearly avoided making the same mistake. Indeed, as soon as the Front's power stabilized shortly after the revolution, it began pacifying the bulk of the population by cutting working hours and increasing wages. Opposition parties accused the Front organizations of hijacking Western aid and distributing it in the name of the Front during the election campaign. For the great majority of Romanians the Front, and above all its president, Ion Iliescu, was synonymous with the overthrow of Ceauşescu and the restoration of economic justice.

The margin of the Front's victory in Romania's parliamentary and presidential elections was staggering. Among ethnic Romanians the opposition comprised essentially the two so-called 'historical parties', the Peasants and the Liberals, who together managed to win just over 8 per cent of the vote. In fact, the Liberals, the stronger of the two, did not even succeed in winning second place in the parliamentary elections despite having some 15 million ethnic Romanian voters to appeal to. Instead the Democratic Association of Hungarians in Romania (RMDSZ), with almost 8 per cent of the vote in spite of their small constituency of about 2 million, became the senior opposition party. In some counties up to 97 per cent of the electorate voted for Ion Iliescu, the NSF's presidential candidate. Such a percentage is both frighteningly reminiscent of rigged communist elections and an indication of a very unhealthy sociological balance.

The role and nature of the NSF strikes at the very heart of the Romanian political conundrum. It is not so much the traditions of Romanian communism that have been reinstalled in the country as a system of power that probably owes more to local conditions than to the traditions of the international workers' movement. Stalinism was, of course, imposed on Romania by the Soviet Union just as it was elsewhere in Eastern Europe, but only in Romania could it have assumed the form that it did under Ceauşescu. There is much evidence to suggest that the new, omnipotent NSF will not abide by democratic rules. Already the NSF appears to have rehabilitated members of the Securitate who, it seems, are serving in a reconstituted secret police force. Although this new intelligence organization does not enjoy quite such unrestricted power as the Securitate did under Ceauşescu, it still has enough authority to intimidate and cajole large parts of Bucharest's nervous opposition.

A Question of Food

Twentieth-century Romanian history has been dominated by politicians whose nationalist and authoritarian policies have been dressed up in a colourful variety of ideological garments. At important points in their career most of these figures have claimed to draw on the country's peasantry as a source of inspiration. The image of ruddy-cheeked rustics in cheerful dress bringing in the harvest has fired the rhetoric of many a Romanian patriot. Those whose political constituency lay in urban centres, such as the National Liberal Party leader Ion Brătianu, the dominant figure of the first three decades of this century, none the less wooed the peasantry with promises of land reform. Before assuming power all the inter-war prime ministers, monarchs or dictators assured the peasantry of their commitment to the rural cause. They assiduously cultivated the peasantry and expended time and money on winning the peasants' support. Rarely, however, were they able to deliver the necessary mixture of nationalism and progress that the peasants wanted, with the possible exception of the period from 1941 to 1944, when Romania was ruled by the quasi-Fascist military dictatorship led by General Ion Antonescu. The peasantry and working class were never mobilized during the construction of a new regime except for a short period in the late thirties, when the Fascist Iron Guard movement was able to woo large parts of the peasantry away from its traditional political mouthpiece, the National Peasants' Party.

When the Communist Party came to power in Romania it inherited one of Europe's most backward communities. The preponderance of Hungarians and Jews in the party leadership was a reflection of communism's lack of appeal among ethnic Romanians, who had grown used to authoritarian and profoundly xenophobic ideologies. A political philosophy that espoused internationalism combined with the promotion of social and political rights for workers and peasants was simply unable to take root in Romania in the inter-war period. The gradual but effective elimination of Jews and Hungarians from the leadership of the RCP after the war was entirely consistent with Romanian political traditions. Gheorghe Gheorghiu-Dej, Romania's first post-war communist leader, transformed the Communist Party into a mass organization based on the principles of Romanian nationalism and support for the peasantry and the working class.

Within days of the first communist-backed government's accession to power in March 1945 the prime minister, Petru Groza, announced an ambitious programme of land reform and the return of northern Transylvania from Hungary to Romania, thereby synthesizing the two essential principles of Romanian politics. Overall the land reform, which restricted ownership to 50 hectares, had a negative economic effect, but politically it was a success that ensured Groza, if not the support, then certainly the neutrality of the bulk of the peasantry, which was poor and uneducated. There were relatively few *kulaks*, or rich peasants, in Romania.

As Groza was seducing the peasants, Gheorghiu-Dej was winning over the workers. Gheorghe Gheorghiu-Dej was popular among Romania's burgeoning working class. Not only was he a famous strike leader from the 1930s but he was also widely regarded as a Romanian patriot who could counter the influence of the 'foreign' communists who were mistrusted intellectuals, Jews or Hungarians. The last 'free' elections in Romania, in November 1946, were quite clearly rigged on a massive scale, but the combination of the Soviet presence, the absence of independent observers, the concessions made by the Groza government to the peasantry and the working class and the organizational confusion of the historical parties meant that the fraud was not difficult to perpetrate. The only opposition came from a disparate group of urban intellectuals who would quickly be either assimilated by Gheorghiu-Dej's national communist regime or liquidated.

Gheorghiu-Dej soon developed into one of the outstanding Romanian politicians of the twentieth century, displaying the usual hallmarks, nationalism and authoritarianism, although in his case the latter manifested itself as a particularly merciless form of Stalinism. For a brief period, while Stalin was still alive, he destroyed all overtly Romanian traditions that were clearly nationalist. Instead of relying on the support of Romanian nationalist forces, he was content to deploy the ruthless terror that characterized all of the new people's democracies. None the less he made his position unassailable with a unique victory over the Moscow-based communists during the Stalinist trials. (In all other East European countries so-called national communists, like Gomułka in Poland or Rajk in Hungary, were deposed and either imprisoned or executed by the victorious Moscow-backed Stalinists such as Bierut or Rákosi. In Romania the national communists liquidated the Moscow Stalinists.) His control over the party became total, and he was even able to exploit the Sino-Soviet split of the late 1950s and early 1960s to pull Romania away from Moscow's immediate sphere of influence, although it remained a member of the Warsaw Pact and COMECON.

Initially the Romanian communists' adoption of nationalism, first under Gheorghiu-Dej and later, with even greater intensity, under Ceauşescu, played no significant role in the relationship between the party and the working class and peasantry. Later on, however, its role expanded. At the end of the war the Romanian working class was small and weak. It was created in its present form by the Stalinist industrialization programme initiated in the 1950s by Gheorghiu-Dej and developed in the 1960s and 1970s by Ceauşescu. The working class has remained remarkably loyal to the Communist Party. By contrast with the Polish working class, which was a similar creation of communist policies in the 1950s, Romanian workers only once became a focus of opposition under Ceauşescu – in 1977, when tens of thousands of miners in the Jiu Valley region struck and occupied the mines. Ceauşescu broke the strike, first by making solemn commitments to the strikers (which, needless to say, he immediately reneged on after the men had returned to work) and, second, by arresting and spiriting away the strike organizers. The creation a few years later of an independent trade union in Romania, SLOMR, was inspired essentially by intellectuals, although it did win some members among the working class before it was destroyed by the Securitate. There is no doubt that the Romanian working class grew to hate Ceauşescu, especially when he embarked on the policy of paying off the country's external debt by exporting anything, mainly food, that he could sell for hard currency. But, despite the growing antipathy that finally found expression during the revolution, Romania's young working class remains conservative, politically uneducated and ready to believe politicians who give cast-iron promises of social security.

This was the cornerstone of the electoral success of Iliescu and the NSF. They were able to persuade the masses, both in urban and in rural areas, that only the NSF could provide a social transition that would not be traumatic. There is much evidence to suggest that the Front was quite prepared to cheat in order to win. Its firm grip on the media, above all on television, during the election campaign played a decisive role in its victory. So too did the physical intimidation of the two historical parties, particularly in the south of the country. This may not have been directly organized by the NSF, but it certainly benefited its candidates. Dubious electoral tactics are no novelty in Romania. Before the communists came to power at the end of the war electoral mal-practice had been the rule and not the exception. There was no reason to believe that smooth-running, fair elections would emerge overnight. To some extent the fraud on this occasion was only the continuation of practices that some consider inevitable in Romania. More puzzling and disturbing is the matter of why the Front felt it necessary to use intimidation and illegal practices when it was perfectly obvious that it was heading for a landslide victory anyhow.

Iliescu, together with the prime minister Petre Roman and other leading NSF functionaries, have admitted that the margin of their victory is a problem. Just like the governments run by the historical parties in the 1920s and 1930s, the NSF will now have to deliver the goods. It is promising a great deal. It wants a slow transition to the market economy that can guarantee both prosperity and social security (above all the avoidance of mass unemployment). Roman has even claimed that Romania is potentially the most successful economic power in the entire region. He points out that both Poland and Hungary are burdened by enormous debts. (When making the claim, however, Roman ignored Czechoslovakia, which undoubtedly has brighter prospects than Romania.) Ceauşescu had made people suffer unspeakably, but by the time of his downfall he had more or less paid off the country's external debt. Roman's confidence was also born of the diversity of the Romanian economy. If managed correctly, the Romanian economy could certainly sustain a modest standard of living for the entire population – no insignificant feat for a Balkan country. But the NSF's triumphalist predictions ignore the peril-ous economic imbalance that Ceauşescu has left to the country. Although Ceauşescu did diversify the country's foreign trade, Ro-mania was recognized as an unreliable partner. Towards the end of the Ceauşescu era political relations with Western governments, many of which happily ignored Romania's chronic abuse of human rights, deteriorated rapidly because Bucharest's strategic value collapsed in the eyes of cynical NATO strategists. This, combined with Ceauşescu's decision to pay off the country's entire $11 billion debt, led to a concomitant souring of trade relations with the West. Thus in the last few years the Romanian economy has thrown away the head start it had over some of its socialist neighbours and has become increasingly dependent on the Soviet Union and poor countries of the developing world for its trade. This is a weak and dangerous base from which to start the transition to a market economy.

The Front's claim that it can reinvigorate the economic structure without making hundreds of thousands unemployed is simply not sustainable, as Ceauşescu created vast complexes (notably in the petro-chemical and steel industries) that produce goods that can be sold only in the developing world and certainly not for hard currency. If Romania is to compete with its awakening neighbours, much of its industry must be replaced with smaller, more viable concerns. At the moment Romania has the most unresponsive and outdated industrial infrastructure of all East European countries. In addition it will come under pressure, both from abroad and at home, to introduce measures to reduce pollution in the worst affected areas of the country. Outside the 'triangle of death' that links Czechoslovakia, East Germany and Poland, Romania boasts some of the most toxic regions in Europe, particularly the cities of Copşa Mică in central Romania and the notorious chemical plants of Giurgiu on the Romanian–Bulgarian border. But at the moment the Front is preparing to keep itself in power by buying the support of the working class at the expense of the country's economic health. This will without question guarantee the persistence of the political crisis in Romania, provided that democratic structures in the country still exist.

President Iliescu and his strong conservative base in the Front are clearly unhappy about the idea of Western capital providing the foundation for the country's economic reconstruction. The NSF has been very cautious in its promotion of economic reform and has been slow to welcome help from abroad. In Iliescu's case this caution stems from a combination of good old Romanian xenophobia and a deep suspicion of capitalism that he learnt as a cadre of the RCP. Not everybody in the Front feels the same way about foreign investment, and the prime minister, Petre Roman, is an important counterbalance to Iliescu's Khrushchevite socialism.

Roman was educated in Paris, speaks several foreign languages and believes that Romania can emerge from its economic quagmire only with the West's helping hand. None the less his roots remain in Romanian political culture, which means that he is not prepared to oppose Iliescu openly and that he is ready to condone violations of democratic principles in order for the Front to have absolute control within Romania. But ultimately Roman understands that Iliescu's isolationist policies will threaten the political base of the Front. The positions of Iliescu and Roman illuminate the country's essential dilemma. The only way to win power is to promise wealth that is untainted by the hands of diabolical foreigners. The only way to deliver wealth is to deprive the bulk of the population and dance with the devil.

The strength of the Front means that the most decisive political struggles in Romania take place not within parliament but within the elite of the NSF. They may also be channelled in other directions: for example, when Iliescu set the miners on the opposition in June 1990 his aim was to pressure his adversaries within the Front and to justify the creation of a gendarmerie that many believed to be the *de facto* reconstitution of the Securitate. Considerable evidence suggests that supporters of the NSF, Interior Ministry operatives and former members of the Securitate were involved in provoking violence against state institutions, thereby affording NSF leaders the excuse to call on the workers to deal with Bucharest's small and largely defenceless opposition. Iliescu showed no remorse about the violence perpetrated on the opposition leaders and their newspapers, not to mention innocent people. But the suffering was secondary as far as he was concerned. His primary aim was to strengthen his position, which was under threat at the time. Since then various members of the government and the NSF have attempted to reassure not only the West but other East European countries as well that the events of June 1990 were an aberration. Within the Front Iliescu seems to enjoy more authority than any other individual. However, the greatest threat to his power stems from the army, which has for a long time been recognized as an 'unreliable' element of state power. Ceauşescu invested faith and resources in the Securitate at the expense of the army's prestige, while Iliescu justified his appeal to the workers to save the revolution in June by claiming that the army did not respond quickly enough to the threat posed by the opposition. Significantly the army rejected Iliescu's accusations in public a week after the June events. President Iliescu is aware that he cannot humiliate and browbeat the army at will without serious consequences.

ICH DIEN: *the Intellectuals and the Intelligentsia in Romania*

Violence has always stood impatiently in the wings of Romania's political theatre, waiting for the slightest excuse to make its entry. In June 1990, six months after its starring role in the revolution, it burst on to centre stage after President Iliescu appealed to the workers to defend the revolution against what he claimed was a neo-Fascist plot. Twenty thousand miners arrived in Bucharest on special buses and trains and for two days terrorized the city with the support of sections of the population. Their behaviour was bestial; they picked out anybody they suspected of sympathizing with the opposition and beat them senseless regardless of their gender, age or nationality. Some brave voices were raised against this Fascistoid tactic sanctioned by Iliescu, but the events also inspired many intellectuals, in particular journalists and writers, to leave Romania for good. For these people the cry of the miners left an unambiguous message ringing loudly and painfully in their ears – they were still not wanted in Romania, revolution or no revolution. For President Iliescu the departure of a few scribes who accuse him of Stalinism is probably a happy solution to a minor irritant, but for the future of Romania the trend is very disturbing.

While the number of critical intellectuals in Romania is much smaller than elsewhere in Eastern Europe, the intelligentsia – the body of administrators, teachers, doctors, engineers, lawyers and architects that serves loyally and forms an integral part of what sceptical Romanians call the mafia (i.e. political power) – is just as large. This 'massified' intelligentsia, as much a subject of state power as the peasantry or the working class, has its origins in the development of the Romanian intelligentsia in the nineteenth and the first half of the twentieth century, which was dominated by a nationalism whose base was both mystical and metaphysical, suggesting that some unidentifiable spirit linked all Romanians. It was not linked with any particular political struggle until the 1920s and 1930s, when it encouraged and fed upon the growth of extreme nationalism and Fascism in Romania. Above all it was deeply loyal and subservient to a particular ideology, invariably lacking any rational base.

There was one crucial difference between the rule of the Communist Party and the variety of regimes that had controlled Romania before and during the war: for the first time the intelligentsia could identify not just with an ideology but also with the state. The RCP was guaranteed its leading role by dint of Soviet support even after it began to distance itself from Moscow in the early 1960s. Unlike the governments of the Liberals and Peasants before the war, there was no danger of a Fascist or monarchist *coup* once the post-war division of Europe had crystallized. This security allowed both Gheorghiu-Dej and then Ceauşescu to rely on, and to strengthen, the backward traditions of the intelligentsia so that its importance as an instrument in the system of power increased quite dramatically.

The bulk of the intelligentsia was first- or second-generation. Men and women were plucked from a lower social status and given a new and more attractive social role. On the whole they were not confronted by an existing stratum of more capable intellectuals, as happened in most other East European countries with the possible exception of Bulgaria. And, of course, this new body owed its existence and its privileges to the RCP and, above all, to Gheorghiu-Dej and Ceauşescu. The absence of a critical independent spirit throughout the communist period and the creation of a society policed by automatons who carry out specific tasks without questioning their function have ensured that Romania's primitive political culture has remained largely intact as it enters the age of democracy.

The dearth of a critical and independent group of intellectuals, especially in Bucharest and the regions of Wallachia and Moldavia, is the key explanation for the absence of any serious political opposition to the NSF. (Ceauşescu succeeded better than any other East European leader in his attempt to create the 'new man', as conceived by Zhdanov and Stalin. Many people in the country act simply as marionettes who are incapable of independent activity unless somebody else is pulling the strings, telling them where to go and what to do.) It also partially explains the apparent need of Romanians to invest all their trust and political faith in an omnipotent father figure. Gheorghiu-Dej, and above all Ceauşescu himself, filled this role and for a long time Ceauşescu was the object of genuine adoration, establishing as he did a Romania that was largely free from foreign influence. Ion Iliescu has slipped into this role perfectly, and initially he was extremely convincing because he tried to avoid showing his fangs. As the NSF continues to consolidate its power and influence, Iliescu's paternal qualities become increasingly less endearing. But his influence over the working class and the peasantry is enormous and will remain so for a very long time if he is not destroyed from within the ranks of his own organization.

The NSF and Iliescu have inherited Ceauşescu's brutalized intelligentsia. Indeed, it would not be too much of an exaggeration to say that this intelligentsia *is* the NSF and that the men and women who belong to it continue to have a vested interest in sustaining the *status quo*. It is most illuminating to talk at length with intellectuals who are completely committed to the NSF. They find it particularly difficult to express themselves in anything other than thinly disguised Stalinist language. They talk of 'certain foreign circles' that are attempting to subvert Romania's democracy; they refer to 'reactionary conspiracies'; and they are often anti-Semitic. The transition from Ceauşescu's straightforward dictatorship to Romania's novel form of democracy has created a problem for them. Because the ideology that bound them to the state no longer exists they have no alternative but to substitute for their Stalinist vocabulary a hastily constructed lexicon of democracy.

Their task is made easier by the absence of any productive link between the independent intellectuals and the two major Romanian opposition parties, the Liberals and the Peasants. Indeed, these two groups, with their aged, émigré and ostentatiously oppulent politicians, are as far away from Romanian political reality as can be. The most important critical intellectuals in the capital are organized in the Group for Social Dialogue, which publishes the newspaper *22*. But many members of the Group admit that, although they are fine political analysts, there is an enormous gap separating them from day-to-day politics – except, of course, when they are picked out as targets by the country's psychotic proletariat.

Romania will not be able to liberate itself from its intolerant and violent traditions until a large group of intellectuals has emerged that is not dependent on the apparatus of the state or the NSF for its livelihood. This could take several decades, particularly if its growth is actively hindered by the likes of Iliescu.

Transylvania's Real Bloodsucker

Historically it was the Romanian elite in the Old Kingdom, Wallachia and Moldavia, that provided the drive for unification with the northern province of Transylvania. The Romanians of Transylvania were on the whole unwilling to break from the economic and intellectual prosperity of the Habsburg empire in favour of the uncertainty offered by their more primitive cousins. The relative sophistication of the north and west of Romania is still easy to spot. In the elections the vote of the Romanian population in Transylvania was much more varied than was the case in Wallachia and Moldavia. It was here that the Liberal presidential candidate, Radu Câmpeanu, received the overwhelming proportion of his votes, and although the Hungarian Transylvanians backed Câmpeanu solidly, he also did much better among Romanian voters. It was in Wallachia and Moldavia that President Iliescu scored up to 97 per cent of the vote in some areas. Although Timişoara is not quite part of Transylvania, it is the source of both popular and intellectual opposition to authoritarian ideology in Romania. (None the less this must be seen in perspective: Iliescu and the Front won a clear majority in Timişoara.)

Despite the antipathy between Romanians in Transylvania and Romanians in the Old Kingdom, the struggle between Hungarian and Romanian nationalism in the nineteenth and twentieth centuries, led to Transylvania's becoming one of the most sensitive issues within the Balkan peninsula. At the treaty of Trianon after the First World War Hungary was stripped of Transylvania, which Romania administered until 1940, when Hitler allowed Hungary to repossess the area. In the wake of the Second World War Romania, with the approval of the international community, was once again given control over Transylvania. Generations of historians on both sides of the border have dedicated their lives to establishing an ultimate claim on the area, while politicians supporting the minority, whether Hungarian or Romanian, have always denounced the ruling power for trampling on minority rights. This latter claim has invariably been easy to substantiate, although it has, of course, usually been raised within a strategy aimed at restoring control over the area. Each exchange of the territory has been followed by a systematic settling of accounts with the former ruling ethnic group. Romania's most beautiful, most prosperous and culturally most exciting region has been force-fed a diet of poisonous nationalism for much too long.

Ceauşescu made one fundamental contribution to the social constitution of Transylvania that has already had a profound impact on the area and will continue to do so for a long time. A central part of his programme of so-called 'Romanization' was the movement of Romanians from Wallachia and Moldavia into Transylvania. 'Romanization' was very ambitious. In the fifteen years prior to Ceauşescu's fall Tîrgu Mureş/Maros Vásárhely saw the Romanian percentage of the population rise from 32 to 49 per cent (these figures were found at the RCP headquarters in Tîrgu Mureş after the December revolution). This pattern was repeated in several other large towns in Transylvania. Traditionally social relations between Hungarians and Romanians in the area have been cordial. The blood-letting in the area has almost always coincided with larger geopolitical struggles. The majority of Romanians and Hungarians in the area were bilingual, and both perceived themselves as being part of a common community.

Ceauşescu intentionally provoked the break-up of this common community by introducing Romanians from elsewhere in the country. Their traditional xenophobia was encouraged by the new environment in which they were not even able to understand many of their neighbours. By upsetting the traditional Transylvanian ethnic balance in this way Ceauşescu's programme of systematic discrimination against Hungarians (which they themselves call, rather awkwardly, 'cultural genocide') was much easier to implement.

It was not long after the revolution that the veil was lifted from the Medusa to which Ceauşescu had given birth. One of the main complaints made by the Hungarians under Ceauşescu concerned the erosion of Hungarian language classes in universities and schools. Within days of the revolution Hungarian intellectuals had begun to circulate a petition that demanded the founding of a Hungarian university in Cluj/Kolozsvár. As a direct response to this demand and others that were being formulated elsewhere, a group of Romanian intellectuals founded the Vatra Românească (*vatra* is a Slav word meaning 'fire', although VR points out that in Romanian it has the meaning 'fireplace' or 'hearth'). Vatra began as an organization committed to the propagation of Romanian culture in Transylvania. It also presses for the recognition that all people within Romania's borders should, without regard to their ethnicity, consider themselves loyal to the Romanian national state and that members of the minorities should speak fluent Romanian as well as their mother tongue. Later on VR transformed itself into a political party. Much of VR's work is harmless, but in essence it is an extreme nationalist organization with Fascist potential. The Peasants' Party in Transylvania is also characterized by a poorly concealed suspicion of Hungarians. In conversation most Romanians active in VR, the Peasants' Party and now the NSF in Transylvania will maintain that the aim of the Hungarians is the restoration of the region to Hungary.

In fact, the Hungarian population in Transylvania, which is divided between Hungarians and Szekler (the latter were a group of ethnic Hungarians who were selected as border guards at the foot of the Carpathians by the Habsburgs and, in their isolation, developed their own distinct culture), is noticeably less militant in its demands than most people in Hungary proper. Romanians respond to this observation by claiming that the moderate position of the local Hungarian population is merely a cunning tactical consideration, but the genuine antipathy expressed by Transylvanian Hungarians to their relations across the border indicate a widening gap between the two. It is impossible to ascertain how widespread Greater Hungarian sentiment among the Hungarian Transylvanians is, but empirical evidence suggests that it is not a powerful political instrument in the area.

The lumpen element of the Romanian nationalists in Transylvania was unleashed in late March 1990 when its members stormed the offices of the RMDSZ (Democratic Association of Hungarians in Romania) in Tîrgu Mureş/Maros Vásárhely. There followed three days of mob violence that led to the deaths of both Romanians and Hungarians. There were two significant political consequences of the Tîrgu Mureş incident. First, it gave succour to nationalists in Hungary proper while scaring the Hungarians in Transylvania. Second, it led to the collapse of the quiet contacts that had been maintained since the revolution between the RMDSZ and the NSF. The NSF had by then developed its nationalist hue and was concerned that it might lose votes to the Peasants and VR if it did not distance itself from the Hungarians. As a consequence the Hungarians, almost 10 per cent of the Romanian population, voted demonstratively against the NSF in the May elections. After the results were published I asked the Romanian Foreign Minister, Adrian Năstase, a leading member of the NSF, whether his organization was concerned about the fact that it had succeeded in alienating almost every single member of the country's largest minority. Năstase replied, 'It is not the NSF that has alienated the Hungarian minority. The Hungarian minority has decided to alienate itself from the NSF.' Năstase is considered by many among the Western press to be the acceptable face of the NSF. Yet his answer revealed just how deep anti-democratic and racist sentiment runs in his party.

Despite the signs that since the revolution Transylvania has suffered a serious dislocation that threatens the peace, it is not inevitable that the tense relations between the two ethnic communities will continue to flare up in violence. Having won an overwhelming victory in the elections, the NSF has a vested interest in keeping the communal peace in Transylvania. It has already deployed in the area a special police force that is specifically equipped to deal with such outbreaks of violence. It may be tempted to manipulate the situation only if for some reason its own power structure is threatened. None the less the RMDSZ made a strong parliamentary protest about the mob rule of the miners in Bucharest in June 1990 because, as it explained, 'If that is how Romanians treat one another, what can the minorities expect' if nationalism is once again called up from NSF's arsenal of social control? Certainly in the long term the only guarantee of stability and peace in Transylvania will be an extensive range of rights for the Hungarian minority. At the moment this is not the case, and the longer the situation continues, the more resentment it will fuel among the Hungarian population. Of greater import will be the effect it has on the political mood in Hungary proper. If human rights abuses continue in Transylvania until the next Hungarian election, the nationalist vote could begin to play a decisive role in Budapest. Objectively the only people who would benefit from such a development would be the extreme nationalists on either side of the border.

There is a second nationalist issue that will force its way steadily up the political agenda in the next few years. This is the problem of Soviet Moldavia. When reports of political upheaval in the capital Kishinev and other Soviet Moldavian cities first began to appear the Western media demonstrated its unfamiliarity with the area by for ever referring to Moldavian as a language related to Romanian and to Moldavians as a people related to Romanians. Even *Gazeta Wyborcza*, the independent Solidarity daily in Poland, referred to the Moldavian language before hastily admitting its error the following day. Moldavian is, in fact, Romanian. The only substantial, albeit not irreversible, difference between the two languages is that Stalin decreed that 'Moldavian' would be written in the Cyrillic script. Moldavians themselves are Romanians who happened to live in Bessarabia when it was annexed by Stalin during the Second World War. While Moldavians are considered among the most backward and primitive Romanians, this is a cultural and not an ethnic distinction. When the Soviet Union agreed to open the borders between Romania and Soviet Moldavia in early May 1990 it was clear from the torrent of people who rushed across to find their relatives on the eastern side of the border that, despite the artificial distinction between the Soviet and the Romanian Moldavians, there is a considerable homogeneity and sense of identity between the two groups. There now exist organizations on both sides of the border that are demanding the return of Soviet Moldavia to Romania. Bucharest is unlikely to press this issue at international fora, but if Soviet Moldavia succeeds in asserting some degree of independence from the Soviet federation, which seems very likely, the demands for reunification with Romania proper are certain to grow louder and louder. There is, of course, a problem in the shape of Soviet Moldavia's threatened minority Russian population. Because this comprises largely recent settlers, whom most Romanians regard as colonizers, their fate in a reconstituted Greater Romania may be less than happy.

There are few East European countries where Václav Havel's little drop of wisdom about judging a country by the way it treats its minorities can be applied so accurately as in Romania. There has been a massive and irreversible haemorrhage of the German minority. The economic appeal of a new Germany is almost irresistible for most of its members, who are guaranteed citizenship by Bonn. But some are going because they can no longer tolerate the political climate in Romania and because they do not believe that the revolution will alter substantially the position of the Romanian Saxons in the country. The only area where ethnic tensions impinge less uncomfortably is the Banat, at whose centre lies Timişoara, where the mix of Germans, Serbs, Hungarians, Romanians and Gypsies evidently has a calming effect on any problems that arise.

România Liberă?

Within a short period after the revolution Romania, which for a few months enjoyed the sympathy and support of large parts of the globe, was heading steadily back towards its former status of European pariah. After the Bulgarian elections newspapers around the world reported that Bulgaria 'had bucked the East European trend' and voted communists back into power following their defeat in Hungary, Poland, Czechoslovakia, Slovenia and Croatia. Romania was discounted because, ironically, it was the only country that had outlawed the Communist Party. The Bulgarian Socialist Party did not hide the fact that it was, in fact, the Communist Party with a reformist face. The reason why Romania was spared the accusation of having bucked the East European trend was because the NSF pretended that it was not organically a child of the RCP. This is nonsense. The relationship between the two is extremely intimate. But in one sense neither country is guilty of having voted communists back into power – and Romania is the more blameless. The Communist Party in Romania developed a unique ideology that had nothing to do with 'socialism' except that it borrowed its vocabulary as a convenient instrument with which to facilitate its preservation.

The other factor that guaranteed, and under Iliescu still guarantees, this system's continued existence is its ability to integrate most of the population. In the long term, however, its ultimate guarantor is fear, which is why Ceauşescu allowed the Securitate to gorge itself on weapons and power. Iliescu has a choice to make between maintaining power through strength and isolation or losing it while allowing the democratic institutions of a civil society to develop. So far he has clearly seemed to favour the former path, although, in his defence, his decision has undoubtedly stemmed from the mighty logic of the system.

It is essential that Romania should not be allowed to cut itself off from the rest of Europe, but at the same time other states should persist in registering their protests if Romania continues to tolerate wide-scale abuse of power. This means, first, that press freedom should be guaranteed. Regrettably the press law introduced by the NSF soon after its election included a paragraph banning any newspaper that propagates extremist and fascist propaganda. Theoretically there may be some sound practical justification for the inclusion of such a clause, but unfortunately it was passed by the Constituent Assembly little more than a week after Iliescu had denounced a group of harmless hunger strikers and the intellectual opposition as being the front line of an attempted neo-Fascist *coup* that was purportedly being directed by exiled Iron Guard leaders and foreign agents. A number of journalists on the main opposition journal, *România Liberă*, decided to flee the country after the paper's offices were sacked by miners, while the editor-in-chief, Petre Mihai Băcanu, considered staying in Canada, which he was visiting at the time. The president and the NSF can clearly use their press legislation to control freedom of expression. They also have a back-up weapon that is equally effective, in that they are the sole distributors of newspapers and newsprint in the country. As a consequence the newspapers that support the government, like *Adevărul* (The Truth), which many consider to be the new incarnation of the old party daily *Scîntea* (The Spark), have unlimited access to resources.

But the most appealing object of desire in Romania is the television. Before the hunger strikers' protest was broken up their demands had been whittled down to the single request for an independent, private television station. Television has played the decisive role in all the turbulent events in Romania since the revolution. It is widely agreed that Ceauşescu's fate was sealed when he faltered during a speech that was being televised live from the Central Committee building in Bucharest. The broadcast then ceased, signalling to everybody that it was time to take to the streets. Television was also crucial for mobilizing the workers on behalf of President Iliescu, both before and after the elections. With television firmly in the hands of the state and the NSF, Iliescu has the most direct link to the masses, and so far he has demonstrated that he knows how to use it.

Defenders of the president and the government will state quite frankly that Romania is a typical Balkan culture in which the occasional outburst of arbitrary violence and injustice is nothing unusual. They also are quick to point out that no country in the region has had to come to terms with quite such a traumatic recent past as Romania has. And naturally they justify the development of the country since the revolution because of the huge mandate the government won in elections, the result of which certainly reflected the general mood of the population even if the poll itself was not entirely free and fair. But with democratic friends like the NSF, who needs authoritarian or totalitarian enemies? Romania is not struggling to find its place in a new Europe – that will be a long time in coming. It is struggling to understand once again what it means to be Romanian and uncovering a number of gangrenous sores in the process. Elsewhere in Eastern Europe, even in the other black holes of the Balkans, there is usually the potential for a dialogue that will offer the beginnings of a rational solution to profound conflicts. But in Romania there is little room for rational manoeuvre and considerable room for scepticism. If it were to implement its current programme, the NSF will be able to hold on to power in the long term only by continuing to resort to repressive methods in order to solve internal difficulties and eliminate its external enemies. If, however, it decides to abide by the democratic rules, and as the pain of economic transformation begins to bite, it will have to face more powerful organized opposition than the Peasants and Liberals are able to offer at the moment. Whatever path the NSF and Romanian society choose to take when they reach their next major political crossroads, there will still be a long and exhausting journey towards the elusive goal of a free Romania.

5 YUGOSLAVIA
The Tragedy of Revenge

Yugoslavia is the most seductive and beautiful country in Central and Southern Europe. In its present form it is also the most hopeless and, sadly, quite doomed. Despite a common currency and a national football team drawn from all parts of the country, Yugoslavia is in reality seven or eight countries, which eye one another with frustration, envy and resentment. While the peoples of other East European countries were celebrating their great victories, this once proud model of independence had already begun its solemn, pathetic descent into Purgatory.

In the past socialists in both Eastern and Western Europe had looked admiringly towards Yugoslavia and Tito for inspiration. Here was the third way – the construction of a popular socialist economy that was able to resist the terrible inertia of Stalinism and the seductive but exploitative thrills of consumer capitalism. Where others had failed Tito had apparently constructed a multinational state in the Balkans. For East Europeans Yugoslavia's independence vied with the gorgeous beaches of the Dalmatian coast as the country's most attractive quality. As early as the 1960s intellectual life and the media in Yugoslavia skipped easily across some of the rigid boundaries that had been set in its socialist neighbours to the east. As Europe prepared itself for the dramatic events of 1968, Yugoslavia's philosophers provided a meeting point, geographical and intellectual, for revolutionary leaders from both East and West. In the late 1970s and early 1980s the Yugoslav press was in certain respects one of the best in Europe, combining a unique understanding of socialist systems with a hunger for good reporting.

But behind this exciting and progressive exterior a mass of unresolved problems never ceased to ferment. Sometimes Titoist innovations hid this process, but usually they accelerated it. On the many occasions when Yugoslavia's difficulties threatened to spill out on to the surface Tito resorted to force and successfully suppressed them. But he never solved one of the fundamental problems besetting Yugoslavia, nor did he ever commission a systematic examination of the origins of the Yugoslav crisis. While alive, Tito was able to prevent the crisis from undermining the foundations of the state but only through drastic repressive methods. After his death Yugoslavia's slide towards collapse was only a matter of time.

In an attempt to prevent the final collapse Tito sought to replace his unifying role with a complicated system of revolving leadership, so that representatives of Yugoslavia's eight constituent elements would take turns in controlling the most important state and party bodies. While this system prevented any individual from amassing too much power on a federal level, it also ensured that no single figure wielded significant political authority. Tito had already devolved much power to the regions from the federal capital, Belgrade, with the constitution of 1974. When he died the eight state and party bureaucracies were strengthened even further. Most Yugoslavs agree that a curious multi-party system based on the conflicting interests of the eight regional Communist Parties has existed *de facto* in Yugoslavia for several years. Now that the country has agreed to renounce the one-party system, it must not only deconstruct neo-Stalinism but also defuse the tension that exists between eight separate state apparatuses.

Some form of confederation may emerge from the flaky ashes of Titoist Yugoslavia, but the nation could equally well fragment into a number of hopeless small states with a penchant for feuding. In the past Serbia, Croatia, Bosnia and Macedonia have often joined to create a powerful and dangerous vortex with an ability to drag down surrounding states and provinces, as they did most impressively in 1914. Yugoslavia is about to collapse – one can only hope that it will do so peacefully.

The Road to Failure

Tito's federated Yugoslavia cast off the shackles of foreign domination in June 1948, before Stalin had found enough time properly to dispose of the key. The split between Yugoslavia and Stalin's Cominform (Communist Information Bureau) had two important consequences. Practically it denied the Soviet Union access to the Adriatic and the Mediterranean. Politically it destroyed the myth of unity within the socialist camp and the infallibility of Moscow. Although it was a serious blow to Stalin's pride, the break with Yugoslavia did not pose a direct threat to the Soviet leader's security system and position in Eastern Europe. None the less Tito's determination to take Yugoslavia outside the Soviet sphere of influence was a remarkable act of defiance and courage. It also gave birth to Yugoslav nationalism, a healthy young baby that began to sicken at an early stage of its infancy. Tito's stature among Yugoslavs of all nationalities was great during the early 1950s. Despite the privations caused by the virtual economic blockade imposed by the Soviet Union and its East European allies, Yugoslavia survived and its international reputation flowered.

Tito and his Slovene adviser Edvard Kardelj were determined to proffer an ideological explanation for the break with Stalin. This led to the development of socialist self-management, which was a brilliant and seductive theory but a disaster in practice. It was an attempt to devolve power from Yugoslavia's various political centres to the point of production, so that the working class (the repository of all wisdom in Yugoslavia) could determine its own socio-economic fate. Quite sensibly, the working class simply voted itself pay rises when it was given a choice about what to do with excess funds that were either allotted by central government or, less often, won by its own labour. This led to all sorts of economic ills, and it was not long before Tito reshaped self-management into a novel form of the command economy. Despite the apparent availability of goods and the wealth that allows Yugoslavs an unrestricted right to travel, Tito's economic heritage is one of the most rotten in Eastern Europe.

Although Tito had split with the Soviet Union, the structure of the Yugoslav League of Communists (LCY), as the party was renamed in the mid-fifties, remained Stalinist in essence. Tito and the LCY leadership were the arbiters of what was, and was not, correct. Those who disagreed were either isolated or imprisoned.

Yugoslavia's internal security machine was one of the most powerful in the whole of Eastern Europe, as evidenced by the most
popular catch phrase of the period, *OZNA sve dozna* (OZNA
[the acronym for the secret police] finds out everything). In this
respect the trauma from which Yugoslavia is now suffering is just
as profound and crippling as those facing the rest of the newly
liberated East European states.

In another respect it is even more crippling. From the Alpine
comfort of Slovenia to the dusty poverty of Kosovo, Yugoslavia
does not consist only of six republics and two Socialist Autonomous Provinces attached to the Serbian republic: it contains also
dozens of different cultures and languages, three major religions
and a feast of complex historical vendettas. Most East European
countries have one national conflict to solve as they shake off the
dead skin of neo-Stalinism. In Yugoslavia a kaleidoscope of historical patterns, soiled with liberal coatings of blood, is confusing the
country's attempt to transform itself into a democracy – a feat that
is almost beyond comprehension.

The dénouement to the Yugoslav crisis began towards the end
of 1987, when Slobodan Milošević, a bright, young but eerily cold
banker, successfully engineered a *putsch* in the leadership of the
Serbian League of Communists. Milošević had garnered mass support, both within the party and among the Serbian population at
large, by openly playing the nationalist card. The single issue to
which he subordinated all others was Kosovo and the position of
the Serbian and Montenegrin minority in the province. Some
200,000 Serbs and Montenegrins in Kosovo live among 1.8 million
Albanians. Serbs are leaving the province at the rate of about 2,000
a year, while the Kosovo Albanians boast the highest birth rate in
Europe, thirty-four per 1,000. Milošević claims that Serbs leave
Kosovo because they are being driven out by an organized con-
spiracy of what he refers to as Albanian 'terrorists and separatists'.
The aim of this group is eventual unification, so the theory goes,
with the neighbouring People's Republic of Albania, Europe's last
bastion of Stalinism. Those who defend the Albanians in Kosovo
insist that the Serbs are moving out of Yugoslavia's poorest and
least developed region for economic reasons. They also suggest

that Albanians in Kosovo and the republic of Macedonia are being subjected to systematic racial discrimination at the hands of the Slav Serbs and Macedonians.

When he came to power Milošević maintained that both the Yugoslav LC (League of Communists) and the Serbian LC had allowed the security situation in Kosovo to deteriorate well beyond acceptable levels. He also accused the local party organization in Kosovo, headed by Azem Vllasi, of having done nothing to stop the development of Albanian 'terrorism and separatism' in the province. Indeed, he started accusing the Kosovo League of Communists of having encouraged this disease. In order to strengthen his case Milošević orchestrated a series of mass Serbian rallies, which were held in Kosovo, in Serbia proper and in Serbia's other autonomous province, Vojvodina. Partly by applying popular pressure and partly by some well-organized political bullying, Milošević soon forced the collapse of the hostile Vojvodina leadership, which he replaced with his supporters. He thus drove a wedge through the Yugoslav party. At first he was backed by Macedonia and Montenegro. The Slovenes were explicit and vocal in their opposition to his policies. They in turn were backed, albeit rather nervously, by Croatia's mumbling Stalinists, who had perhaps begun to realize that their days were numbered whomever they supported. Bosnia and Hercegovina took a middle course in the futile hope that the whole problem would somehow go away.

With this line-up Milošević then concentrated the power of the Serbian bureaucracy on Kosovo, cajoling and humiliating the entire Albanian population with the exception of a few quislings. The Albanians responded with a series of spontaneous uprisings that increased their confidence enormously but, over a fourteen-month period, left almost a hundred of them dead. Most of those killed were in their teens. Although life for Serbs has become more difficult in Kosovo, no Albanian 'terrorist' has ever succeeded in killing one of them.

Milošević's seizure of power was a watershed for two reasons. First, he challenged the rest of the Yugoslav communist bureaucracy quite openly on the issue of nationalism. Second, he re-imposed strict authoritarian rule in Serbia, purging from the party anyone who publicly disagreed with his strategy and turning the press into a heap of disgraceful, toadying rags. The decline of the Belgrade daily *Politika*, once one of Europe's finest newspapers, was particularly discouraging. Socialist ideology was peripheral or instrumental as far as Milošević was concerned, although he often invoked Tito and the late leader's catch-all phrase 'brotherhood and unity' in an attempt to disguise his nationalist purpose.

Not only had Milošević opened the wound of Kosovo but he had simultaneously scored a deep gash in the skin bonding Serbia with Slovenia. The moderate Slovenian party leadership, for ever under pressure from a confident and courageous young intelligentsia, considered the outbreak of nationalism in Serbia both distasteful and dangerous. The Slovenes also believed Serbia was putting the brakes on any meaningful economic reform. Serbs who favour the so-called unitary Yugoslav state (this is understood by many outside Serbia as a euphemism for a Greater Serbia) feared that Slovenia intended to secede and break up the federation. Popular mistrust developed between Serbs and Slovenes, and the two republics' leaderships declared a pointless but mutually damaging bureaucratic war on each other. By the beginning of 1990 the gulf between Slovenes and Serbs had become unbreachable. The Slovene party left the federal League of Communists and struck out on its own.

The revolutions in Eastern Europe exposed the extent of political decay in Yugoslavia. In response both to the revolutions and to the growing social and national unrest in Yugoslavia, the eight Communist Party organizations agreed in theory that multi-party elections should take place in each republic. Slovenia began its preparations immediately, and to its credit the Communist Party of Croatia, where a group of impressive young reformers had finally, if belatedly, deposed of the crusty, Stalinist time-servers, was also swift to start relinquishing power.

As the Slovene election on 8 April approached, the parties that had grouped together in the opposition coalition, DEMOS, all began to move clearly towards a position of secession. Their ultimate aim was a Yugoslav confederation. But most DEMOS representatives insisted that this confederation could only consist of fully independent states, so Slovenia would have to leave Yugo-slavia before the confederation could be created. On the other hand, the Slovene Communist Party, now inevitably renamed the Party of Democratic Renewal, supported the idea of a confedera-tion without secession. Just as post-war Yugoslavia had evolved from a centralized state into a federation, so now it could develop further from a federation into a confederation. No party compet-ing either in the Slovene elections or in the Croatian elections was able to elaborate precisely what it meant by a confederation; all agreed, however, that it would have to be created by a Yugoslav round table at which the various republics would discuss, and then concur on, the shape of the new confederation. Nice though this idea was, it presupposed agreement between Serbia and Slovenia, Serbia and Croatia and Serbia and Kosovo, and this is a political equation that bends the imagination as much as does time travel.

So in the middle of 1990, while the rest of Eastern Europe was in a state of great excitement at the straightforward prospect of the first free elections in over four decades, Yugoslavia was in a confused mess.

Serbs and Slovenes had become embroiled in verbal battles that occasionally developed into more petty and tiresome types of con-flict, such as the self-defeating economic blockade that Serbia imposed on its more prosperous enemy. The Slovenes had given the opposition coalition, DEMOS, an absolute majority at the elections. If not constitutionally, at least psychologically many Slovenes had broken with Yugoslavia and were daily resembling more and more their smug, uptight friends from across the border in Austria. As one weather-beaten activist from *Mladina*, the youth newspaper that was practising *glasnost* years before Gorbachev had thought of it, remarked to me during the elections, 'The only thing that ever made Slovenia interesting was its membership of the Yugoslav federation. Now that looks likely to go, this is going to be one of the most boring places in Europe.'

Kosovo's Albanians were busily organizing in new political parties, the strongest of which was Ibrahim Rugovo's Democratic Association of Kosovo. According to the Serbian leadership, these parties were illegal, but, largely because of external pressure from the United States and the European Community, they were now more reticent about locking up Albanian activists or deploying the homicidal Serbian special police force in combat against demonstrators. In Serbia itself political parties were also beginning to grow in opposition to the Serbian LC, although the communists enjoyed the considerable advantage of having already appropriated the nationalist vote for themselves. In order to strengthen his political and material base still further Milošević announced the merger of the Serbian LC with the front organization, the Socialist Alliance of Serbia; they became the new Socialist Party of Serbia. Elections were then set to take place in December 1990, although all of Milošević's opponents accused him of having rigged the electoral process in his favour.

In Macedonia, where the communists had dropped their support for Serbia, an unpleasant assortment of crude Macedonian nationalists were proving much more successful than the timid and youthful democratic parties that had recently been formed. In Bosnia and Montenegro, where they had yet to agree on a transition to a multi-party system, people quaked with fear for a variety of reasons.

Thanks to the shrewd policies of the energetic federal prime minister, the Croat Ante Marković, the economy had stabilized considerably. At the beginning of 1990 Marković introduced the *new new* dinar to replace the *new* dinar, although visitors remained horribly confused, as the population still tended to count using the old dinar, of which you needed millions to buy a loaf of bread. Until the end of 1989 the new dinar had been almost valueless. In 1989 inflation topped 2,500 per cent, but by the beginning of April 1990 Yugoslavia registered a reverse inflation rate of -1.5 per cent. Marković's stabilization of the currency, and its transformation into a fully convertible one, had done a great deal to restore confidence in the economy. But although Marković's fiscal policy was almost essential in order to prevent economic collapse, it had serious social consequences. From being one of the cheapest countries in Europe, Yugoslavia became one of the most expensive almost overnight, and the prices of many goods rivalled those in Paris, London or Vienna, threatening not only local living standards but also the country's most important foreign currency earner, tourism. The menacing spectre of mass unemployment began to walk abroad. Although some economic stability had been won, Yugoslavia was in an unholy political mess. The elections in Croatia, the second largest republic after Serbia, have confirmed that Yugoslavia is facing a rough ride. Nowhere is the potential for violent destabilization as great.

Serbia and Croatia: the Heart of the Matter

Croatia's preparations for multi-party elections went ahead largely unnoticed by the rest of the world. The media were resting after a rich meal that included the East German elections as the entrée and the Hungarian elections as the dessert. And very delicious they were too. A few curious hacks made the trip down to Ljubljana for the Slovene elections, but by the time it came to the Croatian elections on 22 April 1990 most editors were tired of East European polls, particularly in Yugoslavia. Newspaper editors do not like Yugoslavia because it is too complicated, and the Croat elections generated less interest than local elections in West Germany, which had been held a few months before. This was quite clearly a mistake, as the Croat elections produced the most dramatic result of all the East European elections – a parliamentary majority for Franjo Tudjman's HDZ (*Hrvatska Demokratska Zajednica*), the Croatian Democratic Union.

The resurgence of nationalism in Croatia during the elections was perfectly predictable. In 1972 Tito ordered the suppression of the *Maspok* (the Mass Movement), which had combined an influential part of the Croatian LC's leadership – notably two figures, Miko Tripalo and Savka Dabčević-Kucar – with the nationalist cultural organization Matica Hrvatska. The aims of the *Maspok* were vague and contradictory, but essentially it sought greater cultural autonomy and political freedom for Croatia. Extreme Croatian nationalists undoubtedly used the *Maspok* as a vehicle for political activity, but it was by no means the counter-revolutionary nationalist movement that Tito and the LCY (League of Communists of Yugoslavia) leadership described it as.

Since then Croatia has been known as the silent republic, cowering in fear of the secret police, who were extremely influential in the republic and brutal when required. Any manifestation of Croatian nationalism, whether in culture or in politics, was nipped in the bud by Tito. The last two decades have engendered great resentment among Croats, who are convinced that the repression was a simple extension of Serbian chauvinism. Twenty years of silence also reinforced among Croats the widespread belief that in both the pre-war and the post-war Yugoslav states their interests have been systematically ignored in favour of not only Serbia but also, more recently, the poorer republics in the south, which depend on hand-outs from Slovenia and Croatia for their survival. If this had not been sufficient to generate a fresh outburst of Croatian nationalism, the appearance of Milošević and the subsequent transformation of Serbian political life along nationalist lines in 1987 and 1988 ensured that the Croatian elections would be fought on the national issue.

So it was not just Tudjman who played the national card during the elections. The communists – renamed, of course, and in this case transformed into the Party for Democratic Change (SKH–SDP) – demanded a confederate Yugoslavia with wide-ranging autonomy for Croatia. The Coalition for National Agreement (KNS), which would have found the backing of Western liberals and social democrats if these had expressed an interest in Croatia, was led by the stars of the *Maspok*, Miko Tripalo and Savka Dabčević-Kucar, whose standing in Croatia was once on a par with that of Dubček in Czechoslovakia. The KNS advocated virtual independence for Croatia within a loose confederation, but despite the pedigree of its leaders and its nationalist message, it was obliterated at the polls by the HDZ.

According to activists inside and outside the HDZ, Tudjman's election campaign was financed to the tune of between $4 million and $5 million by émigré supporters. In contrast to the other Croat parties, the HDZ has active cells in Sweden, Norway, Germany, Canada, the USA and Australia. The campaign was boosted by countless young students, all with perfect Canadian, American or Australian English, who had forsaken the easy comfort of their birth places to join in the reconstruction of Croatia. All of them had the 'look', which one now encounters all over Eastern Europe and particularly in the Balkans. Translated, the 'look' means: 'We are the most oppressed nation in Eastern Europe, but the time has now come to display our superior cultural values. By the way, we know you are a subversive Western liberal determined to slander us with accusations of anti-Semitism and neo-Fascism.'

It is, of course, very difficult to pin accusations of neo-Fascism on Tudjman and his party. In Yugoslavia and Croatia this is a very sensitive issue. The only time that Croats have created an independent state was during the Second World War, when Hitler allowed Ante Pavelić and three hundred of his mad *Ustasha* followers to establish the Independent Croatian State (NDH). Although this was not a popular construction, it did reveal just how unpleasant Croats can be when they are encouraged. Few European regions under the influence of the Nazis were able to rival the bestiality of the *Ustashas* as they set about the task of liquidating the Serbs and Jews who, unhappily, lived in areas under their control.

Tudjman is no Pavelić. A Titoist partisan and later a colonel in the General Staff, he was not a military man but a bureaucrat in charge of cadre questions in the Yugoslav National Army, which placed him in an extremely influential position. He was disliked by his colleagues, however, and suspected of being a Croatian nationalist, for which charge he eventually spent several years in prison during the purge that followed the suppression of *Maspok* in 1972. In the early 1960s he found work as an archivist at the Zagreb Museum of Military History. There he developed his broad knowledge of Croatian history and his obsession with Croatian military figures. His party's paraphernalia is characterized by heroes of Croatia's history, symbols and flags, but he is a shrewd and careful politician who tends not to commit silly mistakes. Within his ranks, however, there are anti-Semites and racists. During his election campaign Tudjman made one serious slip at a rally in the town of Pazin. He told a group of hecklers that there would be no place for them in the new Croatia. His numerous deputy presidents talk darkly about traitors to the Croatian nation, and in general they define good or 'real' Croats as those who support the HDZ.

But the most disturbing aspect of Tudjman's platform concerns the Republic of Bosnia and Hercegovina, which is populated by Serbs, Croats and Moslems. Yugoslavia's Moslems are Serbs and Croats who were converted by the Turks and have now lost their original ethnic identity. In Tito's federation they were afforded the status of a nation, a valuable privilege. In the past Moslems in Bosnia would split their children into Serbs and Croats, as this was the only way of guaranteeing the survival of the line: when Serbs or Croats rampaged they would spare only the lives of those who claimed the same nationality as they did.

According to Josef Zorek, a Canadian student with a particularly intense 'look' who came to Croatia for the first time to help with the HDZ campaign, 'Croatia and Bosnia and Hercegovina together form a bio-geographic, historic, ethnic whole as an indivisible unit of the Croatian nation. Their future is bound together, and through organization it will become a sovereign Croatian state.' The 'organization' to which Zorek refers will come in the form of the plebiscites that the HDZ wants to hold in Bosnia. Unfortunately not everybody in Bosnia and Hercegovina agrees that they belong to a Croatian 'bio-geographic' entity. Many are Serbs or Moslems, and any attempt to annex Bosnia would certainly lead to civil war. Plebiscites and referenda do not amount to annexation, but they would, without question, heighten nationalist tension in Bosnia – quite possibly to breaking point. Josef Manolić, deputy president of the HDZ and once one of the most feared secret policemen in Croatia, stated before the election victory that if the HDZ successfully formed the government, 'the setting up of referenda in Bosnia will be placed high on the political agenda'.

A substantial part of Tudjman's electoral support in urban areas came from Croats, largely uneducated, unskilled workers, who had emigrated from Bosnia to Croatia. Tudjman himself has been very careful not to commit himself to any specific policy other than a vague desire to create a 'sovereign Croatia' (although he mutters about the need for a confederated Yugoslavia). He may well appreciate that an attempt to interfere with the internal affairs of Bosnia would be courting serious conflict with Serbia and the possibility of civil war. None the less he has publicly committed himself to the holding of referenda. Tudjman is not a classic nationalist leader. He is a poor speaker and is almost embarrassed by the large crowds he attracts at public meetings. But he has engendered great expectations among the Croats, and if, for tactical reasons, he wanted to revise his programme, he could well find himself a victim of the leviathan that he has invoked. And he may discover that it is increasingly difficult to resist calls from his supporters to place the question of Bosnia at the very top of the political agenda.

By the summer of 1990 the HDZ had announced its intention of introducing a new constitution that would afford the republic much greater autonomy within Yugoslavia. The constitution spelled the end of federal authority in Croatia. The 600,000-strong Serb minority in Croatia objected strongly to the new constitution, which, they claimed, would discriminate against non-Croats. There is no doubt that the Serbs who organized the campaign against the constitution were supported psychologically and materially by the Republic of Serbia. They decided to hold a referendum among all Serbs in Croatia on the issue of the new constitution. Tudjman and the HDZ rejected this move as illegal and warned strongly against Serbian attempts aimed at destabilizing Croatia. Armed Serbs temporarily took over the major towns of the Serbian minority in Croatia, Knin and Benkovac, but the situation soon stabilized. None the less the incident demonstrated that Yugoslavia has never been closer to civil war since the Second World War, and it was not long before the area once again threatened the peace.

Many Croats will go to great lengths to deny their close bonds with Serbs. They describe in detail the linguistic superiority of Croatian over Serbian. The two languages are, in fact, the same. There are regional differences, but even to call them dialects would be an exaggeration. The substantial difference lies in the Serbs' use of the Cyrillic script and the Croats' use of the Latin one. This is, of course, a cultural and not a linguistic matter. The language issue became intensely political, however, during the inter-war period, particularly after the abolition of parliamentary rule in 1929 in favour of direct rule by the Serbian King Alexander. During the next ten years the kingdom of Yugoslavia developed into a vehicle for Greater Serbian aspirations. One of the most important hallmarks of the Greater Serbian nationalists was their desire to impose on Croats the Serbian variation of Serbo-Croat, including the Cyrillic script. (This would be rather like London insisting that all Scots speak with an English accent and drop local variations of vocabulary and grammar.) The experience of the 1930s has ensured that language remains a seminal political issue for the Croats.

Despite their ethnic similarity Croats and Serbs are divided by a gaping ravine forged between them by their separate confessional and cultural history. Croats are Roman Catholics and perceive themselves to be a Western nation. Throughout most of its modern history Croatia was dominated by the Habsburg empire. Serbia is loyal to the Orthodox Church and evinces many traces of the Ottoman Empire to which it was attached for several centuries. Croats complain that the Serbian majority has systematically stifled their interests in both Yugoslav states of this century. Serbs, on the other hand, live in fear of a return of the NDH (the Fascist Croatian state).

The democratization of Yugoslavia has revived the possibility of conflict between Serbs and Croats. Lev Kreft, a leading member of the Slovene Communist Party (now called the Party for Democratic Renewal), suggested to me that during Yugoslavia's first experience of parliamentary rule in the 1920s popular conflict between Serbs and Croats was transferred from the streets to parliament. Kreft argued that the democratic system defuses the violence that characterizes the relationship between Croats and Serbs. It is quite clear that national conflict in Yugoslavia can be solved only through the introduction of modern democratic processes. However, this is no guarantee. Unfortunately Kreft's argument rather collapsed when I reminded him that the first democratic system in Yugoslavia came to an end when Stepan Radić, the leader of the Croat Peasant Party, was shot dead in parliament by a Serbian member.

It is by no means a foregone conclusion that the two nations will slip back into the hostilities of the past, but a large number of Croats live in Serbia, while many Serbs live in Croatia. It would require only one small incident on either side to ignite in the area a large-scale conflagration that would be guaranteed to spread beyond the two regions' borders. The division between Serbs and Croats accounts for the greatest threat to stability in the Balkans.

Kosovo: the Nightmare Continues

A few days after the first round of the Croatian elections I sat in the first-floor living room of an Albanian house in Priština, the capital of Kosovo. As in many Albanian homes, there were no chairs, just coloured mattresses on the floor around the walls. The atmosphere was solemn and my anticipation great. I was about to meet Adem Demaqi, known among Albanians as the Kosovo Mandela, within a few days of his release after a total of twenty-eight years in prison. During this marathon spell interest in Demaqi's fate outside Kosovo and the People's Republic of Albania was limited to a few human rights organizations in Western Europe and the United States. On his return to Kosovo in April 1990 he was greeted like a demi-god. Albanians travelled from all over Yugoslavia to welcome Demaqi and enjoy the privilege of being received by him for just five minutes. For days there was a constant stream of well-wishers outside his sister's house (the authorities banned him from visiting his own village outside Priština), hoping for a glimpse.

Demaqi is small and very short-sighted, but he speaks with impressive, relaxed authority. Politically he is not representative of most Kosovo Albanians because he is an unreconstructed supporter of the People's Republic of Albania, but the fortitude with which he faced three long spells of imprisonment and the courage with which he defended the rights of Albanians in Kosovo, at a time when nobody outside the province showed the slightest interest in their fate, have won him more respect in his community than any other figure since the war. The comparison with Mandela is entirely deserved.

On the same day that I visited Demaqi all charges were dropped against Azem Vllasi and ten other Albanians accused by the Serbian authorities of fomenting counter-revolution, and they were released from the custody in which they had been detained for fourteen months. As Vllasi walked from the court a free man, normal life came to a standstill as workers, students, housewives, shopkeepers and schoolchildren lined the streets of Titova Mitrovica cheering wildly when he drove back towards Priština.

Vllasi is a curious political figure. He was put in charge of the Kosovo League of Communists following the uprising there in 1981. He faithfully executed the policies of his Serbian masters and was regarded as a quisling by most Albanians. Following the ascent of Milošević in Belgrade, Vllasi discovered that he could not keep pace with the fanatical demands of the new Serbian leadership. He was ostracized by it, and when Albanians began a series of mass protests at the end of 1988 Vllasi was identified as their spiritual leader almost by chance. Milošević used this as an excuse to imprison him and charge him with counter-revolution, a laughable accusation that the Serbs signally failed to prove. On his return from jail Vllasi was transformed from Stalinist quisling to national hero. He is one of the very few leading politicians in Eastern Europe to have enjoyed the privileges of a corrupt neo-Stalinist bureaucracy and mass popular support. Ironically, Milošević is another, albeit very different, example. On his release Vllasi was coy about his political intentions, although he may join one of Kosovo's political parties where he would play a key role in Kosovo's future if he so desires. It is hard to imagine Vllasi throwing in the towel.

The release of Demaqi and Vllasi marked a shift in Kosovo politics. Although special Serbian troops, armed to the teeth, were still evident all over Kosovo, the return to Priština marked the final bankruptcy of Serbian policy in the region. Vllasi described himself as Europe's last political prisoner. While his claim is open to debate, the Serbian leadership clearly seems to have agreed that locking up Albanians in Kosovo creates more problems than it solves. In the space of eighteen months Albanians in Kosovo developed an extraordinary belief in themselves, best expressed by the tremendous support given to the Democratic Association of Kosovo led by the gentle academic Ibrahim Rugova.

In many ways Kosovo corresponds to Western images of the Balkans. There is no sign marking the border between Serbia proper and Kosovo. The most reliable marker is the first *plis*, the egg-shaped white cap that older Albanian men wear. Much of the land is rugged and uninviting, but behind the Western cities of Peć and Djakovica mountains shoot up dramatically from the ground, affording the secretive People's Republic of Albania natural protection from the contamination of Titoism and the outside world. In Kosovo itself Albanians are almost as wary as they are in the People's Republic. The Serbian secret police continues to operate with equanimity, making life unpleasant for anyone who is not protected by his or her name or reputation. Except in the great bastions of Albanian militancy, such as Podujevo and Uroševac, outside Priština most Albanians behave with great caution, particularly towards foreigners. Although their situation is improving noticeably as calls for the introduction of a democratic system in Kosovo increase, they have no guarantee that Serbia will concede these demands. It is easier to understand Kosovo now than it was even three years ago, but it is still a place where life is often not what it appears to be on the surface.

The conflict in Kosovo is political and not confessional, as some people, Serbs in particular, like to present it. The great majority of Albanians are Moslems, but the attraction of Islam among the younger generation in Kosovo in particular is not great. Indeed, there is a serious generational conflict in Kosovo as young people look to the West for their political and social values. No Albanian has ever demanded an Islamic state in Kosovo, and recently agreements to end the system of blood feuds between families and the growing strength of the women's movement among Albanians have testified to the power of Western influences in Kosovo. Quite simply, Albanians want Kosovo to be granted the status of a republic and the right to vote in democratic elections. It is true that many Albanians have only a basic education and that among the leadership of the main political parties some individuals are unable to conceal an intolerant nationalism, but the most powerful current argues for the creation of autonomy for Kosovo within the Yugoslav federation. Even Demaqi has dropped his demand for the unification of Kosovo Albanians with the People's Republic in favour of the granting of republican status.

Serbs insist that if Kosovo became a Yugoslav republic, this would be the prelude to secession, which they cannot countenance, as they consider Kosovo to be the cradle of Serbian civilization. Despite this historical bond, it is striking that few Serbs from outside Kosovo have ever visited the province. They will, of course, spend many hours denouncing Albanians as terrorists, separatists, Shiptars (a derogatory term in Serbian), rapists, primitives and bandits despite never having spoken to an Albanian from Kosovo. Above all, they consider them stupid and uncivilized. In fact, the Kosovo Albanians boast a vigorous and impressive intelligentsia that is largely responsible for articulating Albanian demands and mobilizing the Kosovo population almost as one for the first time in their history. This is the key to Kosovo's development. Along with Rugova, embryonic parties have been organized by three brilliant young Albanians, Shkelzen Maliqi, Veton Surroi and Rexhep Quosi, who have transformed the political map in Kosovo. Already divisions are becoming visible within the Albanian community. Rugovo's organization is assuming a clearly nationalist hue as a reaction to the policies of Milošević. Maliqi and Surroi look, perhaps rather optimistically, for a solution to the Kosovo problem within a pan-Yugoslav opposition movement. If extreme nationalist forces in Kosovo emerge as the more powerful, then calls for unification with the People's Republic may be heard more frequently. The Kosovo Albanians would not support a Greater Albania unless there were a thorough liberalization in Tirana. That, of course, is looking increasingly inevitable. If the option of a Greater Albania did become a serious part of the political agenda in Kosovo, it would almost certainly threaten to provoke civil war in Yugoslavia.

So far the Serbians have refused to give up Kosovo. Present demographic trends indicate that soon after the turn of the century Kosovo will be ethnically pure. Serbs and Montenegrins in the province have a very low birthrate and are emigrating from the area in large numbers. The Serbian leadership is certain to maintain its heavy police presence in the area even after it finally agrees to democratic elections for the republic. Rugovo's Democratic Association will sweep the board in Kosovo, but Serbian nationalist parties are likely to control the government in Belgrade none the less. This means that the political hostility between Belgrade and Priština may still continue after democracy has been introduced, although for the first time local government in Kosovo might be dominated absolutely by Albanians.

Apart from the gun, which the Serbs have not shied away from using in the recent past, the only solution to the Kosovo problem offered by Belgrade is the recolonization of the area with Serbs from the republic proper. Božur, the Serbian nationalist organization in Kosovo, wants to see 2 million Serbs moved into the province to create an equal balance between Albanians and Slavs in the region. This mad plan of colonization, which many in Belgrade take seriously, has no chance of being realized because Kosovo's economy is the weakest in Europe except for the People's Republic of Albania. Serbia will be able to make it work only if it pours billions of dollars into Kosovo, and one resource that Serbia lacks is money. Nevertheless Serbian nationalist plans will ensure that Kosovo remains one of Europe's trouble spots for a long time to come. If the Serbs attempt to impose their will by force, the Albanians now have the confidence, and a network, that are strong enough to match the violence from Belgrade.

Serbia: The Belly of the Beast

In 1988 and 1989 Milošević was the object of a personality cult that had long since gone out of fashion elsewhere in Eastern Europe. While this was greatly encouraged by Serbia's press, the cult was undoubtedly very popular. After suffering under a colourless bureaucracy that always appeared to cave in to the demands of other republics and the Albanian demons in Kosovo, here at last was a man who talked like ordinary folk. Serbian nationalism has been his main platform, but he has also promised the peasants and workers a higher standard of living and economic security as Yugoslavia moved slowly towards a market economy. Milošević's economic programme has turned out to be an unmitigated disaster.

He has benefited from the ruthless determination of the federal prime minister Ante Marković to stabilize the dinar. But Serbia's economy is in a sorry state. For several months now many Serbs have been suffering regular power cuts because cities like Belgrade are so indebted that they can no longer pay the Serbian Electricity Company for its services. As a result, the SEC simply turns off the tap. JAT, the Serbian-based national airline, lives in constant fear of running out of fuel because of unpaid bills. Wages in Serbia are among the lowest in Yugoslavia, and unemployment is once again becoming a painful social evil.

Unable to deliver on the economic front, Milošević's halo has begun to look chipped and tatty. Forces both within the Socialist Party and among the new parties emerging in the republic's tentative democratic awakening are keen to knock the halo off his head once and for all. In response Milošević and the party leadership in Serbia have been stalling on the holding of free elections. Serbia looks like a battered and wounded animal. It has taken a severe political beating in Kosovo and may be about to lose the province once and for all.

When the break-up of Yugoslavia began Serbia enjoyed the consistent support of the Communist Party leadership in Macedonia, the southernmost Yugoslav republic bordering Greece and Bulgaria. This was largely because of Macedonia's fear of burgeoning Albanian national consciousness in Kosovo, as 400,000 Albanians in Macedonia are just waiting for the opportunity to express their political grievances. As Macedonia moves towards democracy, and the influence of the reactionary nationalist movement increases, fears grow (not unreasonably) that Belgrade will take steps to regain Macedonia, which, during the inter-war kingdom of Yugoslavia, was designated southern Serbia. During the same period Belgrade decreed that Macedonian was not a language, merely a dialect of Serbian, which is palpable hogwash. As these disturbing memories from the inter-war period were revived in the course of 1989 the Macedonian leadership more or less dropped its support for Serbia, isolating Belgrade still further. In addition to these two sores, Serbia must now shape up to the rebirth of Croatian nationalism, surely its greatest test yet. It will be impossible for Serbia to master this situation unless it subordinates nationalist politics to a programme of economic and social stabilization.

But whereas in Croatia the reborn Communist Party represents a genuine progressive force for those who have not been infected by nationalism, the Socialist Party in Serbia is one of the powerhouses of nationalism. Farther to the right of the Socialist Party is an organization known as the Serbian National Renewal, whose chief hallmark is its leader Vuk Drašković, a writer who drifts around Belgrade, Christ-like, in long flowing robes that complement his long, flowing beard. Although he projects a dreamier and more entertaining image than Tudjman, Drašković is a serious political actor with radical nationalist ambitions. Both Milošević and Drašković have benefited greatly from Tudjman's victory in Croatia, and already a pattern of mutual provocation between the leading Croat and Serb nationalists has been established. (The Serbs made the opening move by demanding war reparations from the Croats. In this way the nationalists from both sides feed greedily off one another.) The only powerful democratic alternative to the Serbian nationalists is called, appropriately, the Democratic Party. However, this centre-right coalition has been careful not to discuss the issue of Kosovo or Croatia in any great detail, and its critics suggest that, when elections are finally held in Serbia, it too will move towards a nationalist position. The most modern political party to have emerged in Serbia is the Yugoslav Social Democratic Co-ordinating Committee, led by veterans of the human rights struggle in Yugoslavia, like Milan Nikolić. It is the experience of Nikolić and his colleagues that amounts to one of the most depressing in Yugoslavia. For years such people were among the only ones who dared to speak out against the Stalinist methods of the LCY and its secret police system. Now many of those people who before watched in silence as such men and women were jailed for political offences are attempting to isolate them and, above all, denounce them for rejecting Serbian nationalism.

During a full-scale mobilization of Balkan nationalism it is easy to forget the depth of the mistrust and resentment of all Yugoslavs towards the country's corrupt and self-seeking bureaucracy, which is responsible for the economic crisis – which in turn goes a long way towards explaining the national crisis. There have been many signs in Serbia in particular that nationalism is not sufficient to distract workers and peasants from the pursuit of their social and economic rights. Soon after the victory of Tudjman in the Croatian elections Milošević and the Communist Party leadership tightened their belts as rumours that Serbian banks were on the verge of running out of money began circulating, meaning that salaries would no longer be paid. Until 1990 Serbia, with the support of federal funds gleaned largely from Croatia and Slovenia, could to some extent afford to ignore its reputation abroad. The West was highly critical of Serbia's policy in Kosovo, and in addition it did not trust the Yugoslav banking system to invest foreign loans properly. The decisions to release Vllasi and Demaqi and to lift the state of emergency in Kosovo in April 1990 were almost certainly related to Milošević's urgent need to brush up his image with the West. If Milošević, Drašković or any other nationalist leader fails to revitalize the Serbian economy, they will fall irrespective of the toughness of their posture on Kosovo.

The economy is both the breast plate and the Achilles' heel of Serbian nationalism. By provoking separatist tendencies in Slovenia and Croatia, Serbs are damaging only themselves. Although Slovenia is much more dependent on Serbian markets than some Slovenes will admit, it is Serbia that benefits the most, economically, from the Yugoslav federation. Almost the first move by DEMOS after it was elected in Slovenia was to close down Krško, Yugoslavia's only nuclear power station. Serbia, which suffers from a permanent energy shortage, complained bitterly, alleging that Krško was a Yugoslav project and that therefore Slovenia could not shut it down unilaterally. Practically, however, Serbia could not even claim compensation for its investment in Krško. Slovenia accounts for a mere 8 per cent of the Yugoslav population but for 15 per cent of the country's GNP. Together with Croatia, Slovenia dominates Yugoslavia's trade with the West. The bulk of Serbia's foreign trade is with East European countries and the Soviet Union, which are profoundly unsatisfactory commerical partners even during periods of political stability.

One Ring to Bind Them

Dinaric Yugoslavia is a beautiful strip of wild mountainous territory that stretches for about 100 miles just in from Croatia's Dalmatian coast. The villages that are scattered down the Dinaric mountain range enjoy a reputation similar to that of the Gallic village where Astérix and Obélix lived. Feuds are endemic in the area – within families, between families, between villages and, of course, between national groups, since the region is one where there is a rich mix of Serbs and Croats. Dinaric people with money like to show it off in a rather gaudy way. Colloquially such characters are referred to as cowboys, while their slow, plodding counterparts from the rest of Bosnia, Serbia and Croatia are known as the 'peasants'. Eighty per cent of the leading politicians in Croatia were born there, while the number of Serb leaders who hail from the area is wildly disproportionate to the small concentration of Serbs. Tudjman is the exception that proves the rule. The influence of Milošević, the federal prime minister Marković, Tudjman's deputy Manolić, Miko Tripalo, Savka Dabčević-Kučar (all Dinaric) and many others is out of all proportion to the small area from where they come. Back in their home villages most of them have built themselves grand villas and enjoy nothing more than basking in the acknowledgement that they receive from their loyal friends and family.

The cowboys have transferred this Dinaric feuding to a national scale with unhappy consequences for the plodding peasants. Such petty quarrelling has seriously hampered Yugoslavia's development for a long time. The best example of this in post-war Yugoslavia has been the saga of the *autoput*. The foundations of the main trunk route through southern Europe, which carries millions of lorries, holidaymakers and *Gastarbeiter* traffic every year, were laid in the 1940s by an ominous combination of idealist youngsters and imprisoned members of the bourgeoisie. About three-quarters of the main stretch connecting Zagreb with Belgrade lies on Croatian territory. The main beneficiary of the development of the 130 kilometres that are still single-lane into a motorway would be Serbia. Croatia has always demanded a contribution from Serbia for the completion of the motorways programme. Serbia refuses this, claiming that Croatia must pay. As a result nobody pays; the *autoput* remains both the most dangerous and the slowest road in Europe; and every year hundreds pay for Serbo-Croat bickering over it with their lives.

It will be a miracle if the 250 miles that separate Zagreb from Belgrade are ever covered by a two-lane motorway. Yugoslavia is breaking up along the same axis that divided the Habsburg Empire from the Ottoman Empire. In theory a confederation of Slovenia, Croatia and Bosnia–Hercegovina would be a viable state. The idea that Serbia, Montenegro, Kosovo and Macedonia might form an equivalent confederation is much less convincing, partly because of national tensions between Serbs, Albanians and Macedonians but also because such a configuration would be desperately weak economically. Even if two such state formations did emerge, their creation would inevitably stumble on the rock of Serbian and Croatian enmity. The Slovenes seem to have realized this, and the desire for complete separation from Yugoslavia to avoid becoming embroiled in a conflict between Serbia and Croatia has been growing rapidly since the victory of Tudjman in the Croatian elections.

It seems laughable, even absurd, that as the end of the twentieth century approaches the cluster of states that makes up Yugoslavia, and that in the past has created so many difficulties, should once again be displaying their spectacular nationalist feathers in anticipation of a fight. Reason, one hopes, will surely prevail – but that is to fail to appreciate how intolerant and brutal the Balkans can be.

Myriad images from Eastern Europe have been branded on my consciousness in the last ten years. The strongest of all is not that of Havel and Dubček on Wensceslas Square or of Ceauşescu's and Elena's pathetic bodies lying dead on the concrete. On a warm late spring evening in 1989 I was in Vučitrn, a small town north of Priština in Kosovo. In the square a Serbian communist was denouncing Albanian terrorists wildly. In front of him about a thousand Serbs, most of whom had been bussed in from Niš and Kragujevac, were chanting furiously, '*Srbija je ustala*' (Serbia has arisen). Flanking the entire proceedings in bemused silence were thousands of Albanians (95 per cent of Vučitrn's population is Albanian). For the first time in my life I experienced the atmosphere of the 1930s, the age of wild, unco-ordinated nationalism. Almost two years later I was in a Zagreb housing estate on a miserable April afternoon, surrounded by the same faces wearing the same denim jackets and flags that only experienced Yugowatchers know are slightly different. As Franjo Tudjman took the stage I saw the same look on the faces in the crowd that I had seen in Vučitrn. Only one thing was different – the chant: '*Hrvatska je ustala*' (Croatia has arisen).

6 ALBANIA

The Final Frontier

Albania is a collage of fantasies – Balkan, visual, Stalinist, rural, even Rousseauesque. The dream begins as the border guard slowly draws back the heavy iron gate that is adorned by one of Europe's most powerful heraldic symbols, the double-headed black eagle of the Kastrioti family, the line of the greatest Albanian leader, the fifteenth-century Prince Skënderbeu. The gate separates Albania from the rest of the world. But the vigilance that spawned the countless grey pillboxes that are at first so conspicuous but soon blend into the scenery has lost its intensity. The manner in which border guards and policemen raise their right fist to the shoulder in the Hoxhaist salute is now friendly and welcoming. Their Maoist caps are no longer an expression of commitment to the extreme intolerance of Albania's cultural revolution of over two decades ago. Instead they signify the bearers' identification with the real state ideology – Albanianism.

Tucked away in the south-west corner of the Balkans, Albania's mystery is enhanced by the magnificent mountains that cover 75 per cent of the country. The soil and rock of the mountainous areas are blood-red, which creates a majestic contrast with the deep green of the foliage growing on the steeply inclined sides. As you travel through the mountains, your journey is frequently interrupted by sightings of poorly dressed young Albanians who seem to slide down the mountainside from some secret perch in order to observe the foreigner in greater detail, although they invariably maintain a careful distance. The intimate relationship that many rural dwellers enjoy with the mountains provides a partial explanation for the Albanian name of the country – Shqipëri, Land of the Eagles.

As the only European state that still adheres to the principles of revolutionary socialism, Albania is, of course, peculiar. The changes that have swept the rest of Europe have been prevented from flooding Albania by an apparently impregnable dam built of imposing rocks of ideology and tradition. But these boulders are beginning to show signs of serious erosion. While wary of rejecting its distinct history, Albania too will soon discard the intense neo-Stalinist system that has made it the object of distant fascination for many years. The need for change in the country is palpable, but even more critical for Albania's future will be the speed and nature of that change. For in most respects Albania bears little or no comparison with other European countries, and confrontation between the state and the people could lead swiftly to a situation that may even overshadow the violence of the Romanian revolution.

Albania is the poorest country on the European continent. It enjoys a living standard comparable with those of small, modestly successful countries of the developing world. In addition, the isolation that the ruling Albanian Party of Labour has enforced on the country for several decades has accentuated social and psychological differences, separating Albanians from other Europeans. Albanians from the southern Yugoslav province of Kosovo will occasionally comment on the almost unbridgeable gap that divides them from the people of Albania proper – and this despite mutual fascination and respect, in addition to ethnic ties. 'The rift is now too great,' one Kosovo journalist visiting Albania in early 1990 remarked to me. 'They are mainland China and we are Hong Kong. Even if we were now forced together, this would not disguise the fact that we come from different worlds.' The impact of a swift reintegration into European culture could have seriously adverse effects on a rich and most mysterious country.

But despite the country's almost mythical isolation, Albanians have in recent years become better acquainted with the rest of Europe as the short-wave transmissions in Albanian by the Voice of America radio station have been enhanced by Italian, Greek and Yugoslav television, which most Albanians receive. The ruling Albanian Party of Labour is finding it increasingly difficult to stifle the desire for exploration and experimentation, particularly among urban youth and the intellectuals. Indeed, there are signs that a powerful reformist wing in the party actually welcomes, and even covertly encourages, some popular dissatisfaction in order to strengthen its hand within the Central Committee.

Darkest Albania

Albania's post-war isolation was determined by its geography and its traditions. Albanians claim that they are descended from the Illyrians, who lived in what is present-day Albania, Kosovo, some parts of Montenegro and some parts of Greece. They speak an Indo-European language but one that forms a language group of its own. The major cities of the lowlands, Tirana, Shkodër, Gjirokastër and others, were clearly influenced by European and, in particular, Italian culture during the inter-war years. But the impact of new ideas was felt by only a small number of intellectuals, while most people in the countryside remained firmly bound by semi-feudal socio-economic relations and attitudes. This passive population was mobilized for the first time during the Second World War. Most joined Enver Hoxha's partisan movement, although some were attracted by two other movements, including the army of the nationalist *Balli Kombëtar*. Later in the war the *Balli* cooperated with the Nazi occupiers against the Partizans in a civil war that paralleled the struggle between the Chetniks and the Partizans in Serbia, Montenegro and other parts of Yugoslavia. The success of Hoxha and his military commander, Mehmet Shehu, was all the more remarkable because Albania was the only country in Eastern Europe where not one Soviet soldier fought during the National Liberation War. The Partizans received important material and logistical support from the Allies, in particular the British and the Americans, but their army fought alone. This, of course, was of exceptional importance both in establishing the legitimacy of Hoxha's rule and in determining the curious independent path that Albanian foreign policy would take in the decades to come.

During the break between Yugoslavia and the Cominform in June 1948 Albania sided vociferously with Stalin and his East

European allies against Belgrade. Marshal Tito had hoped to integrate Albania into his Yugoslav federation after the war, a plan greeted with much suspicion in Tirana. The split in the communist movement and the civil war in Greece provoked Albania to wall itself off from its neighbours, while the Adriatic Sea formed a natural barrier to the west.

Hoxha remained one of Stalin's most faithful allies. He refused to dismantle the Stalinist cult of personality after Khrushchev had denounced the former Soviet dictator at the Twentieth Congress of the CPSU in February 1956. Hoxha's resistance to the Khrushchevite doctrine of peaceful coexistence between capitalism and communism led to increasing, if initially veiled, friction between Tirana and Moscow. In 1961 he warmed to the possibility of sustaining Stalin's legacy offered by the Sino-Soviet split in the late 1950s and early 1960s. Together with the Chinese, he helped to define the novel Leninist concept of 'social imperialism', the epithet with which he would denounce the Soviets for years to come. None the less, after a period when all relations between the Soviet Bloc and Albania froze, strong trade links were later revived, and the country remained a sleeping partner in the Warsaw Pact until 1968, when Tirana used the excuse of the Soviet invasion of Czechoslovakia to leave the military alliance. The events of 1968 highlighted Albania's major ideological contradiction – the liberalism of the Prague Spring represented all that was antithetical to Hoxha's politics, as it contained a concealed threat to the leading role of the party. But although the Soviet invasion of Czechoslovakia was ordered by Brezhnev in order to save this the most sacred of Hoxha's cows, the idea of a big country violating the sovereignty of a small country was more than any Albanian could stomach. This led to Albania's curious denunciation of Soviet aggression, which it qualified by adding that the devious reactionary policies of Czechoslovakia's leadership had duped the Czechoslovak people into following an extreme revisionist path that had provoked the social imperialist anger of the Soviets. Hoxha's idiosyncratic policies often resulted in such rhetorical tail-chasing.

Albania's close relationship with China lasted until the mid-

1970s, when the Gang of Four was ousted and Deng Tsiao Ping's revisionism resulted in Tirana's closing most contracts with China and sending back the countless Chinese technical advisers in the country. Since then Albania has been regarded as unique save for its passing resemblance to North Korea.

Enver Hoxha – Hero and Villain

I first heard those five dear letters at the dawn of my life.
Ever since, your name became as dear to me as my paternal home,
As precious as socialism,
As lofty as the mountains,
As vital as light . . .
We shout ENVER!
 And the sky seems to us loftier than ever,
 The space around us vaster,
 The sun bigger,
 And our perspectives ever more magnificent.
We shout ENVER!
 And our days take on colour and meaning
 As they fall in like soldiers
 Into the great ranks of the revolution.

An understanding of Enver Hoxha, one of Eastern Europe's last great Stalinist dictators who died in 1985, is essential to the unlocking of Albania's secrets. He was without question the most important man in Albanian history after Prince Skënderbeu. Indeed, underneath the extravagant clothing of Hoxha's Stalinist rhetoric lay a barely concealed desire to be recognized by history as the second Skënderbeu, the only man to create and sustain an independent Albania a full five centuries before Hoxha. Skënderbeu drew together Albania's four main noble families, which until then had been involved in a series of rather futile internecine struggles that cost much blood and facilitated Ottoman tutelage of the Albanians. Skënderbeu directed the Albanian warriors in a united struggle against the Turks that was characterized by a number of breathtaking and quite unexpected military victories. His rule coincided with an attempt by the Ottomans to push across into what is now

Italy and up to France. As a consequence Albanians regard Skënderbeu not just as a great national hero but also as the saviour of the European order. This has an important echo today because, despite the country's backwardness and the isolation of the last four decades, Albanian intellectuals still consider themselves part of the mainstream of European culture, and the stand against the Turks remains one of the most important symbols on which that conviction is built.

Skënderbeu's heroic exploits were not restricted to foreign and military policy. He also introduced major social reforms within Albanian society. In the short term the most important of these was the banning of the *gjakmarrje*, the blood feuds that seriously retarded healthy social development. The persistence of the *gjakmarrje* (after Skënderbeu's death the convention was quickly revived) was both a cause and a symptom of Albanian society's evident inability to develop in the modern age. Within a few years of Skënderbeu's death Albanians were once again subjected to the Turkish yoke. Although nineteenth-century nationalism sowed the seeds of a movement of national awakening among Albanian intellectuals, these were slower in germinating than elsewhere in the Balkans. As the Ottoman influence in southern Europe waned, Italy emerged as the dominant power in Albania. The inter-war years saw the creation of the self-appointed kingdom of Ahmet Zog, which quickly degenerated into a hideously corrupt extension of unscrupulous Italian economic interests. By the end of the Second World War the desire among Albanians to create a sovereign independent state was very pronounced.

As an orthodox Marxist, an accomplished scholar and a beguiling politician, Hoxha was given to dramatic gestures. His mission, as he saw it, was to rip Albania out of its feudal slumber and hurl it into the twentieth century. In relative terms the social programmes implemented by the Albanian Party of Labour in the first two post-war decades went far beyond any similar projects in other socialist countries. In 1944, when Hoxha established the new Albania, 85 per cent of the population was illiterate (among women the figure was well over 90 per cent), and there was not even a skeletal system of general education. The rates of birth on the one hand and infant mortality on the other were the highest in Europe, while life expectancy for males was thirty-eight years. The standard of living was by far the lowest in Europe, and there was no serious economic infrastructure. In the first half of the twentieth century Albania had been an important source of minerals, notably chrome and copper, but apart from these foreign-owned resources there was virtually no industrial base and mainly subsistence farming.

Complementing the country's economic backwardness was a fragmented and primitive social construction. The *gjakmarrje* had survived quite happily for five centuries since they were revived after Skënderbeu's death, and the blood-letting continued to prevent effective cooperation between the clans into which Albanian society was divided. There was a clear north–south split between the two main Albanian tribes, the Gegs and the Tosks, which still survives on a cultural and linguistic level to this day but in the past was also the focus of tribal antagonism. The clans were very large and run on a strict patriarchal basis. Women were regarded and treated in many ways as a form of life lower than that of animals. Certainly they had no rights and, once married off, were at the mercy of their husbands, who were guided by the medieval Canon of Lek, a set of unwritten laws that afforded men complete dominance over women until the communist victory of 1944. To the Canon of Lek was added the concept of honour, or *besa*, whereby few disputes could be settled peacefully. Some historians claim that the Albanian minority in southern Italy, known as the Arbesh, introduced the idea of *besa* into the *Mezzogiorno*, thus playing a major role in the creation of Italian 'men of honour' or *mafiosi*. Another important source of women's oppression in Albania was organized religion. The majority of the population were Moslems – Albania was the only such country in Europe.

Despite nominal independence since 1912, Albania's social ills had worsened considerably after the progressive Catholic prime minister, Fan Noli, was chased out of Albania by the appalling Zog in 1924. Hoxha was determined to throw off the shackles of Zog's legacy, which had bound the Albanian people to social obscurity for so long, and it is important to acknowledge his staggering achievements. Illiteracy has been virtually wiped out in the country, and Albania now has an extensive system of general education and a university. There is a moderately impressive free health system, and life expectancy among males has shot up to over seventy years. Albania still has the highest birth rate in Europe (thirty births per thousand citizens per year, though the province of Kosovo in Yugoslavia registers thirty-four per thousand), but the infant mortality rate has been reduced dramatically. Every village in the country had an electric power supply by the early 1970s (where before there had been none); indeed, Albania is now a net exporter of electricity. The country has an economic base, from heavy industry (mainly steel production) to light consumer goods (largely textiles).

The Hoxha leadership changed Albania beyond recognition by constructing Europe's most highly centralized political and economic system. One important reason why Albanian Stalinism is proving slightly more durable than its counterparts elsewhere in Eastern Europe is because a command economy and a strict, authoritarian political structure were probably the most effective instruments available to Albanians by which to pull themselves out of the early modern age and into the twentieth century. However, Albania's industry is now in a dilapidated state. The majority of the country's plant and machine tools are obsolete Chinese designs for which it is almost impossible to secure spare parts. In addition to this, Eastern Europe provides Albania with the largest slice of its foreign trade, though during 1991 most East European economies will cease the soft-currency trading now in operation with Albania. Instead they will accept only desirable goods such as electricity or citrus fruits. The restructuring of Eastern Europe's economy and the introduction of market mechanisms will have a devastating effect on the Albanian economy. Although it is unconstitutional for Albania to have an external debt, for the last three decades the country has survived economically on hidden debts provided either by the Soviet Union or China.

Despite the current economic and political crisis, Hoxha was for a long time a genuinely popular figure. However, nationalism rather than Marxism–Leninism was the primary force that allowed him to create a fairly solid social base for his programme. That social base, which has relied heavily on the idealism of Albanian youth, evaporated very quickly in most other East European countries, but in Albania it has remained constant over a long period. There are signs that young people in particular are no longer satisfied with the simple political solutions that Hoxha offered.

Of course, Hoxha could not rely on his historical role alone to maintain power; he also found it necessary to fashion all the repressive trappings of Stalinism. The most recent Albanian constitution, promulgated in 1976, includes in its preamble one of Hoxha's early post-war slogans, 'The Albanian people have hacked their way through history, sword in hand.' His slogan found a certain expression in Albanian political life – Hoxha never suffered hostile elements gladly. In the particular instance of the preamble his language reflected three phenomena: the atmosphere surrounding the National Liberation War, the extreme militancy of Hoxha's rhetoric in general and the violence of Albanian history. Hoxha's uncompromising approach to his enemies, perceived or real, was a toxic, and for some Albanians fatal, cocktail of the indigenous Albanian spirit of violence and a prickly mixer, mature Stalinism. Once in the system, this led to the mass execution and imprisonment of political enemies, including many from the top ranks of the APL, which was regularly purged. The most spectacular of all of these was the suicide of the prime minister, Mehmet Shehu, in 1981. Almost from the inception of the post-war Albanian government he had been Hoxha's most trusted political friend. Many believe that Hoxha engineered Shehu's suicide, and the most lurid account of the affair, whispered over glasses of the country's sweet national drink, Skënderbeu cognac, even claims that Hoxha himself pulled the trigger. The organization that guarded then, and still guards, political orthodoxy is called the Sigurimi, whose activity has successfully prevented the development of any organized opposition in Albania – something that not even Ceauşescu's Securitate could boast.

In one area, religion, Hoxha went further than his colleagues in Prague, Budapest or Bucharest. In 1967, at the prompting of some high-school students in the port of Durrës, Hoxha warmly assented to the abolition of all religious institutions, thereby turning Albania into the world's 'first atheistic state'. Although the ban constituted a straightforward denial of human rights, several authors critical of Hoxha and the APL have pointed out that Albanian traditions offer some explanation for it. The two major Christian denominations, Roman Catholicism and Greek Orthodoxy, and Sunni Islam, to which the majority of Albanians adhered before the war, were all closely associated with foreign control and the subjugation of Albanian nationalism through the ages. They were also linked in the minds of many Albanians with the semi-feudal regime of Zog and, before that, the Ottoman Turks. Younger women, who benefited as a group more than any other from Albania's post-war social development, felt a special antipathy towards organized religion, which they recognized, usually quite rightly, as one of the major sources of the oppression of their mothers and grandmothers. None of this, of course, justifies the crude persecution visited upon clerics both before and after the ruling of 1967.

Another human right that only the East German state denied its citizens with equal rigour was the systematic deprivation of contact with the outside world. Even for privileged members of the elite the possibility of any such contact depended largely on the state of ideological relations with other communist countries. For a long time the great majority of those few Albanians who travelled abroad went to either Peking or Pyongyang.

As the foundations of Europe's most impressive Stalinist bastion solidified, so did the megalomania of Hoxha. It is important to remember that he was the only dictator in Eastern Europe to have enjoyed wide-spread popular support, and the cult that grew up around his personality was not only the fantasy projection of his obsequious colleagues in the Central Committee of the APL but also partially an expression of popular attitudes. None the less, the cult reached staggering proportions, and the word 'Enver' is intoned to this day with bewildering solemnity. The most unforgettable manifestation of the cult is the Enver Hoxha Museum in Tirana, a weird, futuristic building in which a small army of trained Hoxha fanatics nurse and caress the minutiae of his life. In the centre of the museum stands what can only be described as a huge marble throne on which a huge marble Enver sits looking down on his children with that unmistakable expression of East European dictators that effortlessly combines affection and disapproval. It is almost impossible to escape Enver's gaze anywhere in Albania. Surveying the beautiful scenery on top of the mountain city of Berat, the visitor is suddenly arrested by the word ENVER written in huge stones on the mountainside across the valley. Bookshops are still crammed with his voluminous collected works, while outsiders are mildly scolded for suggesting that such institutionalized adoration adds up to a cult. 'He has given us everything,' one guide once told me bitterly after I dared suggest that Albania suffered from a cult, 'so you cannot talk of a cult. This is just our way of thanking him for everything.'

The Genesis of Heresy

The man who assumed Hoxha's mantle after the dictator's death was Ramiz Alia, who is both the country's president and the General Secretary of the APL. Alia is a short, energetic man with a charming smile, fluent French and a diplomatic grace that gives the false impression that he has spent much of his life at embassy cocktail parties. In fact, he is an enormously hard-working politician who played a considerable role in the construction of postwar Albania as Hoxha's ideology chief from the 1960s onwards. None the less, in so far as it was possible to differentiate between Albanian leaders while Hoxha was alive, Alia evinced a slightly more pragmatic approach to politics than others, most significantly in his relationship with intellectuals and young people. After he became the most powerful man in the country in 1985, he adopted a less strident style than his predecessor's. Negotiations with a number of West European states, in particular those with Bonn, led to the flowering of Western diplomatic missions in Tirana. But, following the revolutions in Eastern Europe, and notably the revolution in Romania, Alia went further than this, beginning a reform offensive that disturbed some of the cornerstones of Hoxhaist ideology.

Quite unexpectedly, Alia announced during the Tenth Central Committee Plenum of the APL in April 1990 that Albania hoped to re-establish diplomatic relations with the United States of America and the USSR. Both these states were incarnations of ideological evil during Hoxha's time, and the mere suggestion of talks with Washington and Moscow would have been dismissed as a treacherous plot. Alia's announcement alerted Albania watchers to the possibility of profound change in the country. In fact, his speech contained further bold ideas, including reconsideration of the policy towards institutional religion and towards human rights in general. This was confirmed a few weeks later by the prime minister, Adil Çarçani, when a new government programme included the promise that Albania would soon implement economic reforms similar to those of the days of early *perestroika* and would begin to explore the possibility of joining in the process of European integration.

Alia appears to have recognized that too many pressures were building up in this tightly sealed country. The economy is grinding to a standstill. After several decades of impressive growth the highly centralized five-year plans are now clearly retarding expansion. Albania has to create 70,000 new jobs every year for school and university leavers, and this is beginning to strain its resources. Production is slowing down dramatically, and both the working class and the peasantry are showing signs of growing unhappiness.

Strict Stalinist regimes have been able to cope with such economic pressures in the past, but in Albania these have now coincided with other external events, in particular the revolutions in Eastern Europe. Most Albanians have regular access to foreign television, and the picture of the Romanian revolution had a profound effect on viewers. In addition, the struggle of the Kosovo Albanians against Serbian hegemony influenced young Albanians in the People's Republic. Many Albanians feel ashamed that while their brothers and sisters in Kosovo have faced the guns of Serbian police, they have not yet gathered up enough courage to face the guns of the Sigurimi. But the signs of solidarity with both Romania and Kosovo multiplied in the first half of 1990. Small but significant demonstrations took place in Tirana, and then later in Kavajë, a small town south of the capital. One night in the middle of April the shifts in two sections of the biggest textile factory in the country in Berat struck for eight hours over low wages and poor conditions. This was believed to be the first strike in Albania since the communist takeover. In early July a demonstration was broken up by the Sigurimi together with a recently formed riot police force known as the Sampist. Scores of demonstrators sought refuge in several embassies. As they scaled the walls of the forbidden diplomatic missions police opened fire, and Albania's attempt to slip into the process of European integration received a serious setback. Eventually some 4,000 Albanians were allowed to leave the country to seek refugee status in Europe, the United States and Australia. After they left the tension appeared to die down, although few foreigners were able to enter the country to see for themselves.

President Alia is faced with a number of serious social problems generated or exacerbated by Hoxha. Albania's urban youth is evidently turning against the party and the state. The APL has made a big mistake in allowing the development of hostility among youngsters who no longer see Albanian independence as the top political priority but instead hanker after pop music and democratically elected political representatives. It is young people who have taken their lives in their hands by going out to demonstrate. It is young people who have risked their liberty by talking to Western journalists both about the repression in Albania and, in some detail, about the struggle going on within the party and state apparatus. Most of these proto-dissidents support the attempts of President Alia to reform the country. Almost without exception the discontented youngsters identify Nexhmije Hoxha, Enver's widow, as the main opponent of reform.

If Albanian youth is beginning to look like the engine of rebellion that generated such powerful change elsewhere in Eastern Europe, the intellectuals provide the fuel. One of Hoxha's greatest errors, which Alia has been unable to correct in his time as leader, was to alienate Albania's young intellectuals by periodically purging their ranks and forcing some to undertake the degrading task of self-criticism. In contrast to Romania, Albania has not been able to weld the intelligentsia into the system of the communist *nomenklatura*. Although in the conditions of extreme Stalinism that have prevailed for so long in Albania, few have been prepared to stick their necks out unnecessarily, many have quietly provoked the regime, where possible, in novels, plays and newspaper articles.

In 1990 a number of articles and interviews appeared in the officially controlled press, particularly in the party daily *Zëri i popullit* (The Voice of the People) and the young people's daily, *Zëri i rinisë* (The Voice of Youth), that seemed to prepare the ground. Albania's best-known writer, Ismail Kadare, refuses to admit publicly that his work has immediate political implications, but he has now clearly indicated that the cult of Stalinism in Albania must soon come to an end, while earlier he even suggested that the Sigurimi enjoyed too much power. Another indication of the demise of the Stalinist cult is the demolition of the town signs of Stalin City, the only remaining settlement in Europe that includes the late Soviet dictator's name. The dismantling of the cult of Stalin in Albania is an essential prerequisite for reform. But this particular act of demystification will be easy by comparison with the great ideological barrier that stands between President Alia and his presumed goal of a democratic Albania: the destruction of the reputation of the artful Albanian, Alia's old friend and mentor – the late, great Enver Hoxha.

The destruction of the Hoxha cult will signal the end of single-party rule in Albania, as the cult provides the APL with the very air it needs to breathe. It is difficult to estimate the extent of popular support for Hoxha at a time when the opportunities offered by a Europe that claims to want to embrace all its constituent elements look so exciting. Albanians feel confident and secure in their statehood, but it is impossible to know how closely they identify that independence with the figure of Hoxha. The rural population and the 'partizan' generations probably still hold the old man in great respect, but young dissidents in Tirana are quite certain about what they regard as the greatest obstacle to progress and democracy in Albania – Hoxha. President Alia is doubtless well aware of this too. Of course, Alia must also know that he owes his position and his enormous power to Hoxha. He is faced with the same dilemma that Khrushchev encountered when he decided to confront the criminal legacy of Stalin. It was striking that when Alia acquainted the Central Committee with the first major wave of reform at the Tenth Central Committee Plenum on 17 April 1990 he mentioned Hoxha only four times in a very long and thorough speech. By the standards of the APL this could almost be interpreted as a snub to the great deceased. More realistically it could be interpreted as the preparation of the ground for a reappraisal of Hoxha.

Time is running out for Alia and his reformist friends. The events of early July 1990, when Albanians took to the streets and then to foreign embassies in the most public defiance of the APL, were a signal: reform or go under. The demonstrations were a spontaneous expression of the frustration experienced by Albanians who had been told that fundamental reforms (including the right to travel freely) had been agreed upon but saw that nothing was happening. Together the violent response of the security forces and the fifties-style explanation offered to the outside world by the Albanian media amounted to convincing proof that conservatives still enjoyed considerable influence in the APL and particularly in the interior ministry and in the leadership of the Sigurimi.

All this does not bode well for the immediate future of Albania. The lazy Mediterranean atmosphere of Tirana, combined with forty years of repression can lead to a false sense of security – the traditions of the *gjakmarrje* and the *besa* are just around the corner in historical terms, and these are traditions that could easily be revived. The authorities may continue to insist that the disturbances are the work of 'vagabonds, petty criminals and deceived youths', but President Alia must be aware, in the wake of the East European upheavals, that Albania is now on the edge of a revolutionary struggle. Publicly Alia and all other APL leaders insist that socialism in Albania cannot be equated with the corrupt socialism of Eastern Europe that was imposed on the area by the Soviet Union. It is the Albanian people, so the theory goes, who have chosen the road to socialism. Privately, however, Alia has a choice – to acknowledge the inevitability of fundamental political choice or to drown in the flood. If he decides to try to stem the rising waters, he may find himself drowning not in revolutionary water but in blood. President Alia and his political allies are not in an easy situation. They are being squeezed by pressure from both sides. To move too fast would be to provoke a counter-revolution of the reactionary forces in the party. To move too slowly would lead to further popular disturbances and possibly armed conflict.

In Romania the army played a key role by pitting itself against Ceauşescu and the Securitate. Like all other East European armies, Albania's is a conscript army and, by definition, potentially unreliable. The leadership of the Albanian People's Army has, of course, always been closely entwined with the leadership of the APL. None the less, the APL has on occasions shown itself to be suspicious of the army. It has often intervened in military policy and has purged or disciplined leading officers during periods of tension. There is no available evidence to indicate whether the present army leadership backs one of the two currents in the Central Committee struggle.

The Price of Freedom

The impact of rapid change on Albania could include many negative side-effects. Just as the country was shaken out of its semi-feudal slumber and into the twentieth century by a tough, authoritarian regime, so it must join the rest of Europe and the post-revolutionary states of the Balkans in a controlled and careful fashion. There will be a great temptation on the part of individuals and larger social groups to make money quickly. There is only one economic route open to Albania that would allow this – the expansion of tourism. Albania is one of the last countries in Europe, if not the last, to have a long stretch of beautiful coastline that has been polluted only to some extent by the effluence of Italian and Yugoslav ports and holiday-makers but remains largely unspoilt by the trappings of late twentieth-century tourism. Albanians themselves adore their beaches and usually travel to the coast once a year for their holidays. But they do not stay in large hotels with all the latest facilities or pollute the bays with marinas. With the exception of the major industrial centres, such as Tirana, Elbasan, Berat, the port of Vlorë and Stalin City, Albania is a country that has remained in many respects in harmony with nature. Many areas of it are a dream for the ecological activist. One of the main reasons for this cleanliness, apart from the generally low level of industrial development, is the continuing ban on private cars that was introduced by Hoxha in the 1940s. The country's economy has quite happily experienced an impressive and sustained growth without private cars, and the countryside has benefited enormously from the virtual absence of vehicle emissions.

Albanians have been denied political rights for a long time but the country's ecological balance, which is on the whole impressive, is without doubt a positive legacy of Hoxha's nationalism. If tourism and foreign investment are permitted without restrictions in the future, this balance will be seriously threatened. In the light of this, Albania's maintenance of some of the tradition of isolation may be an extremely important policy. Of course, this will not help economic development, the need for which comprises one of the chief motivations for reform in the country. The conflict between preservation and progress will be an important characteristic of Albania's future.

Politically, a democratic Albania would be the nearest thing to a *tabula rasa* in Eastern Europe, as the only consistent political tradition that managed to establish deep roots before Hoxhaism monopolized political thought in the country was nineteenth-century nationalism. There was a nascent social democratic movement, which Hoxha easily liquidated, and important support among the landed classes and their dependants for right-wing authoritarian solutions. But these traditions have been to a large extent exterminated in Albania, partly through the work of the Sigurimi and the APL and partly by the changing social face of the country and its youthfulness.

For this reason, it is quite likely that religion would not play a substantial role in a new Albania. Although religious traditions in other East European countries have been sustained and even nurtured by periods of extreme repression, the APL has succeeded in transforming Albania into a largely secular society – the urban youth, whether it supports the APL or not, demonstrates this better than any other social group. There is, of course, a clear split between north and south. The Tosks of the south consider themselves more sophisticated and tend to look down on the Gegs of the north. There is still much resentment between the two tribes, although Hoxhaism has gone some way to dissipating any concomitant political tension. The north, with its beautiful main city, Shkodër, is much more Italianate than the south, and it is here that Catholic traditions dominate.

It is hard to predict what political movements will evolve in Albania, although the very absence of tradition may lead to the creation of some form of front organization, similar to Civic Forum or Solidarity, that could play a leading role in any transition. Certainly there are intellectuals and even politicians in the country who enjoy the confidence of much of the population. Kadare himself may deny any political ambition – but so did Václav Havel. It is possible that President Alia could lead a new Albania, as for the moment he enjoys the trust even of many of the small, disparate groups of dissidents. If he were to succeed in this, Alia would be a unique phenomenon in revolutionary Eastern Europe, as the crucial difference between Albania and the other states is its complete lack of organized opposition. One of the great strengths of Poland and Czechoslovakia in the age of democracy is that many of their new leaders have gained years of political experience fighting underground. They may have been excluded from official political life, but once the regimes had ceased executing their political enemies, they could never deny dissidents the learning process. While it is true that in Albania dissidents have multiplied in recent months, they remain unorganized and terrified of the Sigurimi. Lack of political experience could well create difficulties for the builders of a new Albanian state, as it has in both Romania and Bulgaria and probably will in Serbia, Macedonia, Montenegro and Bosnia as well.

Albania now has its industrial infrastructure, but it is one that suffers from all the classic evils of an over-centralized planned economy. One of the major reforms that Alia announced at the Tenth Central Committee Plenum in April 1990 included some devolution of decision-making to enterprise level while at the same time bringing in a mild form of self-financing. Even after the revolution, changing the working patterns and habits of Albanians is going to prove very difficult. In addition to having little, if any, tradition of market principles, Albania is a relaxed, Mediterranean culture, although the desire for improvement and for the benefits of late-twentieth-century Europe is clearly growing in the country. This is not entirely surprising, as average annual wages hover between $500 and $700, and some industrial workers take home much less than that. The knowledge, ability and will to realize these aims may be difficult to find however. Like some of the Yugoslav provinces, Albania may be able to rely on the patriotic support of those Yugoslav Albanians who work in northern Europe (these make up a staggering one-third of the adult male population of Kosovo), but this would be by no means as reliable a source of investment as, for example, the émigré Croatian community is for Croatia, largely because there are powerful economic and political reasons for investing in Kosovo alone.

A Balkan Powder Keg, an Albanian Spark

The future relationship between Albania proper and the 2 million Albanians in Kosovo will be crucial for the development of the Balkans as a whole. Traditionally the leadership in Tirana has severely admonished Belgrade and the leadership of Serbia in particular for discrimination against the Albanians in Kosovo, but it has always expressly denied any desire to expand its territory and create a greater Albania that would include Kosovo. Certainly, there is no historical precedent for such a creation and opposition leaders in Kosovo similarly dismiss the idea. None the less, there has always been a curious relationship between the two Albanian populations. As the domestic crisis deepened in Albania proper during the first half of 1990, the obsession of the media with the situation of the Kosovo Albanians has increased. The APL leadership uses the situation in Kosovo quite shamelessly as a way of deflecting discontent at home. This is a tactic that entails some considerable risk, however. All Albanians in the People's Republic, from the APL downwards, support the attempt of the Kosovo Albanians to be recognized as one of Yugoslavia's official nationalities and to gain the status of a republic. (The Kosovo Albanians have now even lost their status as an autonomous province within the republic of Serbia, a move by Belgrade that was guaranteed to anger Albanians across the border.) Ordinary Albanians in the People's Republic admire the courage of the Kosovo Albanians tremendously. As young Albanians became bolder in their criticism of the APL, the V-for-victory sign, the symbol of Albanian resistance in Kosovo, was raised ever more frequently on the streets of Tirana and elsewhere in the country.

The simultaneous struggles of the Albanian populations have important implications. In the long-term it is unlikely that Serbia will be able to sustain its hegemonic rule over Kosovo, but it will not readily give up control over the area. Serbian nationalists claim that they are prepared to fight for Kosovo. It is hard to ascertain whether that is true or mere rhetorical bravado, but if Serbia does decide to fight, the Kosovo Albanians will have no choice but to respond – and they are ready for armed struggle. As Serbian pressure on the Kosovo Albanians has increased, so has the pressure of reactionary nationalism in Kosovo. While the APL remains in power in Albania proper, it is very unlikely that it would want to intervene militarily in Kosovo on behalf of the Albanians there. However, a post-revolutionary Albania may well adopt a different approach to the struggle in Kosovo and decide to support the armed struggle. In this event, three other areas would immediately be drawn into the conflict in varying degrees – Greece, Montenegro and Macedonia. There are small Albanian minorities in Montenegro and Greece, but in Macedonia, potentially one of Yugoslavia's most unstable provinces, there is an enormous Albanian minority, which suffers discrimination worse than that experienced by Kosovo Albanians and will undoubtedly play a role in the political drama yet to unfold in the Balkans.

There is no country whose future is more difficult to predict than Albania's. This is partly because at the time of writing the revolution is still fermenting and has yet to mature but also because Albania is such an unknown country, whose traditions until the communist revolution were curious even within the Balkan context. Despite the country's historical predilection for violence, it is important to note that Albanians are extremely hospitable and today keen to get to know their neighbours in Europe much better. As the Albanian *Gastarbeiter* in northern Europe and the diaspora in the United States have proved, this nation can be enormously industrious. In New York Albanians are rapidly becoming the largest group of restaurant owners. In Albania itself the knowledge and appreciation of Western popular culture that young Albanians display are impressive. But Albania's people are also yearning to share their culture and lifestyle with the rest of Europe. If its industry were sanitized, and if private cars continued to be banned in a democratic Albania, the country could perhaps even present itself as an ecological model state. The restoration of Albania to Europe will be full of pitfalls and dangers but also of tremendous possibility.

7 BULGARIA

The Delicate Flower

'Bulgaria bucks the trend.' Almost all English-language news organizations reporting the Bulgarian elections used this phrase to describe the result. The elections were held in two rounds, on 10 and 17 June 1990, and saw the Bulgarian Socialist Party (BSP), the renamed Communist Party, returned to power with just over 47 per cent of the vote and a substantial majority over the opposition front organization, the Union of Democratic Forces, (UDF) which polled slightly more than 36 per cent, much less than it had hoped and expected. While Civic Forum, the Hungarian Democratic Forum, the CDU in East Germany and Solidarity were emerging as major new political forces towering over the defeated communists, the Bulgarians were returning the very party whose monopoly they had overthrown six months earlier.

The cliché about bucking the trend was, however, inaccurate. Although the Romanian Communist Party was made illegal during the revolution, a move that brought Ceauşescu down in Bulgaria's northern neighbour, the ruling National Salvation Front assimilated most of the traditions and structures of the RCP. There is a strong case to be made for suggesting that Romania bucked the trend in a much more fundamental way than did Bulgaria. Although the membership of the BSP coincided largely with that of its predecessor, the Communist Party, at the time of the Bulgarian elections, it was already a very different organization, in ideological terms, from the enormous instrument of personal power that Bulgaria's dictator, Todor Zhivkov, had wielded for over thirty-five years until his fall in November 1989.

The Bulgarian revolution comprised a complex and curious sequence of events that passed through various stages and was spun out over a period of months. In some respects the revolution continued after the elections. But to tar it with the same brush as the Romanian experience is unfair, both to the Bulgarian people and to the Bulgarian Socialist Party. After a short period of hesitation the opposition UDF was ready to acknowledge the fairness of the elections. Although some UDF leaders are still not prepared to admit it, they contributed significantly to their defeat at the polls and, given their failure, the concessions they have won from the BSP since the elections are substantial. None the less, the question still remains of why the instrument of political repression in Bulgaria for so many years was able to emerge victorious, given the widespread loathing of Todor Zhivkov himself.

The Sixteenth Republic

Bulgaria is the least known of the countries that left the Soviet sphere of influence in 1989. With a population of about 9 million, roughly 10 per cent of whom are Turkish, it borders Romania and Yugoslavia as well as two NATO countries, Turkey and Greece. During the Second World War the regime of Tsar Boris III, who died in 1943, supported the Axis powers, although it afforded the German war machine fewer privileges than did most of the Axis's other European allies (for example, the Bulgarian government, backed by popular support, refused to deliver up its Jewish citizens to the Nazis for deportation. Moreover, the *coup* that finally put an end to the pro-German regime in Sofia in September 1944 had been the subject of lengthy negotiations between leading members of the Bulgarian military and civilian establishments on the one hand and the Allied powers on the other. Bulgaria's switching of allegiance in the war came as no surprise to either Berlin or the Allies. Soon after, Soviet troops moved into Bulgaria, where they remained until the end of 1947. The presence of the troops ensured the steady growth of Communist Party influence in government and the inevitable erosion of the opposition. The three-year communist take-over in Bulgaria was aided by Western indifference towards the country, encouraged chiefly by Britain, which was prepared to see Bulgaria fall completely under Soviet influence as part of its strategy for maintaining Greece within its own orbit of influence.

Bulgarians were swift to appreciate which way the wind was blowing, and membership of the Communist Party grew from 15,000 in October 1944 to 460,000 less than four years later. In the 1920s the party had been one of the strongest in Europe, and it had been well represented in Bulgaria's parliament, the Narodno Subranie. It was also both a victim and a perpetrator of the violence that became endemic to Bulgarian political life in the inter-war period. Many of its leaders were imprisoned or executed after the party was outlawed in 1924. One radical faction of the BCP wrought revenge by carrying out one of the most spectacular terrorist acts of the twentieth century. A bomb planted in Sofia cathedral killed 128 people, including most of the cabinet. The party (which continued to operate through various front organizations) was forced even further underground after the imposition of Tsar Boris III's royal dictatorship in the mid-1930s but among Bulgaria's small proletariat it continued to command impressive support.

The party's relative popularity was undoubtedly bolstered after the war by its close association with the Soviet party. After 500 years under the rule of the Ottoman sultans and caliphs, Bulgaria had always regarded Turkey, and not Russia, as its traditional enemy. On the contrary, Russia was regarded as a friend and protector of Bulgaria. After the slow collapse of Ottoman rule, and particularly after the Balkan wars, relations between Bulgaria and its Slav neighbour Serbia, Romania to the north and Greece to the south had been badly strained: Bulgaria had territorial disputes with all of these countries. The only country with which it always enjoyed cordial relations was Russia and, after 1917, the Soviet Union, and this state of affairs persisted throughout the period of one-party rule. The close ties between Moscow and Sofia even resulted in Zhivkov's asking the Soviet leader, Nikita Khrushchev, if Bulgaria might be allowed into the Union. From then on elsewhere in Eastern Europe Bulgaria was often referred to scornfully as the 'sixteenth republic'. The relationship that bound Bulgaria to the Soviet Union was one of the diplomatic triumphs of the communist period, although its success can be exaggerated. Bulgaria's dependence on the Soviet Union was determined essentially by three factors, which together made it almost impossible for Sofia to consider any other option.

First, the Soviet Union enjoyed considerable popular support in Bulgaria, and anti-Russian sentiment was never as extensive as it was in all other members of the Warsaw Pact. This was largely for historical reasons, as the Russian Tsar had indeed liberated Bulgaria from the Ottoman yoke, and there had never been a major dispute between the two Slav neighbours.

Second, Zhivkov himself assiduously cultivated Soviet leaders, offering unconditional support wherever and whenever it was necessary. Probably the best first-hand account of Zhivkov's obsequious relationship with Soviet leaders is found in Zdeněk Mlynář's book *Night Frost in Prague*. The Bulgarian leader had travelled to Bratislava, the Slovak capital, at the end of July 1968 to discuss the situation in Czechoslovakia with his Warsaw Pact counterparts:

The Bulgarian leader, Todor Zhivkov, was still relatively young at the time (he was not yet 55), but he was outstanding for his quite exceptional dullness. My years of close contact with many high functionaries had taught me not to have high standards, but observing a living Zhivkov from up close was shocking all the same. When trying to follow what someone else was saying, he did so with the tense concentration of someone who knows that if he doesn't pay absolute attention he won't understand a thing. During the working sessions he sometimes intervened unwittingly to oppose objections with which Brezhnev was getting ready to comply, thus complicating Brezhnev's role. I noticed two or three times in such a situation Brezhnev ignored Zhivkov when he wanted to speak, and then gestured to him to stay out of the debate.

If he noticed such humiliations, Zhivkov was certainly happy to tolerate them for the sake of retaining power in Bulgaria. His main policy goal within the Pact was to ensure that the Soviet Union did not intervene in the Bulgarian leadership, as it did in East Germany in 1971, for example, when Honecker replaced Walter Ulbricht with the encouragement of Moscow. To this end, his relationship with Khrushchev, Brezhnev and even Gorbachev was subservient and unctuous. This did not mean, however, that

Zhivkov always suppressed Bulgarian culture at the expense of an imported Soviet culture. From the mid-1970s onward, he began to permit the development of a much stronger Bulgarian national consciousness, especially among the intelligentsia, which until that time had been afforded very little room for national self-expression.

Finally Bulgaria was dependent on Soviet trade, in particular raw materials and energy, to a degree that no other East European country was. It is almost impossible for Bulgaria to survive without Soviet good will, and that is why the Bulgarian economy is now faced with such enormous problems: although Soviet good will may not have been withdrawn completely, it has certainly been tempered.

Stalinism was imposed on Bulgaria just as it was everywhere else in Eastern Europe. But after the Bulgarian revolution public wrath focused almost exclusively on Zhivkov and the narrow band of his cronies who had been ruling the country since 1954, when he successfully engineered the removal of Bulgaria's great Stalinist first secretary, Vulko Chervenkov. Anti-Soviet feeling remained muted and insignificant as a political force. In fact, one of the curious idiosyncrasies of the Bulgarian revolution was that the hundreds of thousands who celebrated Zhivkov's fall in the streets of Sofia and other Bulgarian cities could find nothing to put in the place of general hatred for him.

The Search for Identity

At the end of the war Bulgaria was still a predominantly agrarian society; over 70 per cent of the population worked on the land. In the 1950s, when all the other countries in Eastern Europe were hastily constructing indigenous industries at the behest of Stalin (except for Romania, whose industrialization was a slight deviation from the role allotted to it by Stalinist planners), Bulgaria was faithfully fulfilling its role within the international division of labour as socialism's market gardener. Whereas other East European countries were moving away from the semi-feudal structures bequeathed by the inter-war period, Bulgaria retained much of its feudal tradition. The most important consequence of this was the development of a system of patronage, which was administered by the regional barons of the party. Bulgaria was divided into a number of fiefdoms, where the regional party secretaries would sit atop a large, corrupt network from which everybody derived some benefit. Those who chose to opt out for reasons of principle suffered material loss. In return for political obedience, the party secretary would represent his constituents' interests on a national scale. Nowhere else in the communist world was the power of the regional party organization so sacrosanct as it was in Bulgaria, while Romania was the only other country in which the system of corruption encompassed such a large proportion of the population.

Belatedly Zhivkov embarked on a programme of industrialization in the 1960s, but the novel urban infrastructure never became strong enough to compete even with those of Bulgaria's socialist allies. The country has remained stubbornly rural throughout its post-war history. Even today between 20 and 30 per cent of the population (the figure changes as a result of seasonal adjustment) works in agriculture. In the inter-war period Bulgaria had quite the most impressive education system in the entire Balkan peninsula, and by the outbreak of the Second World War over 80 per cent of males and almost 60 per cent of females were literate. Importantly, a remarkably high percentage of Bulgarians who went to university were prepared to study technical subjects and not the humanities, which elsewhere in Eastern Europe created a vast pool of unemployable graduates – though these unemployable graduates helped to produce a more spirited independent intelligentsia than emerged in post-war Bulgaria.

Indeed, the absence of an opposition tradition in Bulgaria after the war is striking. The party's political opponents were either forced into emigration or terrorized into silence soon after the Communist Party's take-over. But, in contrast to all other East European countries (including Romania), no democratic opposition movement of any type emerged in Bulgaria until as late as 1988. There was an attempted military *coup* against Zhivkov in the 1960s, although it is assumed that the aim of the *putsch*ists was not to undermine communist power in Bulgaria but simply to remove Zhivkov and his clique. One of the reasons why the army *coup* failed was because of the firm support enjoyed by Zhivkov among the regional communist barons. These owed their power to Zhivkov and the partisan unit that he led during the war, the Chavdar Guard, most of whose leading members sat on the Politburo for as long as Zhivkov was General Secretary. Unlike Ceauşescu, Zhivkov did not create a system of national communism, nor did he have the resources or facilities to construct the consumer communism that characterized the regime of Kádár in Hungary. His state system can best be described as feudal communism. Within this framework the creation of any articulate opposition programme was extremely difficult.

After Mikhail Gorbachev was appointed General Secretary of the Soviet Communist Party, Zhivkov felt he must make an adjustment to the 'new thinking' that began to emerge from Moscow. By East European standards his knee-jerk reaction to the stirrings in the Soviet Union was swift. In July 1987 he produced his Conception on the Further Construction of Socialism in Bulgaria, a mesmerizingly wordy Bulgarian version of *perestroika* whose scope went well beyond what Gorbachev had proposed for the Soviet Union at the time. In private conversations leading members of the Bulgarian party would admit that Zhivkov had no intention of actually implementing any of the far-reaching reforms (particularly in the economic sphere) that were outlined in the July Conception. None the less, some members in the party interpreted its very publication as a sign that Zhivkov was no longer as assured of power as he used to be. In addition, the Soviet leadership had begun to apply indirect pressure on Zhivkov to consider the implementation of reform. One of the most important developments in Bulgarian politics in early 1987 was Sofia's agreement to boost Soviet television signals so that 90 per cent of Bulgarians were able to view the programmes. The impact on public opinion was considerable. From that time on Bulgarians realized that the changes going on in the Soviet Union were fundamental.

Six months later, in January 1988, Bulgaria's first structured dissident organization, the Independent Society for Human Rights, came into being. Despite state repression, a variety of opposition movements were founded in the following eighteen months, though none included any comprehensive programmatic demands. Probably the most advanced politically was Ekoglasnost, led by the charismatic young zoologist Petar Beron. Not surprisingly, Bulgaria had its share of pollution. The town of Ruse in the north-east of the country, on the Romanian border, suffered from what is still one of the gravest environmental problems in Europe. Ruse is an industrial town that produces a great deal of air pollution itself, but it is also regularly enveloped by blankets of gas drifting over the Danube from the Romanian city of Giurgiu. At one point in early 1989 Ekoglasnost and an influential group of party members (these included Sonia Bakish, wife of Stanko Todorov, chairman of the National Assembly) appeared almost ready to attempt to unseat Zhivkov by exploiting the critical issue of Ruse. The environmental movement might have played a central role in the collapse of Zhivkov; it failed because it was simply unable to mobilize large sections either of public or of intellectual opinion even though it, and other opposition organizations, probably enjoyed substantial tacit support.

It became increasingly clear that the only organization capable of bringing the Zhivkov dictatorship to an end was the Communist Party. The opposition would not be able to achieve this. Zhivkov himself threw the entire Bulgarian polity into turmoil when he ordered the acceleration of the assimilation of Bulgaria's Turkish minority in the early summer of 1989. The Zhivkov regime had not acknowledged the existence of a Turkish minority in the east and south of the country since the mid-1970s, when it began referring to them as Bulgarian Moslems. In fact, a 200,000-strong community of real Bulgarian Moslems (known as the Pomaks) already existed. The Turkish minority spoke fluent Turkish and often only halting Bulgarian. In response to Zhivkov's renewed attack on the minority's rights (which was undoubtedly motivated by a desire to deflect growing unhappiness among Bulgarians from the economic situation and direct it towards a campaign of popular racism), the Turks rioted and demonstrated. An indignant

Zhivkov reacted in the only way he knew by sending in the police and firing on the crowd. Dozens of people were killed, provoking both a diplomatic crisis with Ankara and a potentially explosive situation within Bulgaria itself. Too late Zhivkov recognized his mistake and attempted to cut his losses by suddenly giving Bulgarian Turks a passport and allowing them to emigrate to Turkey. The exodus soon developed into the biggest movement of peoples in modern Europe. The whole affair was a dreadful miscalculation. The Soviet Union, involved in a complicated diplomatic game of extricating itself from Eastern Europe, was livid, while leading members of the party, including Zhivkov's long-standing foreign minister, Petar Mladenov, were exasperated by the action, which they were obliged to defend to the outside world. The decision to accelerate assimilation was taken by Zhivkov and his closest friend, Milko Balev, without even consulting the rest of the Politburo. His refusal to consult the party on this issue cost him dear.

Mladenov decided to act by mobilizing anti-Zhivkov sentiment in the party. He was very careful to include the Soviet leadership in his plans. On his return from a visit to China in November 1989 he stopped off in Moscow for a final briefing on the forthcoming dénouement of the Bulgarian leadership crisis. He appears to have been given the final go-ahead, and Zhivkov's fate was sealed, Following a slightly complicated palace revolution, Mladenov replaced a disbelieving Zhivkov during a session of the Central Committee. Before long the party had committed itself to an ideological sea change, following the example of the Hungarian Socialist Party by adopting the sobriquet 'a modern party of the European left'. The new leadership (Mladenov was backed by one of Bulgaria's most talented politicians, Andrey Lukanov) also announced that the country would move towards multi-party elections and guarantee the rights of all Bulgarian citizens, including members of the Turkish minority.

The opposition was completely disarmed because the party had conceded most of its major demands before it had even had time to articulate them. Hastily the main opposition groupings (new ones were springing up every day) amalgamated to form the front organization, the Union of Democratic Forces (UDF). From the beginning the UDF was poorly structured (naturally, it had none of the resources available to the BCP/BSP initially) and ideologically completely chaotic. The younger, more dynamic activists, like Petar Beron, were forced out by a lacklustre group of older men led by Zhelyu Zhelev, an honest but rather slow-witted writer whose main claim to fame was as the author of a comparative study of Fascism and communism in the early 1970s, which was banned by Zhivkov when it was published in 1980.

From the beginning the UDF was its own worst enemy, riven with factional fighting and simply incapable of formulating a clear policy that could translate into an effective election campaign. Throughout the six-month period leading up to the election the UDF was unable to come up with its own coherent policy for rescuing Bulgaria's chronically sick economy. Early on, the UDF leadership also made the grave error of expelling from its ranks any movements that were based on ethnic principles. This immediately alienated the best-organized group within the opposition, the Movement for Rights and Freedoms, which was headed by Ahmed Dogan and whose primary aim was to defend the rights of the Turkish minority (according to Dogan, by June 1990 the MRF had a membership of 140,000, of whom 3,000 were Bulgarians and the rest Turks). The decision to expel the MRF and the movement of Macedonians in Bulgaria (Ilinden) not only demonstrated the profound stupidity and tactical incompetence of the UDF leadership; it was also an undeniable expression of the racism that permeates the opposition in Bulgaria, just as it does the BSP. When Zhivkov resorted periodically to bullying the Turkish community, he was not plucking a prejudice out of thin air. He was playing on what he knew to be a deeply felt suspicion of the Turks among many Bulgarians. The first evidence of this was provided on a bitterly cold December morning in 1989, when speakers at a mass opposition demonstration in Alexander Nevsky Square in Sofia proclaimed that the opposition must defend the rights of the Turkish minority in Bulgaria. They were greeted with boos, catcalls and the chanting of anti-Turkish slogans.

The opposition's equivocation on the issue of the Turks was seized on gleefully by the conservative party barons in the provinces, who were desperate to cling on to their feudal rights. They successfully organized anti-Turkish riots and strikes as a way of undermining the opposition in January 1990. Since the revolution the conservative elements in the opposition and the hard-line faction in the party have used the Turkish issue regularly as a way of unsettling the electorate. In the first two months after the palace revolution, however, it appeared that the party hard-liners were benefiting from this and not the opposition. Indeed, at the beginning of 1990 it already looked as if the UDF was heading for electoral embarrassment.

The *coup* against Zhivkov was both a symptom and a cause of a critical power struggle within the BCP/BSP. The issue was, quite simply, to reform or not to reform. Essentially at the time of the palace revolution there were two major currents within the Central Committee. One was the modern technocratic elite whose most important representative was Andrey Lukanov. The second current was Zhivkov's old friends based on the Chavdar Guard, Grisha Filipov, Milko Balev, Pencho Kubadinski and other assorted villains who had made up the Politburo for as long as Zhivkov had been General Secretary of the party. Although the feudal barons were enormously powerful in their own areas, they were dependent on Zhivkov and the Chavdar Guard for their existence. In addition, the power structures that guaranteed their privileges were clearly threatened by a group that wanted to modernize Bulgaria and bring the party into line with the 'modern European left'. At the same time they respected whomever it was who controlled the Central Committee, so once Mladenov and Lukanov gained the upper hand in the party's highest executive body, a huge public split divided the party from top to bottom. The anti-Turkish riots in January 1990 were the first major manifestation of this. The split soon turned into a bitter dogfight, and the two factions had become six or seven by the time of the elections.

For a short period the reformists and conservatives buried their differences. This was because the Agrarian Party (which had been a Communist Party stooge throughout communist rule) showed sudden signs of reviving remarkably and undermining all support for the BSP in the countryside, the most important constituency outside the party's own bloated bureaucracy. The Agrarians initially agreed to consider the possibility of a government coalition with the UDF. By this time the UDF had become closely associated with the West and in particular the United States. The link between the Agrarians and the UDF was to devastate Agrarian power in the countryside, as the peasantry, like its counterpart in Romania, was by far the most conservative social stratum. The BSP launched an extraordinarily successful campaign against the Agrarians, claiming that their association with the UDF was in preparation for a take-over of the Bulgarian countryside by foreign, and in particular American, capital. At the elections the BSP crushed the Agrarians, who began with over 20 per cent in the opinion polls but had to content themselves with a depressing 8 per cent of the final vote. This slightly unexpected domination of the countryside was the key to the BSP's victory.

The size of the victory boosted the position of the conservatives in the party. Lukanov himself had not wanted the party to win such a large majority. Instead he had hoped that the party and the UDF would each win about 40 per cent of the vote, so that they would be forced to govern Bulgaria in a grand coalition. Lukanov and the party technocrats had been watching developments in Romania very closely. They observed that the dominance of party conservatives was bound to ensure the maintenance of backward, xenophobic policies that, they believed, would damage Romania in the long run and, if copied in Bulgaria, would have the same effect. In addition, if the BSP formed a coalition with the UDF, it would not be considered solely responsible for the difficulties that Bulgaria was certain to face in the next few years.

Uncle Sam's Cavalry

It was not only the political forces in Bulgaria itself that monitored the growing strength of the BSP in the first half of 1990. The United States and its embassy in Sofia paid closer attention to the political development of Bulgaria than of any other country in Eastern Europe. By February Washington, it seems, had decided to act by sending in what can only be described as a diplomatic

SWAT unit in an attempt to bolster the UDF campaign and contribute to the defeat of the BSP. The Sheraton Hotel (by far the most luxurious in Eastern Europe) was filled to overflowing with American advisers whose only contact was with the UDF. In other East European countries American advisers spread their gospel evenly. In some cases they were even prepared to talk to the Communist Party. (Despite their excellent cocktail parties, it was sometimes difficult to ascertain what particular pearls of wisdom local politicians from Alaska and Iowa could bestow on the emerging democracies in Eastern Europe.) But in Bulgaria the advisers, armed with a total of $1.3 million, were there for one reason and one reason alone – to ensure a UDF victory.

The money was totally misused, and the selling of the UDF during the campaign was a disaster. Ironically, the BSP, which had employed a British advertising firm to run its campaign, ran a much more successful, American-style campaign, handing out T-shirts, adopting a teddy bear wearing American-style sneakers as one of their mascots and generally creating a carnival atmosphere that contrasted most favourably with the UDF's dour news conferences. But the BSP played fair. It did not deny the opposition access to the media, as had been the case in Romania, and there was no evidence of a dirty-tricks campaign despite many unsubstantiated accusations made by the UDF. In public the BSP also scrupulously avoided attacking the role of the United States in the election. It refused to resort to the Stalinist and xenophobic language used by the NSF, although Bulgarians could see for themselves that the interest taken by the US in the UDF was hyperactive. The nearest that Lukanov came to criticizing Washington was in a discussion with a visiting American diplomat, to whom he allegedly said, 'The UDF is not the opposition. You are the opposition.'

The role of the United States, and in particular its embassy in Sofia, during the election was an absolute disgrace. It also benefited the UDF very little, if at all, as Bulgarians could see quite clearly that the organization was cooperating closely with foreign forces. It would appear that the US did not want the victory of a party that, although committed to the transition to a market economy, was not prepared to relinquish its autonomy and accept dictates as to how that should be achieved. That being said, unlike the NSF in Romania, the BSP did not promise Bulgarians a rise in living standards and freedom from unemployment as the country made the transition to the market economy. It stated quite baldly that unprofitable factories would have to close and that it would not be a comfortable ride. So why was the United States government prepared to interfere in the Bulgarian campaign when it decided against similar intervention in the affairs of Bulgaria's northern neighbour, Romania? True, the US denounced the NSF's use of violence against the opposition, but it did not bolster the opposition Peasant and Liberal parties either with handouts or with its diplomatic SWAT unit.

The obvious answer concerns Bulgaria's foreign debt, which stands at around $11 billion. In March 1990 the government became the only one in post-revolutionary Eastern Europe to announce a moratorium on debt repayments. Bulgaria had simply run out of money. In addition, the Soviet Union was negotiating a 20 per cent cut in oil supplies to Bulgaria. Until 1990 Bulgaria had helped to service its debt by selling surplus Soviet oil, which it bought for soft currency, on the open market for hard currency. Rather than negotiate a bridging loan as Poland and Hungary had done, which would have involved introducing an austerity programme, Bulgaria's BSP government decided that it would simply not pay the debt. There is no doubt that this unilateral action infuriated the US government, but the interference in the Bulgarian election campaign had begun in earnest one month before the moratorium was made public.

The Revolution Delayed

After the elections the UDF, together with its friends from the US, was shell-shocked. Although there had been some irregularities in the voting, no party that had participated in the elections felt that the incidents were serious enough to warrant another poll. The BSP had won 211 seats in the 400-seat Narodno Subranie, while the UDF received 144. The Agrarians were allotted sixteen seats but were forced into fourth place by Dogan's MRF, which won twenty-three seats.

The opening ceremony of the democratically elected parliament took place in the medieval Bulgarian capital, Veliko Turnovo, a gesture designed to mark symbolic continuity between two sovereign Bulgarias. It was marred by anti-Turkish demonstrations, which, it was suspected, had been organized by conservative groups within the BSP. Ahmed Dogan was prevented from taking his seat in the parliament and from giving his opening address. Dogan himself has bent over backwards to reassure Bulgarians that the MRF does not threaten Bulgarian territorial integrity. He has also agreed that Bulgarian should be the language of state, merely asking his fellow citizens that Turkish be recognized as an acceptable language of discourse for the Turkish minority (one of the indignities suffered by Turks in Zhivkov's Bulgaria was to be punished even for saying 'good day' in Turkish). The MRF's problems are exacerbated by both the BSP in the countryside and the UDF. There have been calls by some UDF leaders to ban the MRF, which is quite appalling for an organization that is so heavily backed by the Americans as the great democratic hope for Bulgaria.

All this looked ominous as far as the reform mastermind of the BSP, Andrey Lukanov, was concerned. He offered to form a coalition with the UDF, but Zhelev refused on behalf of the opposition. This was another error on the part of the UDF, although it may still be rectified if a coalition can finally be agreed on. Instead the UDF launched a revival of the revolution, spurred on by a large body of Sofia's students. This led to the creation of the City of Truth (a Bulgarian equivalent of the Neo-Communist Free Zone 'Hooligania', which was just about to be destroyed by the miners in Bucharest). Hundreds of people camped out in central Sofia, demanding an end to the BSP monopoly on power. Sofia students also went on strike and soon new Cities of Truth were founded in other Bulgarian cities. The Cities were an important extension of the revolution. Because the party had pre-empted so many demands of the opposition immediately after Zhivkov's fall, ordinary Bulgarians (particularly those who lived in urban areas) had been denied an opportunity to express fully the anger and outrage that had welled up over a period of four decades. These had deepened in the period since the revolution, as the media had started the harrowing task of uncovering the extent of Zhivkov's crimes, which ranged from the mass slaughter of concentration-camp inmates in the 1950s to the development of an atrocious system of nepotism that benefited such dreadfully vulgar personalities as his son, Vladimir. The Cities of Truth had a cathartic effect and eventually pushed the BSP towards more concessions, helping moderates in the party to weaken the hard-liners.

The Cities amounted to by far the most effective gesture yet made by the opposition. Its success can be explained partly by its spontaneity and partly by the Mladenov affair. Petar Mladenov, the former Foreign Minister who had replaced Zhivkov as president, had been caught by a video camera saying in the Narodno Subranie that 'the best thing to do is let the tanks come' as a way of dealing with opposition demonstrations. This was not very convincing proof of Mladenov's commitment to democracy, and the opposition insisted that he should step down. Although Mladenov denied the authenticity of the video tape, claiming it to be 'a primitive montage', the BSP did not stand behind its president, and eventually he was forced to resign. This was simultaneously an important victory for the reformists in the BSP and the opposition.

Following this the BSP, which controls a majority in parliament, permitted the election of Zhelev to the office of president. The ruling party capitulated on a series of other opposition demands as well, including greatly improved access to television. Everything that the NSF refused to tolerate in Romania the BSP permitted in Bulgaria. This has gone a long way to diffusing the political tension in the country, which at one point almost threatened to explode into an orgy of violence that would have pitted town against country.

The UDF continues to be coy about forming a coalition with the BSP, fearing that this may stain its democratic reputation. If the UDF did agree to go into government with the BSP, the benefits for Bulgaria would be enormous. The UDF itself would benefit from the experience of government, while the hard-liners in the party would be delivered what might be a fatal blow. The Lukanov wing of the BSP has already made substantial concessions to facilitate the construction of a coalition. The reformists in the party do not want Bulgaria to drift towards isolation in the manner of Romania. They have made it clear that they see their future not as part of a rotting Balkan mire but in a prosperous Europe.

Despite the attempts made both by the BSP and the UDF, Bulgaria's traditions, which made it one of the most violent countries in the Balkans during the inter-war period, forced themselves on Sofia in late August 1990. Demonstrators led by two members of the militant Civil Disobedience organization ransacked, and then set fire to, the headquarters of the Socialist Party. Inside the building the demonstrators found ham, sausages and toilet paper, goods that had disappeared from the shops because of chronic shortages. All the tension that had plagued Bulgarian society – between BSP and UDF, between town and country, between intellectual and worker – exploded on the evening of 27 August. Zhelev responded quickly with an authoritative statement, while the government decided sensibly against using strong-arm police tactics, which would have led to a rapid escalation of violence. How these tensions are to be resolved in the long term is hard to predict. On a straightforward political level both the BSP and the UDF had shown a preparedness to talk, discuss and make concessions on issues in a way that was totally absent in Romania. But this was not sufficient to stem the rising tide of violence in a Bulgaria that is economically still on its knees. The resuscitation of the economy must remain a priority not only for Bulgaria but for the rest of Europe and the United States. The West will have to offer Bulgaria substantial economic aid if it is to avoid a slide back into the 1920s and a senseless bout of political vendettas.

Empty Coffers

The United States may have interpreted Bulgaria's decision to place a moratorium on debt repayment as a hostile action, but, more than any other East European country, Bulgaria had no option. The country is more or less completely bankrupt, making the need for a political solution to the country's problems extremely urgent. Already the population is having to cope with rationing of many basic goods, while production of the country's major exports (tobacco and soft fruits) has yet to recover from the exodus in 1989, of Turks, who are the most industrious farmers in Bulgaria's most fertile areas. Living standards are collapsing, as is the country's economic infrastructure. The imposition of UN sanctions against Iraq following Baghdad's invasion of Kuwait in August 1990 was a massive blow for Bulgaria. The government in Sofia agreed to stop trading with Iraq almost as soon as the UN Security Council had passed its resolution. Iraq owes Bulgaria $1.2 billion, which is now almost certainly lost. The reduction in oil supplies from the Soviet Union has begun to have serious effects on industry, leaving the country on the edge of a major recession.

The appointment of Zhelev to the presidency has altered the atmosphere. The United States embassy in Sofia welcomed the move, and the American ambassador declared his certainty that 'the situation in Bulgaria will now improve'. Despite the moratorium the IMF agreed to begin talks with Bulgaria, and these went on through the autumn. But the West must bear in mind that Bulgaria is completely penniless, having spent all its hard-currency reserves.

If the economic situation were to deteriorate still further, the demagogic spirit of the regional party bureaucracy (known colloquially as the 'mafia') will be able to reassert itself. This could have grave consequences both for Bulgaria and for some of its neighbouring countries. Tension between Bulgarians and the Turkish minority would undoubtedly increase. This issue is the one that generates violence most swiftly in Bulgaria, although the emotion usually travels only one way, with the Turkish minority having to defend itself against irrational attacks. Moreover, mistrust towards the United States and Western Europe would grow, allowing reactionary forces inside the country to nurture the isolationist tendencies that clearly exist among much of the peasantry and some of the proletariat.

Although the country is suffering from a dearth of technology and the inertia of over four decades of deplorable management, Bulgaria has traditionally been a more prosperous society than its Balkan neighbours, Romania and Serbia. As one distinguished historian of Central Europe, Joseph Rothschild, has pointed out, the Bulgarians pride themselves on 'sustaining a *rabota*–work culture, in contrast to the Serbs' *haiduk*–hero culture or the Romanians' and Greeks' alleged mercantile–ingenuity culture . . . The Bulgarians are, on balance, rather impressively utilitarian and hard-headed, with little of the romanticism or mysticism of other Slav peoples.' In an area where romanticism and mysticism render rational conversation almost impossible, these hard-headed utilitarians are welcome and refreshing. It would be most distressing to see their country fall into the mess of Balkan violence that their neighbours seem unable to shake off.

8 CONCLUSION
The Rebirth of History

Western Europe and the United States recorded a great ideological victory in 1989. The historical enemy was defeated in a series of stunning revolutions that sought to throw off the burden of a socialism that claimed to be based on scientific principles. In the year of these revolutions an American historian, Francis Fukuyama, elaborated his theory of the 'end of history'. If the theory were to be applied to the new Eastern Europe, it would predict the emergence of a free-market economy combined with a two-party democracy by the end of this century. A number of well-respected commentators from Western Europe and the United States concurred in the view that the see-saw political balance of social democracy and Christian democracy would now prove irresistible to the new state orders in Eastern Europe. The historical continuum was slowing down as it prepared to berth in its final resting place. In fact, since the war Eastern Europe has been quite stable, judged by the yardstick of its own history. Stability has been bought at the expense of the democratic development of the area. Four decades of dictatorship have left the countries of Eastern Europe neurotic and confused. The goal of modern Western democracy may be appealing in theory to most East Europeans, but they are concerned first to ensure a basic standard of living for their children. This fundamental consideration is something that policy makers in Western Europe invariably overlook. Far from coming to an end, history is being reborn.

The Rise and Fall of Central Europe

Together with the break-up of the USSR itself, the revolutions of 1989 represent one of the most important historical cycles of the twentieth century, rivalling both world wars, the Russian Revolution, the Nazi take-over of power in Germany, the collapse of colonial power and the post-war development of a divided Europe. The political map of the continent, which has been stable and predictable for an unprecedented number of years, is now changing beyond recognition at a remarkable speed. The sheer bulk of events renders it almost impossible for an observer to monitor Eastern Europe in the way he or she may have become used to. The political fragmentation of the Soviet Union's former allies was swift, while any discussion of Yugoslavia involves consideration of eight more or less completely independent political entities.

As they began the exploration of dormant political traditions and the construction of new, peculiar structures, the ties that used to bind the East European countries loosened almost overnight. Before the revolutions the peoples of Eastern Europe showed no great concern for the personal fate of their neighbours, but they were always attentive to their political fate. Everyone recognized that there was a sensitive relationship between what happened in Hungary, for example, and events in the rest of the bloc. Thus the imposition of martial law in Poland in December 1981 was greeted by the official media of East Germany and Czechoslovakia with undisguised jubilation. The opposition in both countries naturally interpreted the events as an enormous blow to their work. This taut relationship became especially marked just before the revolutionary wave that swept the area in the autumn of 1989. The leaders of the GDR, Czechoslovakia and Romania felt it necessary to forge a reactionary axis in an attempt to fend off the influence of the increasingly popular reforms in Hungary and Poland, which by the middle of 1989 looked as though they might well lead to a major shift in the development of East European politics. It was a decision made by the Hungarian foreign minister, Gyula Horn, a reform communist, that lit the fuse leading to the East German revolution. In September 1989 he opened Hungary's border to the West, provoking the most serious crisis ever faced by the Politburo and Central Committee of East Germany's Socialist Unity Party (SED).

But popular awareness of conditions prevailing in other socialist countries was usually expressed at a more mundane level. Thus while ordinary Czechs may have used the usual stereotypes to describe East Germans, Poles or Romanians, they would always know where the standard of living was highest in the bloc, giving concrete examples of which goods were available at what price. They would generally know in which countries political discrimination was more or less intense. It is hard to imagine an Italian being able to offer a similar comparative study of the lifestyles of the Danes and the Belgians.

Once the Romanian revolution had been completed, the shackles of repression that had bound these countries so tightly for forty years started to dissolve. During the communist period some countries had developed particularly close relationships that now lost some of their intensity as collaboration against a common oppressor faded while competition for Western financial and political attention increased. The friendship between Hungarians and Poles, for example, which was rooted in the nineteenth century and which always found some form of expression during the political upheavals of the last forty years, has lost its voice since the revolutions.

The distances separating the new democracies since the end of 1989 have never been larger. A new political culture is evolving in each country, and despite their common fate after the war each culture is entirely distinct, which reinforces the observation that Eastern Europe, and indeed Central Europe, has only ever existed as a geographical entity and a very imprecise one at that. The idea that a certain set of values binds these countries and some of their neighbours would be appealing if the values were not usually restricted to a small pool of intellectuals. During the communist period the oft discussed idea of Central Europe as a distinct political entity proposed that the small countries sandwiched between Germany and the Soviet Union* had a unique contribution to make

---

* The debate about Central Europe has been one of the most fruitful of the last twenty years but also one of the most complex and verbose. Much time has been spent on trying to identify what area constitutes Central Europe (or *Mitteleuropa*, as it was originally called by the Germany geo-politicians who sought to give the cluster of regions between Germany and Russia a name). In recent years it has often

to European politics and culture. Above all it stressed the role of a civil society in which citizens, on their own initiative, would create democratic institutions to compensate for the failure of state power to provide them. This had enormous implications for Eastern Europe, where the state was committed to destroying independent political activity. To a significant extent the ideas of 'civil society' and 'Central Europe' became the ideology of the opposition, which eventually spearheaded the assault on communist power.

Political 'Central Europe' extended well beyond its geographical barriers and developed into a rich exchange of ideas and political experience between a wide spectrum of ideologies, Eastern and Western. Thus the philosopher Roger Scruton and Norman Podhoretz, the tenaciously right-wing American commentator, would be received by representatives of Charter 77, Solidarity and the Hungarian Democratic Opposition with the same courtesy as that accorded to the left-wing historian E. P. Thompson or the sociologist and END activist Mary Kaldor. Later on the concept of the 'new movements' within the Western left, which saw the development of individual pressure groups as a new political vanguard, began to influence the opposition in Eastern Europe (notably in Slovenia and Hungary), and a process of differentiation began within 'Central Europe'. But ultimately 'Central Europe', almost contrary to its intentions, developed into a successful ideology of peaceful revolution.

In as much as 'Central Europe' existed as a coherent political concept, however, it could be sustained only while the Soviet Union or its quislings continued to dominate the area. Once that coercive force ceased to play a pivotal role, the only attraction

---

been used in a narrow East European sense to refer to Poland, Czechoslovakia and Hungary, whose opposition movements made strenuous attempts to co-ordinate their work. East Germany was regarded as an occasional, honorary member, while Romania and Bulgaria were somehow regarded as outside 'Central Europe's zone of operation. Yugoslavs, mainly from Slovenia but also from Croatia and Serbia, chipped in with the occasional contribution. However, many people still understand Central Europe in a wider sense as embracing virtually all the former lands of the Habsburg Empire plus those parts of modern Poland not under Habsburg control, plus much of Germany.

binding the new states was the nostalgia of an intense recent experience. Certainly, President Havel recognized that the return to Europe of Poland, Czechoslovakia and Hungary would be made easier if the three countries could establish some form of co-ordination. But attempts to consolidate this relationship, despite the personal ties between many leading figures in the three new democracies, have met little success. If 'Central Europe' does continue to exist beyond its uncertain geographical limits, it will do so only with the emergence of a new European security system. The new foreign ministers of Czechoslovakia and Poland have set about the task of devising just such a system, which would guarantee an equal role for the Central European nations, but despite their sterling efforts, when negotiations begin in earnest they are likely to find themselves among the objects of negotiations between more powerful interested parties.

None the less, pre-revolutionary Central Europe has fulfilled its political role in remarkable style. The revolutions of 1989 were unexpected but essential victories of the rational over the irrational, the democratic over the totalitarian and the market over the plan. Human dignity proved more forceful than the arrogance of power. Gorbachev's policy of self-determination for the countries of Eastern Europe was a precondition for the revolutions, but even without the enlightened General Secretary the revolutions would have erupted – not quite so soon, admittedly, but could anybody envisage Polish workers remaining passive when faced with the combined evils of economic collapse on the one hand and Brezhnevism in an advanced state of senility on the other?

The people's democracies were doomed from an early age, though force of arms ensured that their time on earth would be a memorable and critical historical interlude. They were mutant political constructions that looked all the shabbier for their utopian aspirations. The one promise that most of the communist states lived up to throughout their existence was the guarantee of freedom from unemployment. However, the working class, allegedly the controlling force in society, quickly recognized that the political and social privileges it could savour outside the restricted sphere of guaranteed employment were limited, if not negligible. With the exception of the extremely under-developed areas that came under communist control (in particular Albania, Serbia, Macedonia, Montenegro, Bosnia and Romania) after the Second World War, the East European countries' record on health, education, housing and a range of other social services has been atrocious.

Despite overwhelming evidence, the Communist Party leaderships refused to admit that the working classes lived in more squalid conditions, breathing in more damaging air and drinking more toxic water, than Western working classes. They trampled on the democratic rights of anybody who threatened the structure of Stalinist power, which for so long appeared to be fashioned of galvanized steel but finally revealed itself to be as brittle as matchwood. When the most rabid national Stalinist of all, Nicolae Ceauşescu, was executed and the regimes appeared to dissolve before our eyes, many of the dazed but ecstatic revolutionaries asked themselves one question: why? (Or, as the banner carried by two men in late middle age demanded of the former Czechoslovak president during the revolution, 'Husák! Give us back twenty-one years.') Unfortunately for those who suffered, there is no answer to the question that does not sound absurd. The daily experience of 'actually existing socialism' was invariably petty and unnecessary, appearing to benefit nobody.

With communism finished in Eastern Europe, the revolutionaries were able to set about the creation of some form of political plurality. The emergence of huge popular movements before and during the revolutions in almost all countries was determined by the will to defeat the common enemy, the Communist Party in power. By the end of 1989 these movements had carried out their initial task, in some cases quite brilliantly. During the second phase, the period between revolution and elections, fragmentation took place to varying degrees. In Hungary the opposition umbrella separated into a number of identifiable parties. In Czechoslovakia several currents began to crystallize in Civic Forum and Public Against Violence, while those who left the movement, such as the Catholic philosopher Václav Benda (who joined the electoral alliance known as the Christian Democratic Union) still maintained close contacts with Civic Forum. In Romania factions within the centralist FSN began to form behind the scenes, while those who broke with it completely, such as Doina Cornea, left for good to help form an opposition movement. Solidarity, of course, began its slow and bitter break-up before Poland had held general elections.

With the exception of the FSN in Romania, which called itself a centre-left organization, all groupings, regardless of their political heritage, immediately announced that they were forces of the 'political centre'. Everybody was centrist, and nobody dared to admit to being either left or right – except for the old or reformed Communist Parties, which insisted that they were all carrying the torch of the 'modern European left'. Needless to say, whenever called upon to define the 'modern European left' their representatives were at a loss. The Hungarian Socialist Party (the former HSWP) was helped in this respect by being accepted into the Socialist International, although its chairman, Rezsö Nyers, firmly denied that the reformed party was social democratic. By retaining its name the Communist Party of Czechoslovakia clearly rejected social democracy and indicated that there was life in the old ideological dog yet, while in Poland the pompous Social Democracy of the Republic of Poland, as the party dubbed itself, seems to have adopted its name in order to prevent any other political formation from capitalizing on the social democratic sobriquet. But, apart from the Communist Parties, none of the new formations felt the slightest inclination to identify itself with the left, and even the reformed social democratic parties felt the burden of their names. Despite strong traditions in the area, no social democratic party emerged as a serious political force after the revolutions.

The right was equally coy. Even the Republic and Freedom parties in Czechoslovakia, whose programmes planted them firmly on the radical, non-Fascist right of the European spectrum, made sure that the language they used during the election campaigns was bland and 'centrist'. Poland is able to boast a plethora of extreme nationalist and right-wing parties that are less embarrassed by their position. However, most of them, though not all, are for the moment politically insignificant. The GDR remains a special case, as most of the parties that gained seats in the Volkskammer (the East German parliament) at the March 1990 elections were sister organizations of the main West German parties, the most important exception being the former Communist Party, the PDS.

All of these new programmes spoke of the need to create stable, democratic structures, to introduce a market or social market economy and to become part of an integrated Europe. Given that socialism had been pulverized politically during the revolutions, it was striking that no party spoke explicitly of the need to re-introduce capitalism, except as part of the joke that defines social-ism as a road that leads from capitalism to capitalism. Socialism was, of course, assumed to be unacceptable, while no programme spoke specifically of the 'third way'. The absence of any definition of the proposed socio-economic development apart from the ubiqui-tous market or social-market economy, and hence the obsession with the 'centre', can partly be explained by the deep aversion that many East Europeans feel for any discussion of the traditional political spectrum. 'We are neither right nor left,' 'We cannot be categorized into any sort of left–right schema,' 'The old ideas of right or left no longer hold any meaning for us' are quotes picked at random from political leaders of Solidarity, Public Against Violence and the governing DEMOS coalition in Slovenia.

This refusal to be identified by old political symbols extends to the economy as well. While the introduction of market mechanisms is almost a *sine qua non* (Romania provides a possible exception), most of the ruling organizations view the process with considerable trepidation and conservative misgivings. Thus the programme of the MDF in Hungary says of the economy that the party 'rejects any form of experimentation with the people and expects the renewal of the economy to come not from restrictions but from *modernization** ... The inevitable price of economic moderniza-tion will be unemployment, but this can be mitigated by the

---

*I stress 'modernization' because it implies that Hungary will develop and adapt the existing system (with its absolute commitment to full employment) as a means of creating market mechanisms.

establishment of a state scheme to retain workers and by the co-ordination of factory closures with the opening of new places of work.' Civic Forum too revealed in its electoral programme its fears that unrestricted capitalism might have profoundly negative effects on the economy: 'In view of our present backwardness we will have to work harder than others, limit the consumption of the products of our work in order to increase our investments. Otherwise, due to the conditions of tough economic competition, we could again lose the ownership of our home; the selling off of our national assets would make us paid labourers in our own country.'

Clearly, when discussing the market economy most political forces in Eastern Europe are talking about capitalism. None the less, for political reasons they consider it prudent not to mention the word. Moreover, almost all political parties in Eastern Europe devote much energy to explaining those policies that are aimed at softening the blow that economic reform will deal to all social groups (the number of people whose existing wealth will provide adequate shelter from the coming economic storm is negligible). This is hardly unexpected. Market mechanisms are not being introduced into economies with smoothly functioning infrastructures, visible growth areas and export potential. They are supposed to inject vitality into economies that simply cannot sustain the living standards of the population and, in some cases, are in a state of complete collapse.

At the beginning of 1990 the Balcerowicz plan was inaugurated in Poland. Everybody realized that it would seriously threaten the economic well-being of many Poles, in particular the working class. None the less the Mazowiecki government enjoyed enormous popular trust. The plan was essentially a fiscal austerity programme (it did not, in its key initial phase, tamper with the state's ownership of industry) that was considerably more thorough, and in the short-term more damaging, than anything that Gomułka, Gierek or other Polish communist leaders had dared to introduce. Despite the popular support for the Mazowiecki government, within five months the Balcerowicz plan had caused such hardship that strikes and other forms of industrial unrest began to proliferate.

The bold Polish plan, which had received accolades from the West, threatened to destabilize the country's polity. Economic failure in the new Eastern Europe does not lead to calls for the resignation of cabinet ministers – it swiftly translates itself into unrest.

The Whip of the West: Economic Policy in Eastern Europe

Before the revolutions the bulk of the East European countries' foreign trade took place either within COMECON's cripplingly bureaucratic plan for an international division of socialist labour or between individual East European countries, regulated by bilateral treaties. Even Yugoslavia, which as an associate member of COMECON enjoyed special trade privileges with the bloc, was heavily dependent on the Soviet Union as its most important trading partner. The West imposed between itself and the East a variety of restrictions and trade barriers that kept a tight lid on commercial ties. The best-known of these was COCOM, a body that was created in the late 1940s to control the flow of technology from West to East. COCOM was set up to ensure that the Soviet Union was denied easy access to military technology, although particularly during the 1970s and 1980s its orders were often enforced as a way of maintaining political pressure on Eastern Europe. COCOM's policeman was always the United States, which punished countries that infringed COCOM regulations. This often led to conflict with Japan and the United Kingdom as well as with the so-called 'springboard' countries such as Austria, but above all with West Germany.

In addition to COCOM, the United States and Western Europe used political criteria to decide which countries would be granted beneficial trading arrangements. The US would grant and revoke Most Favoured Nation (MFN) trading status as a way of applying differential political pressures on East European countries, depending on its local political interest. Thus in the mid- and late 1980s Romania continued to enjoy MFN despite having the worst human rights record in the bloc, while Poland continued to be denied it despite having one of the best. The extent of Washington's benevolence depended primarily not on considerations of domestic politics within this or that East European country but rather on a particular country's relationship with the Soviet Union. The EC had its own system of tariffs and restrictions, which was motivated less by politics and more by economic interests, although once again Romania was singled out for beneficial treatment. In addition, the EC refused to trade with COMECON as a bloc; it would enter into bilateral agreements only with individual countries.

One of the most powerful aspects of Western influence was the indebtedness of East European governments to the West. The debts were incurred during the 1970s, when Western governments and banks had a substantial credit surplus that they wished to dispose of. Above all, the Poles, the Hungarians, the Romanians, the Bulgarians and the Yugoslavs accepted the offer of large Western credits. Most of the monies were squandered during that decade by the remarkably short-sighted communist leaderships that used the money both to buy political acquiescence by increasing the supply of consumer goods and to commemorate their historical role by investing in pompous industrial projects of little economic value but with grandiose propaganda potential. Naturally the enormous hard-currency debts that were accrued by some countries have developed into forceful political actors on the East European stage.

Czechoslovakia was careful not to incur too high a debt, while East Germany's budget deficit was effectively funded by West German generosity and by its back-door access to EC markets that its special relationship with West Germany made possible. In 1983 Nicolae Ceauşescu decided that Romania, which owed over $11 billion, would divert the bulk of its foreign-currency earnings to the repayment of the debt. By mid-1989, just six months before Ceauşescu's fall, Romania had paid off most of its debt but only at the cost of an appalling squeeze on living standards that had left the population cold, hungry and ultimately ready for revolution. Poland failed to make any headway in the payment of its debt, which had risen to $41 billion by the end of 1989. Hungary, with a population of just over 10 million, had managed to run up the region's highest per capita debt, about $17 billion, by the beginning of 1990. So sensitive were people to the size of the debt that the last communist prime minister, Miklós Németh (whose policies during his short but active period in office revealed him to be by far the most committed capitalist of all the new East European prime ministers), had the difficult task of explaining to the Hungarians that successive governments in the Kádár period had lied about the size of the debt, claiming that it was between $4 billion and $6 billion less than it actually was. In Yugoslavia the presence of the debt, combined with the awesome incompetence of the country's political leadership, has made both a mockery of any attempted reforms and an important contribution to the country's fragmentation. Almost all ordinary East Europeans have suffered severely for debt that was eagerly arranged by a distasteful alliance of vain dictators and greedy bankers.

After their successful revolutions of 1989 the peoples of Eastern Europe tore down the political barriers that had blocked the development of trade and cooperation between them and Western Europe. Democracy and political pluralism, whose installation were considered essential by the West if there were to be a fundamental revision of policy towards Eastern Europe, were in place. One of the fastest methods of injecting some stability in the region would have been to reduce the debt burden and substantially to improve trading facilities. However, since President George Bush's path-breaking visit to Poland and Hungary in July 1989, when he disappointed both governments by not offering any debt relief or substantial capital assistance, the West has made it clear that the debts will have to be repaid in their entirety. Indeed, far from loosening economic restrictions on trade with Eastern Europe, the West is imposing strict and damaging conditions on the new democracies in order to influence their socio-economic development. This is a dangerous game which has already affected the taut political situation in at least one country, Poland.

The bulk of East European debt has been funded not by private banks but by governments. For example, of Poland's $41 billion debt only $9 billion was loaned by private institutions. The pattern is reflected elsewhere in Eastern Europe. Privately, the new leaderships in Eastern Europe hoped that the West might cancel most of the debt, which was lent during the communist period to corrupt regimes who frittered the money away. It was the ordinary people who had to pay for financial mismanagement. In Romania the loans were translated into considerable suffering, while in Poland and Hungary debts have squeezed the economies dry. Now the West has deemed once again that the peoples of Eastern Europe should pay for the debts, this time with hard currency, which is in very short supply.

At first most post-revolutionary countries talked of the debt problem in cautious terms. In March 1990 one country, Bulgaria, went out on a limb and infuriated the West by imposing a unilateral moratorium on repayments. By then Poland had begun to scream for help. From early February 1990 onwards Prime Minister Mazowiecki raised the issue of relief on the basic debt whenever he travelled to the West. He succeeded in arranging a further rescheduling of the debt repayments, which afforded Poland some useful breathing space but no solution. The IMF and the World Bank, the two primary representatives of the creditors during discussions of the debt, remain unmoved on the issue of debt cancellation. These two intermediaries for the Western governments, the IMF in particular, are linking negotiations for bridging loans with specific changes in economic structure.

Thus Hungary, for example, was negotiating with the IMF a modest $200 million loan in the spring of 1990. The Hungarian government was keen to secure the deal, as a further $1 billion loan from the EC would be released only on the agreement of terms with the IMF for the $200 million. The IMF insisted that all rent subsidies would have to be scrapped as part of the deal, a move that would have incalculable social consequences. The government agreed after some resistance, but parliament refused to accept the condition, so the IMF refused the money.

Western governments and institutions such as the IMF invariably raise the issue of precedent when calls are made for the total or partial cancellation of East European debt. There are already precedents – admittedly those of countries with poorer economic prospects than Eastern Europe's – but in addition there is the key moral point that the money was lent not to democratically elected governments but to a group of corrupt neo-Stalinist leaderships. Despite the tireless rhetoric of Western leaders, which for forty years berated Soviet and East European governments for the abuse of human rights and lack of freedom, they positively encouraged the propping up of these regimes during the 1970s in the misguided hope of swift financial returns. For this reason debt cancellation would be a dignified gesture. It would also minimize the risk to the embryonic democracies, which need more than just the promise of long-term foreign investment in their countries.

The G7 countries have stated at the highest level that there will be no new Marshall Plan in Eastern Europe. Leaving the debt problem aside, if the West were content to allow the East European states to construct mixed-market economies with competitive access to Western markets, Eastern Europe's immediate political prospects might not look so bleak. But even here the West would be linking agreements with specific demands that, in the circumstances, would amount to a form of blackmail. Under tenacious pressure from the West German government COCOM has reduced the number of goods whose exports to Eastern Europe are banned, but only by about half. Although nobody considers Czechoslovakia a security threat any longer, COCOM continues to restrict the sale of critical microtechnology to Prague. Similarly the trade agreements concluded by the EC with post-revolutionary Poland and Hungary place specific restrictions on the export of goods to the Community that include, in Poland's case, steel, coal and textiles, three of its most important export commodities. The Economic Cooperation Agreement signed with Poland in September 1989 stipulates that Poland must afford help to any EC company wishing to start business in the country and that Western firms must be provided with 'investment promotion and protection, including the transfer of profits and the repatriation of capital' by the Polish government. The issue of profit and capital repatriation is one of the most delicate in Eastern Europe as each government attempts to agree on measures regulating the inflow and outflow of foreign capital. But the EC is demanding a controlling interest in these measures in return for a closely defined rearrangement, but not the abolition, of trade barriers.

The West is also trying to phase out the practice of counter-trade, the system of bartering that East European countries short of hard currency and credit depended upon so much before the revolution. The EC agreement with Poland, ratified in September 1989, specifically demands that the Polish government shall not seek to promote counter-trade with EC countries. Finally, at its meeting of government heads in December 1989, the EC defined the requirements relating to East European states applying for associate status of the EC. The Community will consider applications only from those countries in which steps 'have been taken towards systems based on . . . economic liberties'.

The Western economic strategy developed towards the post-revolutionary states in Eastern Europe has clearly been designed to coerce them into the swift construction of a market or capitalist economy along lines preferred by the West. By March 1990 those political forces that were not playing ball had begun to feel the effects of discrimination. The Bulgarian government's announcement that it was slapping a moratorium on debt repayments aroused the wrath of the United States. This anger was further fuelled by the impressive performance of the Bulgarian Socialist Party (née the Communist Party) in the opinion polls prior to the elections of 10 and 17 June 1990. In stark contrast to its policy elsewhere in the bloc (which consisted of parachuting in teams of democratic advisers whose chief function was to organize cocktail parties around the elections and to offer advice to all participating parties), the US government encouraged its embassy in Sofia to intervene quite blatantly in the electoral process in Bulgaria, handing out money and support to the opposition Union of Democratic Forces (UDF). At one point a UDF spokesman said that the British foreign secretary, Douglas Hurd, had told him that if the BSP won the elections, Bulgaria would not receive a penny in aid, although this was subsequently denied by the Foreign Office.

By the summer of 1990 the West appeared to have divided Eastern Europe in two. Just before his spectacular departure from politics in July the British minister for trade and industry, Nicholas Ridley, was in Prague on a visit during which he announced that the UK had decided to make available special 'know-how' funds of £75 million as a goodwill gesture, as he put it. The money was earmarked for the GDR, Poland, Hungary and Czechoslovakia 'because it is precisely these countries which have evinced a determination to join the free world'. The British government has a good case for its punitive action against Romania because of its brutal suppression of the opposition after the elections, but Bulgaria has been left out of the privileged group of nations not because the BSP was accused of electoral fraud (the UDF and other parties have recognized the BSP's victory) but merely because it won the Bulgarian elections. It may have refused to play by the West's rules by imposing a debt moratorium; undemocratic it is not, however.

The use of strong-arm tactics to coerce East European states into the quick creation of market economies has involved a miscalculation that threatens the stability of the area. The example of Poland shows how quickly austerity programmes can provoke an authoritarian response. In May the Solidarity chairman Lech Wałęsa persuaded striking railway workers to go back to work, but everybody realized that the patience of workers in Poland was about to run out. Wałęsa used the crisis to unveil his presidential aspirations (like Havel, he said that he did not want to run for office but that if it was necessary for the country, he would: it is hard to believe either). He also launched a massive and wounding attack on Mazowiecki's government and Solidarity's liberal wing, centred on Adam Michnik. He added that if he were elected president, he would be prepared to rule Poland by decree. It was a very undemocratic, but remarkably effective, intervention.

During this delicate and sensitive period of transition from very weak planned economies to market economies, authoritarian and populist political programmes will inevitably proliferate. From Wałęsa in Poland to Drašković in Serbia, from Iliescu in Romania to the Slovak National Party in Czechoslovakia, there are movements, parties and individuals ready and able to seize the economic uncertainty attendant on the transition. By twisting the arms of East European governments and insisting that aid will be linked with quite specific economic developments, the West is making a fundamental contribution to instability in Eastern Europe that is in nobody's interests; indeed, it is stimulating anti-Western and anti-capitalist popular sentiment. After the Polish affair there were signs that the IMF realized how serious an effect its contractual conditions were having on Polish politics. It is important that the pressure on Poland be relaxed immediately, but the whole strategy of the West must be reconsidered if social unrest is to be avoided in the area.

The Ideology that Dares not Speak Its Name

Western economic coercion is linked with one of the most complex and fundamental political conundrums affecting Eastern Europe – the fate of socialism. As has been noted above, the new political movements have all been furiously claiming the centre ground in the new democratic structures (even the FSN calls itself 'centre left'). The desire for a truly new political order is genuine and popular in Eastern Europe. It has found its most coherent expression in the writings of Václav Havel. The Czechoslovak president hopes to see the emergence of a parliamentary democracy dominated by the personalities of the MPs and not by the ideology of their party. Although many people, probably including Havel himself, recognize the inevitability of Civic Forum's demise as a political force, they hope that in some respects it may function as a model of future political development, an organization in which different ideologies can happily coexist. Understandable though this hope is, given the fear of the ideological labels 'left' and 'right' on the one hand and the genuine pluralism of several of the front movements on the other, it is also ultimately an untenable position. If both the two major Hungarian parties, the MDF and the SZDSZ, insist that they are the political centre, what is there to separate them? Or, to put it another way, how is it possible to have pluralism without plurality? Essentially, what explains the cracks that are beginning to emerge in Civic Forum is precisely an embryonic split between right and left.

During and after the revolutions many people assumed that a strong social democratic movement, fashioned after the West European model, would emerge in Eastern Europe. However, as the elections approached social democracy splintered badly in most countries. In the end the social democratic parties that claimed legitimacy from the pre-communist era held no electoral appeal whatsoever in 1990, being wiped off the map in Czechoslovakia, Hungary, Romania and various Yugoslav republics. Although the social democratic campaigns in these countries were uniformly pitiful, their failure to awake from hibernation was related to the fact that their natural constituency had been usurped by other organizations. In Czechoslovakia Civic Forum soaked up what was probably the largest social democratic vote in Eastern Europe. In Hungary the social democratic vote appears to have split between the MDF, which promised a slow economic transition, and the SZDSZ, whose liberal politics are better suited to the social democratic temperament. In Romania social democrats pledged their support to the anti-FSN opposition forces but collapsed as an organized force well before the elections as the bulk of their potential voters plumped for the FSN. In Croatia there is evidence to suggest that while some social democrats supported the weak liberal Coalition for National Agreement, the majority backed the triumphant right-wing nationalist party, the Croatian Democratic Alliance.

So has social democracy collapsed in Eastern Europe? On the contrary. With the exception of the Communist Parties, any organization that pinned its colours firmly to the mast of socialism was almost certain to lose heavily at the elections. For the majority of the population the vocabulary associated with socialism is identified with economic failure and political repression. Socialism – or, more properly, social democracy – is the ideology that dares not speak its name in Eastern Europe, although across the region it is probably still the most influential. In addition to the linguistic taboo, Civic Forum, the MDF in Hungary, the FSN and the BSP in Bulgaria all campaigned furiously with the notion that a vote for a small party – including, of course, the social democrats – was a wasted vote. In the case of Czechoslovakia one faction of social democracy, led by the well-respected Charter 77 signatory Rudolf Battěk, split from the party and sought refuge under Civic Forum's umbrella. Apart from their electoral victory, the political platforms of these successful political movements, as well as Solidarity in Poland, have one element in common. All of them stress the need for a complex programme of social welfare – above all, they are all committed to combating inflation and unemployment during the transition to a market economy. None of them is prepared to apply a radical free-market economic policy in order to guide their country towards market mechanisms.

This should not come as any great surprise. In most of these countries a strong egalitarian tradition has always existed. Czechoslovakia boasted the most educated working class in the region, which responded quickly and efficiently in support of the students and intellectuals during the Czechoslovak revolution. Workers in Bohemia, Moravia and Slovakia voted for Civic Forum and Public Against Violence partly in recognition of the role that these organizations played in overthrowing communism and partly because of their promise of economic progress with minimal social discrimination. In Poland it was the workers, indignant at the way in which the authorities stripped away their living standards, who formed the majestic foundations of the revolution. The members of Solidarity had cut their fighting teeth doing battle with Stalinism and its repressive network. The tradition of trade unionism has persisted everywhere in Eastern Europe. Most of the political forces that competed in the elections of 1990 stressed the absolute necessity for trade unions to play a central role in the transition to a market economy. The Czechoslovak prime minister, Marián Čalfa, went so far as to say that he could not imagine a healthy Czechoslovakia without a strong trade-union movement. In Poland most people adopted the view that if any capitalist wanting to invest demanded legislation restricting the activity of unions, then he must be a bad capitalist whose investment would be unwelcome. Even in Hungary, which does not have such powerful workers' traditions, the unions gained considerable support during the first half of 1990 with their resolute backing for strikes that included both economic and political demands (which were usually calls for the sacking of communist managers). In Bulgaria, during the period of political vacuum in July and August, it was the political skill of the trade unionists that helped to set a political agenda for the rather inexperienced and apparently incompetent MPs.

In this context it is interesting to note that the Hungarian SZDSZ lost heavily to the MDF in the second round of the elections. Although its membership, and indeed its political traditions, closely resembled those of Civic Forum in Czechoslovakia, the SZDSZ underwent a sea change in early 1990, discarding its protectionist economic policy for one in which the market would determine everything. Most important, the SZDSZ wanted to scrap all the country's controls on the inflow and outflow of foreign capital. The SZDSZ lost not only in the countryside, where the MDF was assumed to be strong, but also in its urban strongholds, including its 'capital', Budapest, where the MDF came out on top. The failure of Christian democracy in Czechoslovakia, with its liberal economic policy, was quite a surprise, especially in Slovakia, where Jan Čarnogurský's KDH was beaten into second place by Public Against Violence, Civic Forum's Slovak ally. Although the FSN felt it necessary to consolidate its already unassailable position with revoltingly undemocratic techniques, its success in the elections rested to a great extent on the promise made to workers and peasants that Romania would not be ravaged by foreign capitalists and that living standards would be stabilized and then increased. Although the FSN's unacceptable human rights record was an important reason why the West reconsidered its aid programme for the country, the FSN's explicitly socialist platform contributed to Western disillusionment.

This social democratic tradition may have found a home in the front organizations, but it shares that political space with many other currents. During the transition to democracy such an arrangement is beneficial to all those involved, though sometimes tensions cannot be concealed. There is a clear struggle within the MDF between Westernizers and Hungarian traditionalists. Running through the middle of Civic Forum is a split between left and right, while Wałęsa has forced the issue of Solidarity's identity under the influence of economic pressure, vanity and his shrewd, if devious, advisers. But it will be a long time before the social democratic bases within the front organizations are able to declare themselves or 'come out'. In the case of Poland, this is something of which Lech Wałęsa is very aware. The programme of Adam

Michnik, the Solidarity leader's erstwhile close colleague turned most influential opponent, is, broadly speaking, social democratic. But this he dares not admit, as especially in Poland social democracy is a commodity that for the moment nobody wants to buy if it carries the brand name. Some representatives of the left within Civic Forum acknowledge that before the 1992 elections they expect to find new political partners with whom they will be able to form a new social democratic organization. While they have a powerful base within Civic Forum, the political landscape outside looks motley.

The failure of the Green parties in the elections is also important. In all countries opposition Green movements made a substantial contribution to the raising of public consciousness about the rottenness of the communist governments. At the beginning of the electoral campaigns many of the Greens appeared to find favour with quite a high percentage of voters. In the Czech lands, Bohemia and Moravia, it was assumed for a long time that the Green party would take second place after Civic Forum. The specific reasons for the collapse of Green support varied from country to country (in Hungary, for example, a sad and painful bout of factional fighting within the movement left it badly maimed), but it is striking how uniformly weak most of their programmes were on the development of a coherent economic policy.

The preference of so many voters in Eastern Europe for a protected transition to the market economy indicates that even the most advanced among the new democracies, such as Czechoslovakia, may be prepared to forgo some of the opulence available to the upper end of the Western social strata in order to build a safety net for the bulk of the population. Certainly, if the economic programmes of most ruling political parties in Eastern Europe are implemented, considerable financial resources will have to be diverted from investment and towards the maintenance of a complex social security network. Apart from the moral imperative to do this, which is upheld by many of the new governments, influenced by the movements that opposed communism, there are sound political reasons as well. If some degree of stability is not guaranteed in these countries, forces much darker than social democracy will cast an ever longer shadow over Eastern Europe's political stage.

Nationalism in Eastern Europe

There is no political or social force that can match the power of nationalism in Eastern Europe. The revolutions of 1989 were social in character, but in the process a variety of national communities buried their historical differences to destroy the despotic power of the Communist Party. Cooperation between nationalities, although greatly significant, was a secondary force within the revolutionary struggle, however. It was none the less accompanied by moving symbols of national liberation because, although the foreign oppressor, in this case the Soviet Union, had already made it perfectly clear that it was ending its political and military occupation more or less of its own free will, the peoples of Eastern Europe wanted to compare publicly their profound national pride with the hollow usurpation of that tradition by the local communist leaderships. The only time the Czechoslovak national anthem was sung with any passion before the revolution was at international football matches. When military bands struck it up at official communist ceremonies, nobody sang – it was an embarrassing reminder of the gulf between rulers and ruled. When the curtain came down on these artificial celebrations of power, national symbols that had been adapted by the Communist Party, as in East Germany, Hungary or Romania, were restored to their original form, shape or name. Red stars, mathematical dividers, hammers, the qualification 'People's' or 'Socialist' disappeared from flags and titles, while overnight images of Lenin faded and the old, familiar faces of Masaryk, Mickiewicz, Kossuth or Prince Michael were restored in their place.

Nineteen eighty-nine was the finest hour of East European nationalism, when the natural desire for liberation was expressed through a reassertion of national identity. At the point of revolution this threatened nobody except the existing power structures, and for a short period it created an unimaginably warm sense of community that extended beyond national barriers. For a few days Masaryk's dream of a single Czechoslovak nation came true; Romanians and Hungarians embraced one another in Transylvania; Turks and Bulgarians took to the streets to celebrate Zhivkov's fall.

Although the revolutions began as beacons of piercingly sharp light, they have become dull, almost invisible glows behind the dark cloud of nationalist intolerance whose shadow swamps the region's history. In one country, Yugoslavia, the collapse of communist power was accelerated by nationalist conflict. To dismiss the threat of nationalism in Eastern Europe is to be lulled into a dreamy world of harmonious European integration. The assumption that, following the liberation from communism, there will be a rational way to resolve the more bitter historical disputes in Eastern Europe suffered some mortal blows within weeks of the revolutions: in Transylvania four Hungarians and three Romanians died after extremely violent clashes in Tîrgu Mureş/Maros Vásárhely; in Bulgaria there were pogrom-like rampages and riots protesting against the local Turkish community's attempts to organize itself politically; rabid anti-German groups were galvanized in Poland during a by-election in Silesia, where the (mainly Polish-speaking) German minority put up a candidate; radical separatist organizations were founded in two Czechoslovak regions, Moravia/Silesia and Slovakia, both of which won seats in parliament; in Kosovo dozens of ethnic Albanians were shot dead by Serbian security forces; in Croatia and Serbia nationalist organizations emerged, most of which include territorial expansion in their programme. Why is the return of militant nationalism apparently so irresistible in Eastern Europe?

With the exception of hostility towards the Vietnamese, Cubans and other national groups who came to Eastern Europe as students and *Gastarbeiter* from fraternal states in the developing world, none of these nationalist conflicts is new. Of course, they manifested themselves in much more flamboyant fashion before the war and during the nineteenth century than they did during the communist period, but, despite being relatively inconspicuous, their influence on politics in the post-war period was very extensive. This goes a long way to explaining why nationalism in Eastern Europe now represents such a threat to regional stability.

As we have seen, the Communist Parties after the war claimed that nationalism and other such social conflict could no longer exist because its root cause, class antagonism, had been eradicated. This claim was nonsense, as witnessed by the nationalist dispute between Yugoslavia and the Cominform in 1948, the year of revolution. Within twelve months of the victory of communism some of the CPs followed Stalin's lead by adding an especially virulent strain of anti-Semitism to their concoction of repressive bacilli. The influence of nationalism on the nature of Stalinism became ever stronger until in 1969 the Soviet Union and China became the first two states proclaiming the doctrine of socialist internationalism to engage in military combat over a border dispute. In Eastern Europe the patience of the Hungarian and Romanian establishments was severely strained on several occasions, but tension never developed as far as open warfare. Indeed, nationalism appeared in a variety of rather strange guises in Eastern Europe.

Gustav Husák's most consistent political commitment was to the establishment of Slovak political rights within Czechoslovakia. During the Stalinist show trials in the early 1950s he was tried as a 'bourgeois nationalist'. Husák was no friend of the bourgeoisie, but he was a nationalist. The Communist Party leadership was dominated by Czech nationalists who decided to try Husák because of his principled support of Slovak interests within the highly centralized state. Later Husák's line remained consistent. After he was installed to oversee Soviet political power in Czechoslovakia following the Prague Spring he behaved like a model Stalinist, but it was no surprise that the one part of the reformist programme of 1968 that he chose to retain after ousting the Prague Spring's leader, Alexander Dubček, was the federalization of Czechoslovakia. Husák's nationalism, like most East European nationalism, was superbly adaptable.

Ceauşescu's immense power was obviously conferred on him by his control of the Romanian Communist Party. But his ability and desire fully to exploit that power, and in particular his transformation of an ideology based on class into one that relied heavily on ethnic criteria, were surely a reflection of a specifically Romanian heritage. The programme of Romanization and the contaminated nationalism that he fed his intelligentsia during the 1960s and 1970s were curious, highly bureaucratized variations on the ideology of the Fascist Iron Guard or the Peasants' Party of the 1920s and therefore presumably found some support among certain sections of the Romanian population. It is no coincidence that on a visit to Cluj/Kolozsvár, I was told by a leading local member of the Vatra Românească, the extreme Romanian Nationalist Party, 'Of course, he [Ceauşescu] was a terrible man who did terrible things, but you have to acknowledge that he did promote and maintain Romanian culture in Transylvania when it could have come under serious threat.'

That Vatra activist is an exception who proves a fascinating rule about the expression and reception of nationalist politics during the communist period. Although both Ceauşescu and Husák acted in harmony with the historical aspirations of the national groups to which they belonged, they were hated by that same group of people. Any changes for which Husák and Ceauşescu were responsible were embraced by nationalist forces as being just, but the two leaders were not identified as their architects or executives.

Husák was regarded by Slovaks as a double traitor, first as a Soviet stooge and second as someone who, once installed as General Secretary and later president, spent too much time in Prague ignoring Bratislava. And yet under Husák the balance of economic and political power quite clearly increased in Slovakia's favour. Indeed, one of the frustrations that has bolstered Slovak nationalism since the revolution is that, with the election of an unstintingly energetic Czech president, the decisive issues of the state are once again exclusively a Prague affair, now apparently the exclusive domain of a group of ex-Czech dissidents. Although care has been taken to ensure a national balance in the Czechoslovak government, the advisers at the *Hrad* are almost all Czech.

In less than twenty years Ceauşescu achieved something for which Romanian nationalists have been clamouring for decades. The core of his 'romanization' policy was the transfer of the Romanian population of the Regat and Moldavia to Transylvania. His initial target was to top up the Romanian population in every major settlement so that it would eventually comprise 50 per cent. Having effected this extraordinary movement of population, he had laid the foundations for a permanent Romanian majority in Transylvania. But he had also changed the social composition of the Romanian population in the area, so that the relative sophistication of the Transylvanian Romanians was diluted by the arrival of their more primitive compatriots from the south and east.

Husák and Ceauşescu were able to achieve their aims by using the enormous power at their disposal. There have been many nationalist governments and rulers in Eastern Europe but few have controlled the state as totally as the communists did. If Ceauşescu had not been quite as dreadful to Romanians as to everybody else, he could have consolidated his dictatorship with a relatively wide popular base. None the less, his nationalist achievements will be written into the history books of Romanian chauvinists.

Despite the occasional achievement of long-term nationalist goals, nationalism was invoked by most East European leaders as an instrument of control that rarely entailed the active participation of the masses in a struggle against a well-identified national enemy or danger. Mass mobilization is the great spring of East European nationalism, and almost no Stalinist dictator ever risked unleashing such a force, as this would inevitably have threatened his own power. This explains why Ceauşescu and Husák were not thanked for their nationalist achievement – there was no mass political participation and so nobody, except Ceauşescu, Husák and a few lieutenants, could participate actively in the hysteria of the nationalist experience.

One communist leader, Slobodan Milošević, broke the mould and channelled the growing sense of frustration in Yugoslavia's largest republic, Serbia, into his struggle for the leadership of the Serbian League of Communists. This was a calculated shift of political position on Milošević's part, as he had come up through the liberal ranks of the Serbian party sponsored by those whom he eventually overthrew in 1987. Using most of the organs of power at his disposal, he risked awakening a slumbering giant and orchestrated a campaign of mass rallies at which the symbolism of both Serbian and Yugoslav communism was fused with the icons of Serbian nationalism and the Orthodox Church to form a weird ideological alloy. The Serbs' external enemies were the Albanian community in Kosovo and anybody who happened to support the Albanian cause or to encourage the dissolution of the Yugoslav federation. Paradoxically, Milošević's decision to tap the richest lode in Serbia's political mine was the first step on the road to the collapse of Yugoslavia. But personally it was a very shrewd move.

Milošević may be a communist in name, but his only real political commitment is to the wielding of power, and he anticipated the shift in Balkan politics from national communism to nationalism that has made the post-communist struggle for power in Serbia much more difficult. Vuk Drašković, Vojislav Šešelj and other anti-communist nationalist leaders have already proved that they have the necessary charisma to drum up considerable nationalist support. But the Milošević tide, although it has begun to ebb, still rises higher than anyone else's. In Croatia, although the reformed League of Communists–Party of the Democratic Change identified itself with the rebirth of Croatian patriotism, it did not choose the nationalist option, as Milošević had done in Serbia. The Croatian Democratic Alliance, the most obviously nationalist organization competing at the elections, won a stunning victory because there was no nationalist opposition. In Serbia the nationalist vote may well split, but Milošević is almost bound to survive as one of the leading political forces.

The path taken by Milošević offers the most convincing proof of the fact that nationalism can pay. The political dividends tend to be highest in the Balkans. After a few months of calm, Bulgarian hostility towards the Turkish minority revived and almost became violent when the Turkish leader, Ahmed Dogan, claimed his seat in parliament. The readiness of Romanian society to reach for the gun and shoot from the hip was well documented in the first year of the new order. But as the anniversaries of the revolution approach it is the maze of conflict in Yugoslavia that could reacquaint Europe's prosperous peace with the iniquities of war. The breakup of Yugoslavia began in earnest at the end of May 1990, when Milošević responded to the Slovene declaration of sovereignty by announcing that 'the question of Serbia's borders is now open'.

Serbia already claims total control over Kosovo, so the statement will have worried political leaders in Skopje, the capital of Macedonia (which in the inter-war years was known as Southern Serbia), and in Zagreb. Here the new Croatian leadership may also have furtive designs on Bosnia, the object and likely theatre of any war between Serb and Croat. If the Slovenes continue to play their cards right, they may escape the vortex of violence that appears to be sucking in Croats, Bosnians, Montenegrins, Serbs, Macedonians and Albanians. The potential for destabilization in Yugoslavia and the implications of a conflict should not be underestimated.

It was easy to predict the problems facing the Balkans, as the nationalist tensions in the area were already present before the revolutions and the political culture of the area is simply less highly developed than elsewhere. But nationalist politicians have emerged everywhere in Eastern Europe, including Czechoslovakia, generally agreed to be the most sophisticated country in the region. So is the nationalist agenda a permanent feature of the entire area? And how serious is the threat posed to the immediate community and the rest of Europe? There are two aspects to these questions – the political and the economic.

Stalin was satisfied with the post-war borders within his East European zone of influence. He intervened in the Czech/Polish dispute over Těšin immediately after the war, but following that neither he nor his successors had any reason to punish or reward the East European allies by ordering any revision of their borders. Now that a reunited Germany has pledged that the Oder–Neisse line will form its definitive eastern border, none of Eastern Europe's western or southern borders is disputed. To the east there are only three border issues.

The first is a curiosity. Czechoslovakia lost its easternmost region, known as Sub-Carpathian Ruthenia, at the end of the Second World War. It has no wish to seek the return of this backward and unproductive protuberance. However, within what is now part of western Ukraine there is a movement that wants to return to Czechoslovakia (presumably to reap the economic benefits while sparing itself the political pain of transition in a much more backward country). We may possibly face a situation in which an area demands to be attached to a country that refuses to accept it. This is the cutest border conundrum in Eastern Europe, and it bears no comparison with the second disputed eastern border, in Romania. Romanians have a strong case for the annexation of Soviet Moldavia, but such a move would exacerbate tension in the country still further with the addition of yet another large national minority. Finally, there are Poland's eastern lands, which were annexed by the Soviet Union in 1939 and now belong variously to the Ukraine, Byelorussia and Lithuania. There may be some justification for Poland's territorial claim over parts of the countries that are emerging from the husk of the Soviet Union. One would hope, however, that Warsaw will recognize that the benefits of a major campaign for the restitution of these areas to Polish control would be easily outweighed by the disadvantages.

Apart from the two latter issues, which remain open, the geographical perimeter of Eastern Europe is more or less fixed. The problem lies not around but within the region. Every border in Eastern Europe has been at the centre of a nationalist dispute at some time in the twentieth century, and borders remain the focus of attention. Whatever their public utterances, Hungarians who do not consider the Felvidék, southern Slovakia, to be part of Hungary belong to the rarest of species. Even the most enlightened and open-minded Slovaks perceive the Hungarian minority to include a fifth column. Similar suspicion pervades the area around most borders, with the exception of the Czech–Polish border, the only instance in which Stalin personally intervened.

The roots of the nationalist problem draw succour from the imprecise and often arbitrary definition of borders, combined with the identification of individual national groups (in Czechoslovakia's case it was two groups, Czechs and Slovaks), at the time of the creation of nation states in the region during the break-up of the Ottoman, Austro-Hungarian and Russian empires. Members of a minority can participate in the state structure only if they accept the rules, the most basic of which is to learn the language of the majority. But even that degree of assimilation may not be enough. President Havel, for example, has proposed the creation of a vice-presidency. Havel explained that the vice-president should not belong to the same national group as the president. Thus in Havel's case, as he is a Czech, the vice-president should be a Slovak. This expedient, however, would prevent a member of the Hungarian, Romany or Polish minorities from taking up either post. Indeed, the complicated national balance that exists between Czechs and Slovaks would be upset by the acceptance of any highly sensitive office by a member of a minority. Because of his or her mother tongue an individual is the object of discrimination and thus a potential *causus* if not *belli* then certainly of disquiet.

The majority population regards the minority as different. However accommodating they may be, Hungarians living in Transylvania will always say when asked, 'I am Hungarian.' They may then add, if particularly enlightened, 'with Romanian citizenship', but they may well neglect to mention it. If they do forget, Romanians immediately assume that they are questioning Romanian sovereignty in Transylvania. With the exception of the cosmopolitan intellectuals in the Group for Social Dialogue the entire Romanian political spectrum agrees that members of the minorities are Romanians first and members of a minority second. The correct answer, from their point of view, would be, 'I am a Romanian,' after which 'whose mother tongue happens to be Hungarian,' may be added. A prior commitment to a language or national group implies an attack on the state's right to exist in a particular geographical form.

Such tensions are generated by the presence of minorities whose historical claim on a region is invariably as old, and therefore as uncertain, as that of the majority national group. Local historians spend much of their working life attempting to prove that their particular national group settled in an area at an earlier date than the cohabiting national group. This leads to some scholarship of rare fantasy whose main aim is not the search for eternal truth but the stoking of contemporary political fires.

Antipathy between Serbs and Albanians in Kosovo is palpable. But the most effective fuel firing this conflict is not race or confession; it is economic decay. That different linguistic or national groups can live in harmony is evidenced by countries like Finland and, above all, Switzerland. Wealth is of critical importance in guaranteeing social peace in Switzerland, but it is clearly only one of many criteria defining the militancy of national consciousness. None the less, the nationalist movements throughout Eastern Europe all owe much of their appeal to the chronically sick economies of the area. Sometimes the economy plays a specific role in individual conflicts. Thus in the case of Kosovo Serbs leave the province because the economic prospects there are so weak. No Serb actually wants to live in Kosovo. But in a strange, metaphorical sense the Serbs preserve an image of Kosovo as their own land of milk and honey, which is being raped by the Albanians. Without Kosovo, the cradle of Serbian civilization, Serbia dries and shrivels. In fact, Kosovo is a substitute, designed to replace the reality of economic decay that is devastating Serbia itself. If the economy of the area began to bloom, Serbs would quickly forget about their brothers and sisters in Kosovo; and, indeed, as the infrastructure in the area itself improved, the birth rate of Albanians would fall and the rapid social change would slow down and stabilize. But as nobody is interested in injecting money into the area (certainly no other part of the Yugoslav federation, as communist bureaucrats have been squandering millions of dollars on useless, unproductive projects in Kosovo for a decade), the struggle for land that is at the heart of the Serbian/Albanian dispute will continue.

If the Romanian state were able to provide the Hungarian minority with a standard of living comparable with that enjoyed by Hungarians in Hungary proper, then of course the possibility of nationalist conflict in Tranyslvania would be dramatically reduced. The Hungarians complain about the treatment of their minorities in the Soviet Union, Romania and Czechoslovakia, but they never feel it necessary to raise their voices in defence of the Hungarians in Austria's Burgenland because the Burgenland Hungarians enjoy a living standard higher than that of Hungarians across the border. Indeed, if a movement emerged in Hungary demanding the restoration of parts of the Burgenland, the Burgenland Hungarians would doubtless oppose it vigorously. Austria may not be paradise on earth, but it is vastly more appealing than the poorly economic stripling that is Hungary.

It is precisely in this respect that Western economic policy towards Eastern Europe could have disastrous consequences. The adamantine refusal of the West to give way on the issue of debt relief, and its cautious and even punitive approach to the negotiation of trade agreements, will ensure that living standards in Eastern Europe remain low for many years to come. The uncertain economic atmosphere is the perfect breeding ground for nationalist and populist ideologies. The swift lurch of Poland towards right-wing populism is the clearest example of this so far. A right-wing authoritarian government in Poland, driven on by nationalism, is an unhappy prospect at a time when Lithuania, Byelorussia and the Ukraine, three Soviet republics with Polish minorities, are breaking away from Moscow and attempting to find their political feet with less experience than Poland and on very labile economic foundations. Similarly, a separate Slovak state would contribute to confusion in the region and greatly increase the possibility of a crisis between Hungary and Slovakia. It is perhaps too late to save Yugoslavia, but an injection of capital into the worst-affected republics at the very least could for once reverse the displacement process and deflect the population's interest from nationalist struggle and towards rewarding economic activity. It remains to be seen whether Western policy makers will have the intelligence to recognize the connection between political instability and poverty in the Balkans. So far the signs are not very optimistic. Once a war is sparked off in Yugoslavia, it will be too late; in all probability, time has already run out.

As long as borders exist and as long as the belief prevails that national groups have freehold rights over particular areas, there will always be a pretext for nationalist conflict in the region. Realistically, this probably means that nationalist tension in the area is something that Europe must live with. While the blind nationalism of many East Europeans inspires despair, it must also be remembered that there is no part of Europe that has such a dense and rich cultural heritage. If East European nationalism could be diverted from irrational political activity, it could be of enormous benefit to the region and Europe. At the moment such a project appears laughably utopian, but however insuperable the problems may appear, solutions must be sought. Because borders and an unshakeable commitment to freehold rights will prolong nationalist tension in Eastern Europe, the nation state outside all other constitutional bodies will be of limited value in guaranteeing human rights.

The most enduring political solution to the national question is the creation of a large regional confederation, or perhaps two such formations, in the areas, of north-central and south-eastern Europe. There has been no serious attempt to create such a zone in Eastern Europe, and the experience of Yugoslavia indicates that federations are no solution. But a substantial reason why Yugoslavia has failed in its two twentieth-century incarnations is because the problem of equality was subordinated first to the interests of Serbia and then, after the war, to the interests of Communist Party bureaucracies that were frequently prepared to abuse their privilege precisely to curry favour with one ethnic or national group. In the present circumstances the proposal for one or two confederations is little more than a pipe-dream, but it should none the less be a matter for urgent consideration at international fora.

No country should be forced into such a confederation, which could function properly only if backed by popular consent. Participating countries should raise all trade barriers within the confederation and guarantee citizens complete freedom of movement throughout the area. (Already Romanians are being blocked from travelling not only in much of Western Europe but in most of Eastern Europe as well.) All minorities in member states must be given absolute guarantees, recognized by the United Nations and the Helsinki process, concerning their rights. Countries should raise conscript armies, with an exclusively defensive function, that would cooperate with the security forces of other confederation members. Any disputes between states within the confederation should be solved without recourse to secret, bartering diplomacy. Instead they should be discussed in public and be judged by a confederative council. During such deliberations a moratorium on any action related to the dispute should be enforced.

This is but a small contribution to a debate that as yet, regrettably, does not exist. It is a debate that must, however, be kindled if Western and Eastern Europe are serious about the integration of their continent. It is also a critical model for the emerging states of the Soviet Union. If Eastern Europe could provide an example for the fractious people of the Soviet Union, perhaps some bloody conflicts there could be avoided. If it cannot, we may face the prospect of half the continent being disrupted by sporadic but intense nationalist feuding.

Back to the Future

'Our main aim,' stated the Civic Forum election manifesto, 'is to return to Europe.' If the phrase 'back to Europe' was not used first by Václav Havel in a speech, it will almost certainly be attributed to him in years to come. The concept is central to Havel's philosophy, and its importance is recognized by many other East Europeans, although they invest it with a slightly different meaning. In itself it is an optimistic, emotive slogan. 'Return' suggests arriving somewhere after a long period away from home, even from exile, perhaps coming in from the cold. Europe, for so long depressed by its potential as a theatre of war, now contains many different, more positive ideas. But a united Europe remains firmly in the minds of people. It is a long way from being realized.

A return to Europe also implies that Europe existed in the same form at the time of departure as it does today, on the eve of the return. But that, of course, is not true. Havel himself offered the definitive explanation at the Bratislava summit meeting between the leaders of Hungary, Czechoslovakia and Poland:

In practical or, if you like, political terms it means that we don't want to, and we can't, go back to the Europe of preceding decades, that is, to the Europe divided by two walls into two opposing power blocs. If we want, so to speak, to return to Europe, we have to return to a Europe quite different from the one we lived in until not long ago. In other words: to ponder our return means for us to ponder a whole Europe, to ponder the Europe of the future.

Or, in other words, back to the future.

In a profound sense many people in Eastern Europe are keen to join a community in which human rights are respected, academic scholarship is valued and not directed to political ends, the cross-fertilization of literature and art is by definition welcome and ordinary people can exchange personal experiences without incriminating themselves in the eyes of the security services. Such a European community has never properly existed, but theoretically its construction could now begin – although it is likely to remain a dream for a long time. In practical terms the East's return to Europe means that it must join up with Western Europe. The new democracies in Eastern Europe are not merely supplicants craving the generosity of the West. They genuinely believe that the creation of an integrated Europe will be of inestimable value to Western Europe. But they do recognize there is much catching up to do before they can consider themselves part of a new 'spiritual' Europe. To attain this semi-divine status, there is much temporal work to be done.

The new leaderships in Eastern Europe are aware of their own weakness. They do not have any levers by which to apply pressure to West European states. In small but psychologically significant ways they have already started building firm bridges to Western Europe. A number of West European countries have scrapped the visas needed by East European citizens. The ability to travel around Europe freely is a dream come true for most young East Europeans, and the intense mutual fascination of East and West will undoubtedly lead to a deeper understanding. Predictably, the United Kingdom shows less interest in abolishing visas. The idea of hordes of impoverished East Europeans looking for casual labour on the scepter'd isle is too much for the Foreign Office to cope with. All borders are equal, but some are more equal than others.

London's conservative policy highlights a problem that few know how to deal with. Since the revolutions Austria and West Germany have been swamped by East Europeans. Vienna is once again the Babel it was during the Habsburg empire. Most visitors arrive for a short visit, their first peek at the consumer paradise. Many simply want to emigrate, unwilling to sweat further for few rewards during the period of transition. Many are prepared to stay for a period of time to earn money for a family back in their home country. Some employers are happy to take them on, but states do not want them. West Germany has forced Poland to accept the return of thousands of Polish *Gastarbeiter*. Austria hurriedly introduced compulsory visas for any Romanians entering the country as a flood of refugees swept across the Hungarian border in early 1990. All of Western Europe assumed that, except in the case of Albania, the problem of human rights, and therefore political refugees, would simply evaporate. Serious abuse of human rights is still being practised in Romania and parts of Yugoslavia, and the blanket assumption that the problem no longer exists is likely to play into the hands of state organs responsible for this abuse. Clearly West European states find it much easier to exclude what are now referred to as 'economic refugees' from Eastern Europe, but over the next five years it will be necessary to co-ordinate some form of pan-European policy to cope with emigration within the continent.

Necessary though such co-ordination is, Eastern Europe cannot stand and wait for pan-European strategies to be developed. There are two ways for the new democracies to enter Europe – individually or within the framework of a collective. Immediately after the revolutions Poland, Czechoslovakia and Hungary in particular began discussions aimed at the creation of some form of united organization that would co-ordinate negotiations with the EC and other European bodies. The Poles, and to a lesser extent the Hungarians, responded brightly to the suggestion of President Carter's National Security Adviser, Zbigniew Brzezinksi, that the three countries should form an economic and political confederation. But Czechoslovakia is not interested in such close cooperation because of the disparity in the three countries' potential – the last thing Prague wants is two washed-out economies hanging on to its coat tails. This is a fine example of the point at which the mutual interests of 'Central Europe' come to a grinding halt.

None the less, Czechoslovakia has encouraged dialogue both between the three states and within a notionally expanded framework of the Alpine Adriatic community. Alpen Adria, as it is known, is an organization comprising sixteen provinces (Bavaria from West Germany, five from Austria, four from Italy, four from Hungary and two from Yugoslavia) that co-ordinates regional policy on the environment, sport and leisure, the media, health, traffic and other issues. There is no authoritarian centre to Alpen Adria, and although its scope is modest, it has been a successful venture. President Havel recognized the value of Alpen Adria when he invited the foreign ministers of Italy, Austria and Yugoslavia to Bratislava for the tripartite talks with Hungary and Poland. Czechoslovakia would now like to cooperate with Alpen Adria, a move that would also create a bridge between Alpen Adria and Poland.

Alpen Adria itself may not be a suitable forum for co-ordination in Eastern Europe, but some confederated structure based on membership of provinces and regions, as opposed to countries, could go a long way towards solving one of the two major obstacles to the co-ordination of a European policy. As states begin the search for expanded fora in which to negotiate the return to Europe, they are feeling the pressure of separatist demands. A substantial body of opinion in Slovakia believes that the republic should negotiate its own way into Europe without the help of Prague. One of the slogans of the Croatian Democratic Alliance during the election campaign was 'Croatia into a Europe of Regions'. The FSN and other parties with a largely ethnic Romanian base maintain that they want Romania to become part of Europe, but, as one Peasant Party leader in Cluj/ Kolozsvár explained, 'as an independent Romanian state where our laws and our culture apply'. Nationalist jealousy is working busily against a co-ordinated Europe, but it can be combated by a free union of states and regions. Perhaps more likely is the crystallization of two units, one comprising Poland, Czechoslovakia and Hungary, the other including Romania, Bulgaria, the Yugoslav republics and, at some point in the future, Albania.

The rewards for returning to Europe are substantial, and they have led to competition between the states that is undermining moves towards cooperation. This was evident at the very beginning, when the East European states with greater economic potential rather ignored developments in Romania, Bulgaria and

Yugoslavia, although this was also partly due to the reasonable obsession with events in the Soviet Union. In the middle of 1990 Hungary announced unilaterally that it would seek EC membership at the earliest possible date. Rather than being seen as an expression of Hungary's undying European commitment, this move has been regarded as Budapest's cunning attempt to get out of the East European ghetto. Once Hungary had voiced its intention, Czechoslovakia was quick to follow suit. They will now, it seems, be pursuing their goal independent of other countries, thus reinforcing Poland's insecurity. Of course, the EC does not yet know how its policy towards East European states and their membership should develop. In the first place, there is a queue of states waiting to join, headed by Turkey and Austria. The applications made by Austria, Turkey, Cyprus and some EFTA countries are in varying degrees very problematic. There is no question that any country from Eastern Europe will be allowed to jump the queue (with the exception of East Germany, which was automatically afforded membership on unification with West Germany), so it will be a long wait. None the less, it would be valuable to know whether the EC wants the new democracies to become members of the community. In the long run, if the West is committed to a united Europe, it will have to allow the East European countries into the Community. But for the foreseeable future the idea of the EC being joined by a motley crew of lame economies hoping to plunder the regional development fund is, of course, distinctly unappealing. Although these economies should stabilize within the next decade, there is no evidence to suggest that they will catch up with the rest of Europe. Czechoslovakia has a chance of achieving this, but it is slim. At the moment Eastern Europe seems much more likely to develop a 'second world' economic system that will fence it off quite clearly from Western Europe. Eastern Europe has embarked upon the final leg of its return to a future Europe. It could be one of the most hazardous of all.

Security – the One Word

During high-level negotiations between the Warsaw Pact allies in May 1990 the Soviet delegation, led by Foreign Minister Eduard

Shevardnadze spent hours disputing the joint communiqué that the Pact intended to release. Finally the Soviet delegation came up with its own version, which at first looked identical to the suggestion made by some of its allies until one of the foreign ministers spotted that one word had been inserted at a crucial juncture, which changed the emphasis of the document substantially. The word was 'security'.

The collapse of the security system that has regulated European development since the war has raised myriad questions. The Soviet Union no longer poses a serious military threat to the West. It is generally agreed that the likelihood of a military *coup* in the Soviet Union and the construction of a hostile anti-Western defence policy is slim. The Warsaw Pact itself is breaking up, and Soviet troops are being withdrawn from all over Eastern Europe. Within three to four years the last troops will leave the territory of what used to be the German Democratic Republic. With the exception of Hungary, the new leaders in Eastern Europe have not tried simply to pull out of the Warsaw Pact and run. Largely under the influence of Poland, Czechoslovakia and, until recently, the GDR, the East European states have attempted to use their presence within the Pact to exert a calming influence on the Soviet military while the Soviet Union begins the painful process of breaking up. To ignore the Soviet Union and leave the Warsaw Pact, they argue, would be to isolate the country's military leaders, who are already feeling badly neglected and undermined by the enforced departure of Soviet troops from Eastern Europe as well as the collapse of their domestic authority. Just as nobody outside Germany wishes to see a neutral Germany unattached to international organizations, so the East European leaders do not want to see a psychologically unbalanced Soviet leadership without some type of controlling, or at the very least consultative, body. Therefore the plan to be realized by the end of 1990 is to turn the Warsaw Pact into a political consultative body that will be convened to discuss security matters.

Eventually, when Europe's new system of security has been decided, the Warsaw Pact will, in Marx's elegant phrase, 'wither away'. Hungary, it is reported, has played an exclusively negative role in discussions about the Warsaw Pact's future. Budapest now wants to end its membership of the organization, and there is a vocal lobby in the government that would like to apply for membership of the other military bloc, NATO. The collapse of the Soviet Union takes up most of the working life of East European foreign ministers. Above all they are concerned to prevent a reactionary backlash and to contribute to the orderly constitution of a new confederation or state system where the Soviet Union once was. Just as Western Europe has had to adjust to a sudden influx of East Europeans, so too will Eastern Europe have to cope with a new movement of the labour force from the Soviet Union looking for work. There is also the danger of conflagration to the east of the new democracies. Poland, Romania and, to a lesser degree, Hungary will all be watching the fate of their own ethnic minorities in the Soviet Union with considerable care.

Although the Soviet Union will be able to send shivers down the spines of Eastern Europe for a long time, realistically it is no longer a threat to the region. Indeed, the government of Poland, where anti-Russian sentiment has traditionally been more fully developed than elsewhere in Eastern Europe, does not want the Red Army troops stationed on its territory to leave in any particular hurry. Once the treaty guaranteeing the Oder–Neisse line as its Western border is signed, it may feel slightly different. But just as the Soviet Union is no longer a threat to Eastern Europe, neither can it be considered a serious opponent of NATO. So who is NATO's enemy? Why does NATO need to exist?

During their years in opposition many of the dissidents who are now running Eastern Europe came close to activists inside END (European Nuclear Disarmament) and other peace organizations. A rich cross-fertilization of ideas took place, based on the premise that the division of Europe by Churchill, Roosevelt and Stalin at Yalta was a bad thing. The positions of the Western peace activists and the East European opposition were rarely identical – East Europeans often felt that the Western activists' criticism of NATO's strategy was exaggerated – but they respected one another. Both groups objected strongly to the existence of two military blocs as a reflection of an ideological divide. Indeed,

Czechoslovakia's current foreign policy initiatives on European security can be traced back to the Prague Appeal, a document formulated by Charter 77 activists that was submitted to the END Convention in 1985, in which the Czechoslovak opposition called for the abolition of both military blocs. Therefore, as it became clearer at the beginning of 1990 that the revolutions in Eastern Europe would lead to the eventual dissolution of the Warsaw Pact, East Europeans began to mutter about the possible end of NATO. Václav Havel explained the unacceptability of NATO most eloquently when he addressed the Council of Europe in May 1990:

Above all it [NATO] should – in the face of today's reality – transform its military doctrine. And it should also, in view of its changing role, soon change its name. This for at least two reasons: first because contemporary changes are the result of the victory of historical reason over historical absurdity and not the result of a victory of the West over the East. The present name is so closely linked to the era of the Cold War that it would be a sign of a lack of understanding of present-day developments if Europe were to unite under the NATO flag.

In January 1990 James Baker, the American Secretary of State, visited Prague on his way to the Soviet Union. When he met President Havel, instead of being welcomed as one of Czechoslovakia's spiritual liberators, he was questioned intensely by Havel and his security adviser, Jiří Křižán, about Washington's intentions concerning its force deployment in Europe. Baker curtly explained to Havel that such security issues were no concern of Czechoslovakia. Havel had the last laugh. A month later he addressed both Houses of Congress, where he spoke of the need, *inter alia*, for a Europe free of military blocs. Such a view is music to the ears of some American Congressmen who would like to see 'their boys' out of Europe as quickly as possible. It does not, however, coincide with the strategy of the Bush administration.

The plan, devised largely by Havel and his foreign minister, Jiří Dienstbier, is warmly supported by many in Eastern Europe. It envisages the creation of a new set of institutions in Europe that will regulate the security of the entire continent. This plan sees the

Helsinki process, the Conference on Security and Cooperation in Europe (CSCE), as providing a starting point for the development of these new fora (again, this idea could be found in the Prague Appeal of 1985). Dienstbier has suggested the creation of a European Security Commission, which would develop into a treaty organization prefacing the confederation of the continent. Basing the plan on CSCE means that it would include the United States and Canada (both belong to the CSCE group of states). However, North America would not enjoy any special controlling interest, as it does in NATO, but would be on equal terms with all other states in the system.

The United States has invested enormous sums of money in the post-war reconstruction and defence of Europe. It does not wish to be pushed out by idealistic little Central European nations. They are of secondary concern to Washington, whose mind is focused sharply on a single country – Germany. Now that the Soviet Union is no longer an important player in the security game and Germany is united, the threat to American interests shifts clearly to the West. This is why it was essential for NATO that a united Germany be a member of the organization: it had to be under the control of the West. The East Europeans assented to that happily because of the historical threat that a powerful Germany has posed. No other state wanted a neutral Germany that had exclusive responsibility for its own security policy. For the future it may be valuable to remember that, although before unification both German governments agreed to NATO membership without demurring, in the opinion polls taken in the first half of 1990 between 55 and 70 per cent of the population in both Germanies supported a neutral status for the new country. Tension between the United States and the United Kingdom on the one hand and Germany on the other will be the springboard for most discussions on security within the new Europe.

Eastern Europe's security interests do not coincide with either of these positions, however. The long-term existence of NATO as a political–military alliance in Europe is unacceptable to most East Europeans (although Hungary remains an exception), who have three security concerns. The first is a united Germany that may at some point turn malevolent (although all governments in Eastern Europe welcome a united Germany as a positive contribution to the search for lasting European peace). The second is the revival of a powerful Russian state (although this is believed to be a remote prospect). Finally, they fear instability within their own region, and they would like to see some form of collective security system that could isolate and neutralize any local conflicts. This last issue is one that NATO is simply not addressing, but it is important to the East Europeans, who would like to see the continent develop a European security system in which *all* states have a stake and in which *all* states play a role. A dispute between Romania and Hungary over Transylvania could then be referred to the collective security system. If Hungary has its way and is permitted to join NATO, a military conflict with Romania over Transylvania would take on a very different character. But however energetic the new East European leaderships, and in particular the Czechoslovak one, may be in defending their interests in the debate about the construction of a new security system, one issue to which the East Europeans are particularly sensitive, the role of Germany in the new Europe, towers over all others.

The German Ideology

There may be a curious and awkward period of adjustment, but for the citizens of what used to be the German Democratic Republic, there will be no long-term struggle for economic and political stability. A minority of East Germans regret this. Ironically, a surprisingly high percentage of that minority led the revolution of October 1989. They had hoped that after the revolution the GDR, as a sovereign country, would alone decide how its future should be shaped. Many of those who organized New Forum, the East German equivalent of Civic Forum, indicate that they feel regret and are even envious of their counterparts in other East European countries who are now in leading positions and enjoy far greater political and moral authority than leaders of countries as small as theirs could usually expect. To the surprise of most observers, East Germany was the key country in the revolutions of 1989. Its people understood the implications of change in Poland and Hungary and forced these to their logical conclusion in their own country. Once Honecker's authority had collapsed in the SED, the days of the one-party state were numbered. Once Stalinism was finished in East Germany, it was a matter of weeks before the revolution began in Czechoslovakia, and even the cowed and beaten Romanians then took their cue from the two countries that had been Ceauşescu's most important allies before the revolutions.

The leaders of East Germany's political revolution were very disappointed that it was quickly transformed into a national revolution. This happened partly because New Forum was slow-witted tactically and partly because the irresistible machinery of West German party politics bulldozed its way through the debris of the wall and 'death row' as soon as the SED began pulling them down. Instead of joining the new democracies that are emerging from hibernation, the people of East Germany have willingly accepted the imposition of an older, more experienced democracy. They have a part to play in the rebirth of history, but their role is secondary. It exists only within the larger context of the creation of the German Colossus in Central Europe. Their contribution cannot be identified as a uniquely East German one.

The new Germany will have an enormous, even a decisive, influence on the structure and prospects of the new Eastern Europe. This initiative will emanate, not surprisingly, from what used to be West Germany. It will be some time before economic and industrial power evens itself out in the new Germany. Indeed, even within the unified country the former territory of East Germany may well be permanently disadvantaged. West German industrialists and politicians have considerable advantages over their European partners when it comes to working in and with Eastern Europe, thanks to the dual policy towards the area developed at the beginning of the 1970s, the *Ostpolitik* of the former Chancellor, Willy Brandt. The process of *rapprochement* with the East was aimed chiefly at the Soviet Union and the GDR, but it also benefited Poland, Czechoslovakia and other East European countries. West Germany was in principle committed to the restitution of democratic rights in Eastern Europe, and it was constitutionally committed to the unification of Germany, but Bonn did not allow this to damage economic relations between West Germany and Eastern Europe. Instead it signed with the Soviet Union, Poland and East Germany a number of pioneering agreements that eventually paved the way for the opening of the Helsinki process in 1975.

While West Germany was affected by the resurgence of the Cold War (especially with regard to its relationship with the GDR) at the end of the 1970s and the beginning of the 1980s, its politicians again attempted to shield West German industry and finance from the negative consequences. As the 1980s progressed West Germany began to explore substantial projects suitable for cooperation with the Soviet Union in particular but also with other East European countries. The investment of West German firms and banks in Eastern Europe was small as a percentage of its total foreign investment, but with the exception of Austria, which developed an extensive economic network in Central Europe and Yugoslavia, it was by far the most influential economic power in the region.

West Germany's commitment to the human rights issue was half-hearted. In 1988 West German diplomats in Prague were still minimizing the importance of Charter 77. They considered Charter to be a mere extra on the Czechoslovak political scene, which had no realistic chances of contributing to the machinery of politics in the country. Dissent was a side issue for West Germany unless it involved ethnic Germans, as it did in Poland, Romania and the Soviet Union. Here, rather than make a big human rights issue out of the treatment of German minorities, the West German government simply offered to buy or to take ethnic Germans who wanted to leave Eastern Europe. Tens (if not hundreds) of thousands of East European Germans took up the offer. Some Eastern European leaders, like Nicolae Ceauşescu, were only too pleased to be rid of members of a troublesome ethnic minority.

The American and British governments linked economic co-operation quite closely with the question of human rights (provided this was in their security interests). Geographically it was more awkward for Western countries (except, of course, for West Germany and Austria) to launch a major investment programme in Eastern Europe. So when the revolutions occurred, although the British, American, Italian, French and Dutch embassies had been in close contact with Solidarity, Charter 77 and the Hungarian Democratic Opposition, they were not well equipped to boost their economic presence in the country. West Germany was. The Czechoslovak, Polish and Hungarian opposition, many of whose members are now in government, doubtless remember the extremely supportive, and on many occasions brave, roles played by British and American diplomats before the revolutions. But what they need in large doses now is economic cooperation, not nostalgia. West Germany's recognition of the new politics has been swift in coming. Indeed, its Prague embassy, which once cold-shouldered the opposition, now has a regular *jour fixe* organized by an energetic young diplomat. The entire spectrum of the new Czechoslovak élite has moved in and out of these drinks parties, and almost all influential Czechs and Slovaks in Prague are now known to the West German embassy staff personally. The same cannot be said of either the British or the American embassies despite the flamboyant presence of Shirley Temple-Black as ambassador at the latter.

The governments of Mazowiecki, Čalfa and Antall all welcome foreign capital, which plays by the rules regardless of its national origin. Publicly they say they want to encourage as much industry from developed countries as possible to counterbalance what they recognize as an inevitably strong German presence. But privately they admit that German capital will play the decisive economic role throughout the region during and after the transition to a market economy. American business has a higher stake in Hungary, partly because the reform communist government that came to power in 1988 made a point of wooing American industry. This process was encouraged by Mark Palmer, the American ambassador to Budapest, who was probably the most energetic diplomat in the entire region. (Some critics even thought that this role went beyond what was proper for a diplomat.) Palmer and others encouraged American investment in Hungary as a bridgehead from which an economic assault on the Soviet Union could be launched. As the Soviet Union begins to open up to foreign capital, the United States will have some advantages over West Germany.

But unless there is a concerted effort by other Western states, Poland, Czechoslovakia and, to an extent, Hungary will become economic fiefdoms of the new world giant, a united Germany. Czechoslovak economists maintain that this will not affect their economy in an adverse way. They believe that their economy is potentially strong enough to absorb German influence but develop independently. In Poland there are more misgivings. In politics Poland attempts to behave towards Germany with friendly, dignified respect, but in economic terms West Germany has tended to discuss matters with Poland in a rather authoritarian fashion. The sight of Jacek Kuroń, one of the fieriest dissidents in Eastern Europe, having to bow and scrape over the issue of the illegal Polish workforce in West Germany was one of the most sobering since the revolutions. Among radical nationalist groups and some of the social democratic formations there are fears that Germany aims to treat Poland as a form of economic *Lebensraum*. They point in particular to the possibility that Germany may pay Polish companies to store toxic chemical or nuclear waste. Certainly, in the past West Germany favoured selling its toxic waste to East European countries if they would take it, and as the need for hard currency increases there is some reason to believe that the Germans will want to continue with the trade.

But on the whole the prospect of German economic domination in Eastern Europe does not concern the new democracies. They are prepared to open their doors to anyone who wants to invest. If other Western countries are anxious about the level of German investment in Eastern Europe, they always have the option of increasing their activity in the area. If the desire is there, other Western countries should concentrate on establishing bases while Germany is still coping with the integration of what used to be the DDR. Although in the long term reunification will be an enormous boost for the West German economy, in the short term it will create tremendous problems that, if not handled carefully, could lead to domestic unrest, particularly on the former territory of the GDR. As far as East Europeans are concerned, German economic control in the region will become controversial only if it is accompanied by political instability.

The two countries most closely affected by the emergence of a united Germany are Poland and Czechoslovakia. Popular suspicion of Germany is widespread in Poland. Although the Soviet Union assumed the role of external enemy after the war, reconciliation between Poles and Germans proved much more difficult than it did between Germans and Czechs, for example. This can be explained partly by the destruction wrought by Germans in Poland during the Second World War, which was much more extensive than in Bohemia and Moravia. The relative affluence of East Germany during the communist period led to considerable friction between the two countries. Poles regularly went on shopping sprees in East Germany to buy goods unavailable in their own country. Given the client role of the Polish economy, Poles were frequently involved in the black market in East Germany, and many worked there in temporary jobs. East Germans developed a strikingly contemptuous attitude towards Poles, who later became obvious targets for the racist skinhead and neo-Nazi organizations that proliferated in East Germany as authority in the country began to collapse prior to the revolution.

Simmering resentment between Germans and Poles found ample room for expression early in 1990 after the death of a senator resulted in a by-election in Silesia, the home of the German ethnic minority. The size of this minority is unknown. At certain times during the post-war period the Polish authorities refused to acknowledge the existence of a German minority while revanchist organizations in Germany claimed it was over 2 million. When the election was called Henryk Krol (or Heinrich Kroll, as he is now known) stood as a candidate for the German Circle of Friends in Silesia. There were attempts to prevent Krol from standing on a German ticket, but they failed; indeed, he won the first round, although as he had not won over half of the votes cast, he had to face a run-off. It was then that racist slurs, used by extremist groups as an electoral tactic, became central to the campaign. In the end a Polish nationalist vote was successfully mobilized and

Krol lost. Poles consider the existence of a German minority in Silesia to be a concrete threat to Polish statehood. Even with Germany's recognition of the Oder–Neisse line as the definitive border between the two countries, many Poles still believe that in times of political or economic stress Germany may set its territorial sights on Silesia and eastern Prussia.

Not surprisingly, the Polish government is much more aware of the importance of maintaining good relations with Germany than ordinary people are. The foreign minister, Krzysztof Skubiszewski, was persistent in his demands for Polish participation in the 'Two plus Four' talks on German unification where these affected Warsaw's interests. All members of the Polish government and parliament monitored Chancellor Kohl's willingness to agree to the Oder–Neisse line very closely, and although the Mazowiecki government is now quite satisfied with the arrangement, the fear persists that an aggressive Germany could tear up any agreement about borders if it so decided.

Officially everybody has welcomed the unification of Germany as a positive contribution to the search for a new, stable Europe. But Czechoslovakia and Poland stress above all else that a unified Germany is valuable only within the context of a unified Europe. Without the target of what would ultimately be a pan-European federation, Germany appears to be a different and much more dangerous creature. For this reason Czechoslovaks and Poles find it difficult to understand the British government's reticence about joining in the process of European *political* integration. The argument that by participating in this process states will help to fulfil Germany's hidden desire to become the only controlling voice in Europe is regarded by Prague and Warsaw as preposterous. The only way to guarantee a safe Germany, they maintain, is to create institutions to which all European states belong, so that any revanchist tremors can be silenced as they begin.

Eastern Europe in the Age of Democracy

Witnessing the Czechoslovak revolution was without question the most moving and satisfying experience of my life. As I was the

BBC's chief radio correspondent in Prague during the revolution, it was essential that I should keep my emotions to myself. There were moments, however, when I could allow myself to be shamelessly swayed by everything happening around me. On the afternoon of Friday, 24 November 1989, Alexander Dubček, whose sad smile had remained imprinted on the minds of most Czechoslovaks for over twenty years as a reminder of what could have been, stepped out on to a balcony in the middle of Wensceslas Square. Over half a million Czechs screamed his name in unison as he began his first public address in the Czechoslovak capital for twenty-one years. I stood about ten yards behind Dubček, watching his back as he spoke. Together with the Voice of America correspondent, Jolyon Naegele, I had met and spoken with Dubček for the first time a year before at his home in Bratislava. Although our conversation was strictly off the record, he told us that we were the first journalists (*ne jenom vase ale i nase* – not only from the West but from the East as well) to whom he had agreed to speak for many years. For both Jolyon and me it was a staggering moment. Now a year later, as Dubček started to charm Wensceslas Square with his mellifluous Slovak, Jolyon and I stood just behind him, incredulous that the revolution, which we had both known would happen at some point, was with us so soon. A young girl who, I judged, must have been born after Dubček's fall from grace in 1969 smiled before tears began to slide slowly down the sides of her face. That was when professional considerations were set aside, as far as I was concerned, and for a good five minutes I cried. It was the only way to comprehend what I was witnessing – the rebirth of a history that the forces of reaction thought they had killed off for ever. The incident was so charged with irony that no fictional account will ever do justice to the poetry of the moment.

But we cannot allow the electrifying moment of revolution to obscure the enormous task that lies in store for Poland, Czechoslovakia, Hungary, Romania, Bulgaria, Yugoslavia and Albania – not to mention the Soviet Union. There are only two things that unite these countries, apart from an unwanted common history – poverty and economic distress. From Warsaw you can travel to Tirana across central Slovakia, eastern Hungary, Transylvania, the

Regat, south Morava in Serbia and Kosovo. By Western standards it is a stretch that is virtually uninterrupted by the twentieth century. In some areas the situation has been made worse by forty years of communism. The further south you travel, however, the greater the support for communism becomes, especially in rural regions, where the party liberated people from even more depressing feudal drudgery.

None the less the perceptions and aspirations of even the poorest people in Eastern Europe have changed substantially in the past few years. The widespread desire for political change has been motivated in part by a desire for material change – popular discontent in Albania began to increase after the Romanian revolution, but it was fuelled by several years of Western television. The Albanians know that they are the poorest and most deprived nation in Europe. Their need to explore and to improve themselves is about to spring the rusted manacles of Hoxhaism. But, like every other East European country that has successfully forged democracy from the single-party state, Albania will be faced with economic problems that will seem insurmountable. For occasional visitors the problem is smothered by charm, beauty and the desire of those few who are monied to strut and display their wealth. A weekend in Prague is a breathtakingly romantic experience, while to stroll down the rather regal boulevards of Budapest for the first time is quite thrilling. On a summer day in Belgrade the cafés are full of apparently affluent Serbs who are unconcerned about the latest batch of depressing economic statistics, and the Adriatic coast of southern Albania could almost be paradise. But behind these easy romantic images lies widespread deprivation, which in most cases is now properly visible for the first time but is likely to be accentuated within the next few years.

It is essential that the millions of people in Eastern Europe whose life is a daily economic struggle should be provided with some form of compensation for the hardship they are certain to face over the next decade. For the stability of Europe and, indeed, as a moral gesture, the West should remember that Eastern Europe does not consist merely of Czechoslovakia, Poland and Hungary. There is a marked tendency in the British media, for example, to ignore the Balkans. The exception to this was Romania, a country that until the violent revolution had been largely discounted. Interest in Romania remained keen after the revolution because it had caught the imagination of the media and because there was considerable salacious material to be excavated from the legacy of Ceauşescu's hell hole. In the first half of 1990, however, dozens of Albanians were being killed by security forces in Kosovo. Had anything on this scale occurred in Poland or Czechoslovakia, the Western media would have pounced on it as one of the stories of the year. But because these were poor Albanians (many of them Moslems to boot) and Kosovo is a conflict that always rumbles on and that few people can be bothered to understand, their deaths provoked no great uproar. Indeed, they most probably passed by the consciousness of even the informed newspaper reader. Similarly, the variety and depth of the Albanian intelligentsia or the existence of a man known as Kosovo's Mandela are scarcely likely to pierce the skin of Western perception.

Capitalism will probably survive and later thrive in Czechoslovakia, and perhaps in Hungary and Poland too, but in Romania, Bulgaria, parts of Yugoslavia and Albania, although it will satisfy the needs of some powerful social groups, its effect will be politically divisive. The Balkans may for the moment be of secondary interest to the West, but the region has a nasty habit of shaking the rest of Europe from its slumber by hosting local wars. While the prospect of war in north-eastern Europe seems remote, the stability of the three favoured Eastern nations can easily be undermined. Poland has yet to settle in its new political home, and even when elections are finally held they are likely to be fairly chaotic. If the new Czechoslovak Federative Republic is unable to demonstrate some positive economic gains within the first two years of its existence, the power of Slovak separatism may prove irresistible.

The rebirth of history in Eastern Europe will enable the people to participate actively in determining their own fate, in most cases for the first time in half a century. In the 1920s and 1930s democracy proved unable to harmonize the interests of the complex web of social groups in the area except in Czechoslovakia. These interests, which have been suppressed or distorted for over forty years by the Communist Parties in power, are now emerging with as much force as ever before. The belief that Eastern Europe has overthrown Stalinism with the express purpose of adopting whole-sale a system of Western values is simply wrong. If the democracies prove strong enough, the emerging social systems in Eastern Europe are likely to retain the armour of social security and protec-tionism to shield them from the more brutal aspects of consumer capitalism. In the interests of stability the West continues to differ-entiate between those countries that appear keenest to introduce capitalism (Nicholas Ridley's Gang of Four) and those whose governments consider, for local reasons, the swift introduction of market mechanisms to be inadvisable. Sanctions against the Ro-manian government's abuse of human rights can be justified. To refuse the Hungarian government a bridging loan because it feels unable to risk abolishing rent subsidies or to declare political war on the Bulgarian Socialist Party simply because its policies do not appeal amounts to a serious subversion of the democratic process. Just because both sanctions have been applied in the name of the free market they should not be condoned, although they almost certainly will be.

Marcin Król, the editor of one of Poland's most respected pub-lications, told me that the West has displayed a complete 'lack of imagination' in the development of a policy towards Eastern Europe. Indeed, he was worried by the absence of an overall strategy towards Eastern Europe that is anything other than puni-tive. The great majority of initiatives that aim to co-ordinate the stable transition of Eastern Europe has emerged from within the area itself. However noble these ideas may be, they are foundering on the spirit of competition: in order to succeed economically, Czechoslovakia knows it cannot be too generous to Poland, there-fore a confederation is out of the question. The West's only co-ordinated response to Eastern Europe has been to organize an aid programme, which is made cautious by the variety of strings attached to it. While the 'Two plus Four' talks have been success-fully concluded, providing a smooth unification for the two Ger-manies, nobody has even mooted the idea of creating fora in which to discuss the most effective ways to solve the many political dilemmas facing the countries of Eastern Europe. The idea of a Danubian federation of peoples, one of the few possible escape routes from nationalist violence in the Balkans, is an idea that remains locked inside the minds of students of Otto Bauer, the great Austrian social democrat who went a long way towards solving the national question almost before it was asked. Instead the West deals with each country according to a flexible, sliding scale of merit, which is guaranteed to provoke existing regional tension. This approach invites disaster and, specifically, the restoration of populist authoritarian regimes whose grasp of economic realities is usually as weak as their grasp of social and political realities.

The peoples of Eastern Europe have fought for their existence and for their democracies. Now, with the odds – as always – stacked against them, they must fight for their dignity and stability. History is by no means dead. In Eastern Europe it has emerged dramatically from its artificial hibernation after forty years, and it has much to catch up on.

Index

Political parties are entered under both full names and abbreviations/acronyms. Where page references are few, they are given against both entries, and in other cases against the preferred term as generally used in the text, with cross-references where appropriate.

Index

Index

Index

Index

FOR THE BEST IN PAPERBACKS, LOOK FOR THE

In every corner of the world, on every subject under the sun, Penguin represents quality and variety – the very best in publishing today.

For complete information about books available from Penguin – including Puffins, Penguin Classics and Arkana – and how to order them, write to us at the appropriate address below. Please note that for copyright reasons the selection of books varies from country to country.

In the United Kingdom: Please write to *Dept E.P., Penguin Books Ltd, Harmondsworth, Middlesex, UB7 0DA.*

If you have any difficulty in obtaining a title, please send your order with the correct money, plus ten per cent for postage and packaging, to *PO Box No 11, West Drayton, Middlesex*

In the United States: Please write to *Dept BA, Penguin, 299 Murray Hill Parkway, East Rutherford, New Jersey 07073*

In Canada: Please write to *Penguin Books Canada Ltd, 2801 John Street, Markham, Ontario L3R 1B4*

In Australia: Please write to the *Marketing Department, Penguin Books Australia Ltd, P.O. Box 257, Ringwood, Victoria 3134*

In New Zealand: Please write to the *Marketing Department, Penguin Books (NZ) Ltd, Private Bag, Takapuna, Auckland 9*

In India: Please write to *Penguin Overseas Ltd, 706 Eros Apartments, 56 Nehru Place, New Delhi, 110019*

In the Netherlands: Please write to *Penguin Books Netherlands B.V., Postbus 195, NL–1380AD Weesp*

In West Germany: Please write to *Penguin Books Ltd, Friedrichstrasse 10–12, D–6000 Frankfurt/Main 1*

In Spain: Please write to *Longman Penguin España, Calle San Nicolas 15, E–28013 Madrid*

In Italy: Please write to *Penguin Italia s.r.l., Via Como 4, I-20096 Pioltello (Milano)*

In France: Please write to *Penguin Books Ltd, 39 Rue de Montmorency, F-75003 Paris*

In Japan: Please write to *Longman Penguin Japan Co Ltd, Yamaguchi Building, 2–12–9 Kanda Jimbocho, Chiyoda-Ku, Tokyo 101*

PENGUIN HISTORY

The Victorian Underworld   Kellow Chesney

A superbly evocative survey of the vast substratum of vice that lay below the respectable surface of Victorian England – the showmen, religious fakes, pickpockets and prostitutes – and of the penal methods of that 'most enlightened age'. 'Charged with nightmare detail' – *Sunday Times*

A History of Modern France   Alfred Cobban

Professor Cobban's renowned three-volume history, skilfully steering the reader through France's political and social problems from 1715 to the Third Republic, remains essential reading for anyone wishing to understand the development of a great European nation.

Stalin   Isaac Deutscher

'The Greatest Genius in History' and the 'Life-Giving Force of Socialism'? Or a tyrant more ruthless than Ivan the Terrible whose policies facilitated the rise of Nazism? An outstanding biographical study of a revolutionary despot by a great historian.

Montaillou   Cathars and Catholics in a French Village 1294–1324
Emmanuel Le Roy Ladurie

'A classic adventure in eavesdropping across time' – Michael Ratcliffe in *The Times*

The Second World War   A. J. P. Taylor

A brilliant and detailed illustrated history, enlivened by all Professor Taylor's customary iconaclasm and wit.

Industry and Empire   E. J. Hobsbawm

Volume 3 of the *Penguin Economic History of Britain* covers the period of the Industrial Revolution: 'the most fundamental transformation in the history of the world recorded in written documents.' 'A book that attracts and deserves attention ... by far the most gifted historian now writing' – John Vaizey in the *Listener*

PENGUIN HISTORY

The Penguin History of the United States   Hugh Brogan

'An extraordinarily engaging book' – *The Times Literary Supplement*. 'Compelling reading … Hugh Brogan's book will delight the general reader as much as the student' – *The Times Educational Supplement*. 'He will be welcomed by American readers no less than those in his own country' – J. K. Galbraith

The Making of the English Working Class   E. P. Thompson

Probably the most imaginative – and the most famous – post-war work of English social history.

The Waning of the Middle Ages   Johan Huizinga

A magnificent study of life, thought and art in 14th- and 15th-century France and the Netherlands, long established as a classic.

The City in History   Lewis Mumford

Often prophetic in tone and containing a wealth of photographs, *The City in History* is among the most deeply learned and warmly human studies of man as a social creature.

The Habsburg Monarchy 1809–1918   A. J. P. Taylor

Dissolved in 1918, the Habsburg Empire 'had a unique character, out of time and out of place'. Scholarly and vividly accessible, this 'very good book indeed' (*Spectator*) elucidates the problems always inherent in the attempt to give peace, stability and a common loyalty to a heterogeneous population.

Inside Nazi Germany   Conformity, Opposition and Racism in Everyday Life
Detlev J. K. Peukert

An authoritative study – and a challenging and original analysis – of the realities of daily existence under the Third Reich. 'A fascinating study … captures the whole range of popular attitudes and the complexity of their relationship with the Nazi state' – Richard Geary

PENGUIN HISTORY

The Germans   Gordon A. Craig

An intimate study of a complex and fascinating nation by 'one of the ablest and most distinguished American historians of modern Germany' – Hugh Trevor-Roper

Imperial Spain 1469–1716   J. H. Elliot

A brilliant modern study of the sudden rise of a barren and isolated country to the greatest power on earth, and of its equally sudden decline. 'Outstandingly good' – *Daily Telegraph*

British Society 1914–1945   John Stevenson

A major contribution to the *Penguin Social History of Britain*, which 'will undoubtedly be the standard work for students of modern Britain for many years to come' – *The Times Educational Supplement*

A History of Christianity   Paul Johnson

'Masterly ... It is a huge and crowded canvas – a tremendous theme running through twenty centuries of history – a cosmic soap opera involving kings and beggars, philosophers and crackpots, scholars and illiterate *exaltés*, popes and pilgrims and wild anchorites in the wilderness' – Malcolm Muggeridge

The Penguin History of Greece   A. R. Burn

Readable, erudite, enthusiastic and balanced, this one-volume history of Hellas sweeps the reader along from the days of Mycenae and the splendours of Athens to the conquests of Alexander and the final dark decades.

A History of Latin America   George Pendle

'Ought to be compulsory reading in every sixth form ... this book is right on target' – *Sunday Times*. 'A beginner's guide to the continent ... lively, and full of anecdote' – *Financial Times*

A CHOICE OF PENGUINS

The Secret Lives of Trebitsch Lincoln Bernard Wasserstein

Trebitsch Lincoln was Member of Parliament, international spy, right-wing revolutionary, Buddhist monk – and this century's most extraordinary conman. 'Surely the final work on a truly extraordinary career' – Hugh Trevor-Roper. 'An utterly improbable story ... a biographical coup' – *Guardian*

Out of Africa Karen Blixen (Isak Dinesen)

After the failure of her coffee-farm in Kenya, where she lived from 1913 to 1931, Karen Blixen went home to Denmark and wrote this unforgettable account of her experiences. 'No reader can put the book down without some share in the author's poignant farewell to her farm' – *Observer*

In My Wildest Dreams Leslie Thomas

The autobiography of Leslie Thomas, author of *The Magic Army* and *The Dearest and the Best*. From Barnardo boy to original virgin soldier, from apprentice journalist to famous novelist, it is an amazing story. 'Hugely enjoyable' – *Daily Express*

The Winning Streak Walter Goldsmith and David Clutterbuck

Marks and Spencer, Saatchi and Saatchi, United Biscuits, GEC ... The UK's top companies reveal their formulas for success, in an important and stimulating book that no British manager can afford to ignore.

Bird of Life, Bird of Death Jonathan Evan Maslow

In the summer of 1983 Jonathan Maslow set out to find the quetzal. In doing so, he placed himself between the natural and unnatural histories of Central America, between the vulnerable magnificence of nature and the terrible destructiveness of man. 'A wonderful book' – *The New York Times Book Review*

Mob Star Gene Mustain and Jerry Capeci

Handsome, charming, deadly, John Gotti is the real-life Mafia boss at the head of New York's most feared criminal family. *Mob Star* tells the chilling and compelling story of the rise to power of the most powerful criminal in America.

A CHOICE OF PENGUINS

The Assassination of Federico García Lorca   Ian Gibson

Lorca's 'crime' was his antipathy to pomposity, conformity and intolerance. His punishment was murder. Ian Gibson – author of the acclaimed new biography of Lorca – reveals the truth about his death and the atmosphere in Spain that allowed it to happen.

Between the Woods and the Water   Patrick Leigh Fermor

Patrick Leigh Fermor continues his celebrated account – begun in *A Time of Gifts* – of his journey on foot from the Hook of Holland to Constantinople. 'Even better than everyone says it is' – Peter Levi. 'Indescribably rich and beautiful' – *Guardian*

The Hunting of the Whale   Jeremy Cherfas

'*The Hunting of the Whale* is a story of declining profits and mounting pigheadedness ... it involves a catalogue of crass carelessness ... Jeremy Cherfas brings a fresh eye to [his] material ... for anyone wanting a whale in a nutshell this must be the book to choose' – *The Times Literary Supplement*

Metamagical Themas   Douglas R. Hofstadter

This astonishing sequel to the bestselling, Pulitzer Prize-winning *Gödel*, *Escher*, *Bach* swarms with 'extraordinary ideas, brilliant fables, deep philosophical questions and Carrollian word play' – Martin Gardner

Into the Heart of Borneo   Redmond O'Hanlon

'Perceptive, hilarious and at the same time a serious natural-history journey into one of the last remaining unspoilt paradises' – *New Statesman*. 'Consistently exciting, often funny and erudite without ever being overwhelming' – *Punch*

When the Wind Blows   Raymond Briggs

'A visual parable against nuclear war: all the more chilling for being in the form of a strip cartoon' – *Sunday Times*. 'The most eloquent anti-Bomb statement you are likely to read' – *Daily Mail*

A CHOICE OF PENGUINS

Better Together Christian Partnership in a Hurt City
David Sheppard and Derek Warlock

The Anglican and Roman Catholic Bishops of Liverpool tell the uplifting
and heartening story of their alliance in the fight for their city – an alliance
that has again and again reached out to heal a community torn by sectarian
loyalties and bitter deprivation.

Fantastic Invasion Patrick Marnham

Explored and exploited, Africa has carried a different meaning for each
wave of foreign invaders – from ivory traders to aid workers. Now, in the
crisis that has followed Independence, which way should Africa turn?
'A courageous and brilliant effort' – Paul Theroux

Jean Rhys: Letters 1931–66
Edited by Francis Wyndham and Diana Melly

'Eloquent and invaluable ... her life emerges, and with it a portrait of an
unexpectedly indomitable figure' – Marina Warner in the *Sunday Times*

Among the Russians Colin Thubron

One man's solitary journey by car across Russia provides an enthralling
and revealing account of the habits and idiosyncrasies of a fascinating
people. 'He sees things with the freshness of an innocent and the erudition
of a scholar' – *Daily Telegraph*

They Went to Portugal Rose Macaulay

An exotic and entertaining account of travellers to Portugal from the
pirate-crusaders, through poets, aesthetes and ambassadors, to the new
wave of romantic travellers. A wonderful mixture of literature, history
and adventure, by one of our most stylish and seductive writers.

The Separation Survival Handbook Helen Garlick

Separation and divorce almost inevitably entail a long journey through a
morass of legal, financial, custodial and emotional problems. Stripping the
experience of both jargon and guilt, marital lawyer Helen Garlick maps
clearly the various routes that can be taken.

FOR THE BEST IN PAPERBACKS, LOOK FOR THE

PENGUIN POLITICS AND SOCIAL SCIENCES

Political Ideas   David Thomson (ed.)

From Machiavelli to Marx – a stimulating and informative introduction to the last 500 years of European political thinkers and political thought.

On Revolution   Hannah Arendt

Arendt's classic analysis of a relatively recent political phenomenon examines the underlying principles common to all revolutions, and the evolution of revolutionary theory and practice. 'Never dull, enormously erudite, always imaginative' – *Sunday Times*

The Apartheid Handbook   Roger Omond

The facts behind the headlines: the essential hard information about how apartheid actually works from day to day.

The Social Construction of Reality   Peter Berger and Thomas Luckmann

Concerned with the sociology of 'everything that passes for knowledge in society' and particularly with that which passes for common sense, this is 'a serious, open-minded book, upon a serious subject' – *Listener*

The Care of the Self   Michel Foucault
The History of Sexuality Vol 3

Foucault examines the transformation of sexual discourse from the Hellenistic to the Roman world in an inquiry which 'bristles with provocative insights into the tangled liaison of sex and self' – *The Times Higher Educational Supplement*

A Fate Worse than Debt   Susan George

How did Third World countries accumulate a staggering trillion dollars' worth of debt? Who really shoulders the burden of reimbursement? How should we deal with the debt crisis? Susan George answers these questions with the solid evidence and verve familiar to readers of *How the Other Half Dies*.

Comparative Government   S. E. Finer

'A considerable *tour de force* ... few teachers of politics in Britain would fail to learn a great deal from it ... Above all, it is the work of a great teacher who breathes into every page his own enthusiasm for the discipline' – Anthony King in *New Society*

Karl Marx: Selected Writings in Sociology and Social Philosophy
T. B. Bottomore and Maximilien Rubel (eds.)

'It makes available, in coherent form and lucid English, some of Marx's most important ideas. As an introduction to Marx's thought, it has very few rivals indeed' – *British Journal of Sociology*

Post-War Britain   A Political History   Alan Sked and Chris Cook

Major political figures from Attlee to Thatcher, the aims and achievements of governments and the changing fortunes of Britain in the period since 1945 are thoroughly scrutinized in this readable history.

Inside the Third World   Paul Harrison

From climate and colonialism to land hunger, exploding cities and illiteracy, this comprehensive book brings home a wealth of facts and analysis on the often tragic realities of life for the poor people and communities of Asia, Africa and Latin America.

Housewife   Ann Oakley

'A fresh and challenging account' – *Economist*. 'Informative and rational enough to deserve a serious place in any discussion on the position of women in modern society' – *The Times Educational Supplement*

The Raw and the Cooked   Claude Lévi-Strauss

Deliberately, brilliantly and inimitably challenging, Lévi-Strauss's seminal work of structural anthropology cuts wide and deep into the mind of mankind, as he finds in the myths of the South American Indians a comprehensible psychological pattern.